LONG WAY TOGETHER

LONG WAY TOGETHER

Forty Years, Four Home Grounds and Four Divisions with Brighton & Hove Albion

Robert Townsend

pitch

First published by Pitch Publishing, 2026
1

Pitch Publishing
9 Donnington Park, 85 Birdham Road
Chichester, West Sussex, PO20 7AJ
www.pitchpublishing.co.uk
info@pitchpublishing.co.uk

Set in Adobe Caslon 11.4/16pt

Typeset by Pitch Publishing

Cover design by Olner Design

Printed and bound in India by Thomson Press India Private Limited

The authorised representative in the EEA is
Easy Access System Europe OÜ, Mustamäe tee 50, 10621 Tallinn,
Estonia gpsr.requests@easproject.com

A CIP catalogue record for this book is available from the British Library

ISBN 978-1-83680-441-3

Papers used by Pitch Publishing are from
well-managed forests and other responsible sources

MIX
Paper | Supporting responsible forestry
FSC® C010615

CONTENTS

INTRODUCTION

FOUR DIVISIONS. Four home stadiums. More than 40 years. My life has been inextricably linked to Brighton & Hove Albion Football Club for as long as I can remember, and the journey from the bottom of the entire league to watching my team play in European competition has been pretty bonkers.

Where to begin? Well, there was the year I inadvertently ruined thousands of Brighton fans' Christmases. Oh, and the other Christmas I spoiled on club duty. There was the time a whole stand cheered at how badly I was performing my ball boy duties. Paul Gascoigne once gave me a banana (not a euphemism) and I got Italian legend Toto Schillaci's autograph by accident. I took a former England manager to the pub, and I turned down a ticket to England's Euro 96 semi-final against Germany because of who I would have been sitting next to.

I encountered some very bitey Cardiff fans, experienced two big ball-boying controversies, and had a friend give himself whiplash celebrating a goal which was immediately disallowed. I watched games as the only person in an otherwise empty stand, and was once asked to translate for our new Argentinian striker even though my grasp of Spanish stretched about as far as asking directions to the beach.

With my family also being familiar faces around Brighton & Hove Albion since the 1980s (more about this later), this book documents the ever-shifting dynamic of my lifelong relationship with a wonderful but sometimes calamitous football club through anecdotes, insights, universal truths and a bit of midlife grumpiness. Within all that, I delve into what it was like to work at the club during an era when the fans were at war with the owners, why a penalty shoot-out win sent me into blind panic, and the reason I took strange comfort from Albion blowing the Championship title.

I explain why I got into trouble with the police every matchday just for doing my job, why I spent several years silently watching games alone in the dead of night, the reason I was backstage at London's Shepherd's Bush Empire wishing I was in Hartlepool, and why some of my happiest times were spent in the car park of the club's stadium.

I reveal why half a dozen professional footballers and I sat with our backs to a game watching a crocodile documentary, why the rat who briefly lived in the souvenir shop in the 90s was given a very specific name, and the reason I spent the most important match in the club's history sitting alone in a rainswept park … wearing only one sock.

If you're a Brighton fan, the stories here should stoke your own memories. If you're not, then you'll likely draw parallels with your own team; the silly superstitions, the service-station stops, the unparalleled joy of injury-time winners, and if football isn't your thing, then this book will probably still ring true with your own unhealthy obsessions.

PART ONE:
THE GOLDSTONE

THE BEGINNING

IT STARTED with disappointment. The year was 1986 and I was about to attend my first ever professional football match. It was an FA Cup fifth-round replay featuring the team my father supported, Brighton & Hove Albion. This was my rite of passage.

My puffy, navy blue winter coat swamped me and was proudly decorated with the same rosette my dad had worn to Brighton's only FA Cup Final appearance three years previously. I had a matching blue and white scarf and woolly hat. As well as being suitably attired, I'd obsessively read every snippet of information I could find on Brighton's players and their opponents, Peterborough United. I was nine years old and I was as excited as I had been for anything in my life. But then, that rite of passage was blocked by snow. Heaps and heaps of snow.

It had been a freezing February and as March approached the cold snap showed no signs of abating. The pitch at the club's stadium, the Goldstone Ground in Hove, on the supposed sunshine coast of the UK, was frozen, the terraces dangerously icy. The game was postponed and I was devastated. The match was rescheduled to take place within a week and my parents promised me that I could still attend but, such was my disappointment, they might as well have informed me that it would now be happening in the year 2000. On the moon.

Disappointment is perhaps the perfect first emotion for someone to experience upon being introduced to the world of football. Aside from those who follow the handful of regularly successful clubs, most people soon learn that being a fan can be as much a chore as it is a pleasure, and that moments of triumph can be rare and fleeting. I wasn't aware of this at the time of course, and the match's postponement was disappointing to me because I couldn't wait to enter this enthralling new universe. Had I known it would be 15 years until I'd see my team win a trophy and that the football I'd witness along the way would be largely insipid, would I have been as keen to head along? Probably not.

With this in mind, we tangentially and temporarily time-travel forward three decades, from the south of England to Parramatta in Australia, the home of Western Sydney Wanderers FC, who my Aussie wife, Jayne, supports.

Western Sydney Wanderers are the subject of an interesting story. In 2014, they won the AFC Champions League. That's not especially interesting in itself, but it becomes more so when you learn that the Wanderers were barely two years old at the time. They weren't a rebrand of a previous entity, a moved franchise, or anything like that. They were completely new and, a couple of years after their first ever game, they won the Champions League.

Despite my affinity-by-association with Western Sydney Wanderers, I couldn't help but feel it was a shame that they had won the biggest trophy possible so early in their history. Jayne had tasted the ultimate glory without ever experiencing the hard times. A great philosopher (Dolly Parton) once said, 'If you want the rainbow, you've got to put up with the rain.' Well, Western Sydney Wanderers skipped the rain and slid straight down the side of the rainbow into a pot of gold. Where was there to go after that?

Before I eventually saw Brighton lift some silverware, the club survived winding-up orders, became homeless and forced to ground-share 70 miles from home, faced near extinction, and played a whole lot of absolutely terrible football along the way. There were mass walkouts at the stadium and thousands of supporters marched to Downing Street in protest at the club's owners. The team dropped to the very bottom of the Football League.

There were many, many bleak times. This, however, made success taste all the sweeter when a trophy was finally won. As Jayne celebrated Western Sydney's glory with her fellow red-and-black-shirted supporters, I had to fight the urge to solemnly suggest to her that things probably wouldn't always be this good. Jayne soon found out for herself, though. Western Sydney Wanderers finished second from bottom in their domestic league the following season and have been largely rubbish ever since. A case of the rain following the rainbow. For the nine-year-old me in 1986, the rainbow had been preceded by snow. However, the Peterborough postponement wasn't even my first disappointment as a Brighton fan. For that, we need to time-travel again, back to 1983.

My first ever football memory goes like this; I am at infant school in my home town of Eastbourne, a seaside resort along the coast from Brighton, popular with blue-rinsed tourists. It is the day before the FA Cup Final between Manchester United and Brighton & Hove Albion. At playtime, there is a group of boys marching around the perimeter of the playground shouting 'United, United'. A smaller gathering of boys (actually, just two of them) are walking in the opposite direction shouting 'Brighton, Brighton'. I was one half of this duo. My best friend, David, was the other. David had no interest in football and I think he was just joining in because he didn't fancy the alternative of playing kiss chase with the girls.

I had never been to a football match, yet here I was, stomping around the playground shouting the name of 'my' team, even though I knew almost nothing about the club or indeed the sport. I clearly remember though, the bigger group of boys displaying an air of superiority as they marched. They numbered maybe a dozen, and they supported the most famous team in the world. Every time we passed each other, they laughed at us. Two losers cheering the hopeless underdog. At lunchtime, David and I sat down to eat our sandwiches. After consuming the white, crustless triangles, David pulled a snack from his *Star Wars* lunchbox. It was a United bar, a smallish, chocolate-covered biscuit. I was furious at David's lack of loyalty. A United bar? The day before my team played against Manchester *United* in the cup final! How very dare he?

David was confused by my reaction. He just wanted to eat the treat his mother had packed for him (and United bars had no actual connection with Manchester United, as far as I am aware). David ate his chocolate bar, equally apologetically and bemusedly, while I moaned about it being 'bad luck'. Even having never attended a game, I was already showing signs of irrationality and superstition that all football fans display on a pathetically regular basis.

I watched the FA Cup Final the next day on the telly while my dad attended the match at Wembley Stadium, rosette proudly attached to his jumper. I don't recall any aspects of the game other than the fact that, late in the match with Brighton losing 2-1, my mum said in a resigned tone, 'Let's go for a walk through the woods. By the time we get back, it'll be over.'

The woods ran along the back of my parents' garden. We pulled on our wellies and strolled the mud paths. Dappled light danced through the gaps between the leaves of the grand old trees arching high above our heads. When we returned through the back door into the kitchen some 20 minutes later, my mum switched on the portable radio and was greeted by the tinny sound of live commentary. 'They're still playing!' she exclaimed. 'It must have gone to extra time. Your dad will be having kittens!'

I wasn't sure what extra time was and I certainly didn't know what having kittens meant. I understood though, from my mum's tone, that this was a pleasing turn of events. I don't remember if I watched or listened to the remainder of the 2-2 draw, in which Albion's Gordon Smith missed a golden chance to score a late winner, but I am certain that I didn't see the consequent midweek replay because it took place past my bedtime. The first I heard about the result was my dad waking me the following morning to inform me that we'd lost 4-0. I shed a tear and made a mental note to blame my friend David for eating that United bar the previous Friday.

Albion played little part in my consciousness over the following three years, until my father considered me old enough to go to a game. The postponement of the Peterborough FA Cup tie had been a false start, but the match was finally played a few days later. The UK was still blanketed by snow and it took sheer human determination, in the form of supporters with brooms, to ensure the tie went ahead. Fans gallantly swept the pitch and terraces and, in early March 1986, I attended my first ever professional football match.

I travelled the 40-minute journey from Eastbourne by car with my dad and his mates. We parked a few streets away from the stadium, pulled on our hats and scarves and joined the steady flow of people. With every step that I took along the wide Hove pavements towards the Goldstone Ground, I became increasingly allured. The first glimpse of the floodlights made my stomach jump. They were towering structures, reaching high into the purple sky and pouring out white light. By the time we were directly outside the stadium, I was intoxicated by that football ground smell. What was it? A mix of fried onions and Bovril from the vendors, beer on the breath of supporters, horse dung on the roads and urine from the stadium's disgusting old toilets. I had never seen so many men in one place; cold, white air evaporating in front of their mouths as they spoke. My dad, his pals and I joined a snaking queue at the south-west corner of the stadium. After an age, we eventually made it to the front and I pushed my weight against the heavy metal turnstile. It creaked and clicked as it rotated clockwise before coughing me out the other side.

I was mesmerised by the surroundings. Over 19,000 people were huddled together on cold terraces, all focused on a brilliant green pitch which was bordered by the mounds of snow that had been brushed away from the playing surface. Cocooned by my coat, hat, scarf and gloves, I stood at the front, leaning on the advertising hoardings, squeezed between two boys I didn't know while my dad, a tall man, kept an eye on me from further back.

The game passed in a blur. It finished 1-0 to Brighton. When the goal went in, I cheered and punched the air. I basically just copied what everyone else was doing. When the crowd chanted the club nickname, 'Seagulls', in a slow drone, it was the loudest noise I had ever heard. My most vivid memory of the evening is of exiting the stadium. There I was, a tiny nine-year-old, dwarfed by thousands of men as everyone shuffled for the gates. I felt as though I was drowning in a sea of dark winter coats as the crowd bottlenecked. It was a suffocating experience, yet I fought the urge to yell out for my dad, who I could no longer see. Within moments, I was through the exit gate and on the street, with fresh, crisp air in my lungs and my father and his friends magically by my side again. We walked to the car. They talked about the match and I daydreamed about my first experience of this masculine, adult world.

We got home thrillingly late. My dad told me that I could cut up the matchday programme after he'd read it. I was an irritatingly creative child and he probably thought I wanted to make a collage out of it or something. I had absolutely no intention of cutting up this document, though. Would a Christian return from their first church service and take a pair of scissors to the Bible?

I went to school the next day with a sense of pride at having become part of a very grown-up world; one which few of my peers knew. I was a shy kid and I hated school. Not the learning part, but the 'having to interact with other kids' part. My cheeks would redden if a teacher or another pupil talked to me, meaning I usually kept my head down and ticked off the minutes until it was time to head home and play with my *Star Wars* figures. However, going to the Brighton game had given me a glimpse of something new. I'd stepped through the back of the wardrobe and discovered a land where men smoked and yelled the rudest swear words at the tops of their voices and sang uproarious songs which were somehow tuneful yet cacophonous, witty yet menacing. It was beguiling, and school felt pointless and flimsy in comparison. Just the day before, I had felt moderately frightened by the other kids in my year, yet now they seemed like nothing more than silly little boys. Going to a football game hadn't magically made me more outwardly confident, nor had it instantly initiated me into the school's In Crowd (I don't think I even told many of the other kids about it), but it had given me a strange semblance of internal assuredness.

I had experienced an immediate sense of belonging at the Goldstone Ground, to the extent that school popularity now seemed entirely unimportant. I had 19,000 new friends in Hove.

***

MY FAMILY

My second match at the Goldstone was a bread-and-butter midweek league fixture against Oldham Athletic. There was something very different, however, about my sophomore appearance at the Goldstone. Namely that my dad and I were joined by my mum and, controversially, my sister (cue *EastEnders* drums).

I think my mum had been to games with my dad back in the 70s but for my older sister this was all new, just as it had been for me a few weeks previously. However, I suspect her enthusiasm levels were considerably lower than mine. Seriously, who wants to go to a boring old football match with their annoying little brother? She likely remembers it differently but I'm pretty sure she was only there under duress, because the rest of the family was in attendance and she was still a bit too young to stay home on her own at night.

It felt jarring at first, that the universe I had only just discovered was already being infiltrated by my sister. The posters on her walls were from *Smash Hits*, not *Shoot* magazine. I had literally just found the place where I felt I most belonged, it was *my* secret, yet now I was having to share the experience with *a girl.* If I displayed such misogyny as an adult in the 21st century, I would be ashamed of myself, but it was the 1980s, I was nine and, as far as I was concerned, girls were awful in pretty much every way.

Whilst my childish annoyance was very real and embarrassingly angst-ridden, it didn't even last until half-time. My sister's enthusiasm was soon apparent. She too fell in love with the game, the drama, the atmosphere and the visceral experience. The match was a drab 1-1 draw, yet it proved to be a watershed occasion for the Townsends from Eastbourne. From then on, we would spend many years attending matches together as the definition of a nuclear family. Indeed, as I write these words at the end of 2025, I can say with absolute confidence that there has been at least one member of the Townsend quartet at every Brighton home game from that Oldham match to this very day (aside from when Covid caused matches to be played behind closed doors). There was even a story about us in the deservedly short-lived *Seagull News* (a monthly, Albion-focused newspaper, which sat largely untroubled on the shelves of local stockists at the start of the 1990s). The story was headlined, 'The Complete Football Family'. I mention this anecdotally because the main headline on the cover of that issue was, 'WOMEN ARE NEW FANS'. The accompanying article about an increased interest in football amongst women is anachronistic in retrospect, but I suppose it pointed, if somewhat patronisingly, towards a more progressive attitude in football and a small yet significant step away from the machismo and hooligan terrace culture of the late 70s and early 80s.

By the start of the 1986/87 season, my mum was working in the souvenir shop on matchdays. The role was unpaid. Meanwhile, my dad got a matchday job organising and distributing stewards' wages. I was thrilled. It had been less than six months since my first game, and I had already infiltrated the inner circle! At the time, I had no idea what a life-changing occurrence it would be for my parents to start working at the stadium on matchdays. Over the next

30 years, my mother would continue to play an integral yet unsung role in the day-to-day running of the club. She progressed from this voluntary position to become a part-time member of staff with an actual salary, and eventually worked full-time as (to name a few roles) shop manager, ticket office manager, office manager, and PA to the chief executive. After her retirement from full-time work in the 2010s, she became a part-time member of the marketing team. Meanwhile, my father has worked at the club on matchdays for nearly four decades, and together, my mum and dad still perform various duties together at home games. My sister also worked at the Albion on matchdays for some time, and was also employed at Arsenal FC and talkSPORT.

From the moment my folks secured matchday positions, my burgeoning relationship with Brighton & Hove Albion Football Club changed immeasurably. I was no longer just a kid who had been to watch his local professional football team a couple of times. I was a kid who would spend the rest of his childhood behind the scenes. There was nowhere, aside from school and home, where I passed more hours than the Goldstone Ground. I would come to know every nook of it and, just like my mother, would eventually work in several roles at the club. I started as a ball boy, then worked in the club shop, the lottery department, the administration office, the ticket office, and the supporter services department. I worked at the Goldstone, Priestfield Stadium in Gillingham, when the Albion were ground-sharing there, and at the club's offices/shops in Brighton's city centre. I worked at Albion's 'temporary' ground at Withdean, at Falmer while the new permanent stadium was being built, and, finally, I was employed in the shiny American Express Stadium. For a decade I wrote my own weekly column about the Albion in local newspaper, *The Argus*.

So, if the Peterborough FA Cup game caused me to fall in love with football, then my parents working on matchdays ultimately ensured that Brighton & Hove Albion Football Club would become the single most important institution in both my professional and personal life. I don't know whether I should thank my parents or curse them for getting me so hooked.

***

LITTER ON THE BREEZE

Our matchday would start early and, upon arrival at the ground in the morning, my parents headed to their respective departments, leaving me and my sister to wait for kick-off. Oddly, we were allowed inside the stadium before the gates opened. I have no idea who authorised two unsupervised kids to hang about on an otherwise empty terrace but there we would sit, just the two of us, on the cold, grey concrete for hours (literally hours) while we waited for the turnstiles to open and for the other supporters to filter in. After that, it was only another hour and a half until kick-off!

During this time, I would often just stare out across the Goldstone. The view wouldn't have held much interest to many people. Even most football supporters would likely have found its aesthetic to be somewhat uninspiring; it was a crumbling relic. To me though, it was beautiful. The pitch was the greenest area of grass I had ever seen. From my position, I would stare across at the open East Terrace opposite. It tapered as you looked from one end to the other, to the point where residents at the southern section of the street behind the ground could watch matches from their front gardens. How I envied those people. Imagine opening your curtains to the greatest view on Earth every day.

I gazed at the covered North Terrace behind the goal to my left. It was empty now, but it was the source of the main supporter noise during matches. Thousands of people chanting in unison. When a shot narrowly missed, clusters would involuntarily surge forward as one, a sea of heads flowing like lava.

Directly behind the terrace on which I was positioned, the West Stand housed uncomfortable wooden seats. That was where fusty old fans would sit, very occasionally chanting a slow chorus of 'Seagulls'. The cry would amplify under the roof and spread through the rest of the stadium.

The South Stand behind the goal to my right was covered, seated and favoured by families. The seats in the front three rows were white, the rest blue. A few broken blue seats had been removed, and the club clearly didn't have any replacements of the same colour, meaning a spattering of rogue white seats were dotted around the stand. I wasn't aware of it at the time, but these little white blemishes indicated that money was becoming a little tight at Brighton & Hove Albion.

There is just something about old football stadiums. You can almost feel the ghosts within them, and a completely empty ground creates an eerie atmosphere. Maybe it's because they are in an alien state. We are used to seeing them filled with thousands of animated people, so for them to lie dormant gives rise to these imagined spectres of seasons past. It's different now, in this era of modern super-stadia. Sure, you can be dazzled by their architecture, but they don't have the same aura about them, presumably because, as venues, many of them are still relatively young. When, as a child, I gazed across an entirely deserted Goldstone Ground, I could breathe in its history. For over eight decades people had stood in the exact spot where I was, with the same hopes as those who were there 10, 20, 50 years previously. Aside from churches, there are few such sites in the world, where people return with a common belief and where generations of families experience joy and sadness. It was almost tangible; the atoms in the air, a million memories swirling around the empty stands like litter on the breeze.

***

NEVER GONNA GIVE YOU UP

Albion were hopeless in the 1986/87 season and finished it stranded at the bottom of Division Two (now the Championship), barely winning a match after Christmas. It was grim viewing and I quickly grew to dread the delayed, muffled cheers from the pocket of away fans in the far corner of the ground when their team scored. I learned to immediately look at the linesman when the ball hit the back of our net, hoping that he'd raise his flag for offside. He never did. I found that time accelerated when Brighton were losing and, cruelly, it almost stopped on the rare occasions we were in the lead. I discovered that standing in the winter chill for hours made it feel as though my spine was tied in a knot and that my fingers and toes were going to snap off. The biggest lesson I learned was that watching your team surrender every fortnight with barely any resistance gets old very quickly.

There was no turning back now though. As any fan knows, once you've made your footballing bed, you've just got to jolly well lie in it and, despite my first full season as a supporter being a disaster, by August I was keen for the new campaign to kick off. That's just how football works, isn't it? No matter how awful a season is, the passing of those empty summer months serve to change a fan's expectations from 'quite low' to 'unrealistically optimistic', seemingly for no reason other than if we don't go into a new season with hope then what's the point in any of this? Sure, Brighton had surrendered to relegation but, three months later, football-starved fans were walking the sunny Hove streets to the Goldstone for a Division Three fixture against York City with renewed positivity. It's actually rather reassuring how football resets every summer, offering hope where there had previously been none.

At the end of the 1986/87 season, several key players were sold off to pay the club's ever-increasing debts. It felt strange to have spent the last year watching one group of players and picking my favourites, and now there was an entirely different bunch to get to grips with. It was as though someone had replaced my family with strangers.

One of the most comforting things about football is that it offers routine and, despite the jarring team changes that had occurred over the summer, the Townsend family fell into a regular pattern at the start of the new season. On a matchday morning I'd pull on the same replica shirt, we'd leave our house at the same time, drive the same route, park on the same street and play the same 'lucky' compilation cassette in the car. It opened with Rick Astley's 'Never Gonna Give You Up' and closed with Squeeze's 'Up the Junction' via a couple of Whitney Houston hits, Starship's 'We Built This City' and all manner of jaunty numbers. Music evokes a time and a place to such an extent that I still can't hear 'I Wanna Dance With Somebody (Who Loves Me)' without the image of travelling down Seaford High Street popping into my head, while' Up the Junction' makes me think of turning up The Drive in Hove, past the Queen Victoria statue on the seafront.

One routine that had changed for me and my sister was that, upon arriving at the ground, rather than hanging around on the cold terrace while we waited for the turnstiles to open, this season we were instead plonked in a place called the Seagull Lounge. The lounge sat in the bowels of the West Stand, which also housed all of the club's offices, bars, boardroom and changing rooms. The Seagull Lounge was a smallish, rectangular room in which the match officials, players' wives, injured first-teamers and other guests would have a cup of tea and a biscuit in the early afternoon.

I would sit on the edge of the padded sofa which ran the length of the walls and watch *Grandstand* on the bulky 80s TV, while adults were served hot drinks by two kindly, grey-haired women behind the counter. They were the embodiment of the cliched 'tea ladies' that are forever mentioned by club spokespeople across the land. Again, to this day I don't know on whose authority it was that my sister and I were allowed to be in there, but we were meek kids and perhaps we were so quiet that no one even noticed us. In fact, I was so shy that I spent most of my time feeling uncomfortable, like the imposter that I was, hoping that nobody would talk to me, and half-expecting a club official to kick me out at any moment. They never did though, and it was always interesting to eavesdrop on the match officials or players chatting, as it gave a little peek behind the curtains of their worlds. Even as a kid who knew nothing about anything, it surprised me to hear how ordinary their lives seemed to be. I had previously thought that players and referees were akin to superheroes, but here they were talking inanely about house prices and holidays, as though they were just normal people.

Shortly before the turnstiles opened at 1.30pm, it was always something of a relief for my sister and I to leave this busy lounge and dash round to the West Terrace in order to secure 'our spot' before any other punters nabbed it. This, I now realise, was entirely pointless. We didn't need to claim our position because nobody who arrived for the opening of the ground would have stolen it anyway. Crowds in those days for a run-of-the-mill league game rarely got above 8,000. The Goldstone Ground held 30,000 and you can be sure that anyone keen enough to arrive 90 minutes before kick-off already had their own favourite spot.

Although there was usually plenty of space for everyone, there were occasions during that season when the stadium was packed. In January, Arsenal visited, which was a big deal because I'd seen them play on the telly. On the morning of the sold-out FA Cup tie, my dad decided to park miles from the ground as, by his logic, the further away we left the car, the less likely the windscreen was to get smashed in by London hooligans. Incidentally, this is the same reason that he has never put a Seagulls sticker in the window; in case it provoked the rage of a passing Albion-hater who also just so happened to have a brick in their hand.

As we began our long trek to the stadium, my dad gave me detailed verbal instructions about what to do if I encountered said thugs. The gist of his safety briefing was 'run away quickly' and I was instantly terrified. I wanted to watch a football match, not be attacked by scary grown-ups with shaved heads and tattoos. My mum shot my dad a look which managed to be simultaneously withering and furious, and reassured me that everything was going to be okay. I wouldn't, she promised me, encounter any hooligans.

She was right. The atmosphere was wonderful on a quintessential FA Cup afternoon, with the entire East Terrace being swarmed by 10,000 north Londoners who had taken a winter trip to the seaside. When Albion striker Garry Nelson spectacularly volleyed a goal, the home crowd felt like a single entity, roaring, leaping and throwing arms into the air as one. Similarly, when Arsenal scored, the away fans emitted an extraordinarily loud roar which washed over the entire ground. The stadium had a beating pulse that day and it felt special to be part of it.

Despite a 2-1 defeat, the occasion seemed to spur Albion on for the remainder of the season. Attendances gradually increased and remnants of the malaise that had enveloped the ground the previous season evaporated. In April, seven wins in a row meant that promotion was in our own hands with two games remaining. Sunderland had already wrapped up top spot, but second place was up for grabs because the other promotion contenders, Notts County, were in the midst of a humongous wobble. Two more Albion wins from the final two matches would secure promotion. To anyone who had endured the previous season's dross, it was an inconceivable prospect.

***

CEEFAX

A member of Albion's playing staff that season was Northern Ireland international Gerry Armstrong. The moustachioed forward was legendary for scoring the goal which had eliminated Spain from the 1982 World Cup, and his signing was significant for me because it heralded the introduction of two new friends. Armstrong moved into a flat in Hove with his family and they got to know my parents. Pretty soon his two sons were my best mates. We hung out together all the time. They would come to my house in Eastbourne and I would spend plenty of time at their flat just around the corner from the Goldstone. Their dad's Golden Boot (for Best British Player at the 1982 World Cup) sat on display in the hallway. I used to run my fingers over it when no one was looking and ludicrously dream of one day winning such an accolade. I was barely on the periphery of my school team.

The point of this name-drop is that it was in the Armstrongs' living room that I experienced one of my favourite Albion moments. It was a balmy May evening in 1988, and my family was at their abode. Earlier in the day, Albion had blown a 2-0 lead away to Chester to eventually draw 2-2. The feeling of deflation was almost incapacitating at that point in the season. Our fate was no longer in our own hands. If Notts County won their seemingly straightforward home encounter with Port Vale that evening, they would leapfrog the Seagulls into the last automatic promotion position with one match remaining.

That evening, the grown-ups chatted while us kids watched telly. We put the football-related disappointment to the back of our minds to such an extent that we completely forgot Notts County were in the process of playing an important match. Upon remembering, we frantically searched for the TV remote control in order to call upon our faithful 1980s friend, Ceefax.

Before the internet revolutionised how we consume sport, Ceefax was the greatest tool in the world for a football fan craving instant information, as it was the best and most immediate place you could find scores and football news. These days you can check the train times, team news and weather forecast on your phone on the way to the game and use the same device to find out scores from around the country during the match. Then, on your way home, you can watch highlights, see instantly updated league tables, and even send a DM to your favourite/least favourite player telling them how brilliantly/terribly they'd played. It's quite incredible. But back then you only had the radio and the blocky text of Ceefax on your TV to keep you updated. *The Guardian*'s Barney Ronay once described it, quite brilliantly, as the 'horse-drawn internet'.

One of Gerry's sons pressed the 3, 0 and 2 buttons on the remote control to reveal the main football index. A black screen with blue and white writing appeared, guiding us to the relevant page where we waited for the scores to load. All eyes were fixed to the screen, searching out the result. There it was: Notts County 1 Port Vale 2.

County had lost and Albion were still above them in the table. Everyone in the room went bananas. Seconds previously, it had been like any other living room in the country: kids gazing at the TV, adults talking, but now it was as though a human party popper had been pulled. Everyone was jumping and whooping, cheering and hugging. It was an eye-opening moment for me. I had previously only experienced anything like it within the walls of a football ground, yet here we were, acting in the same way on someone's carpet. I understood for the first time that the feeling of togetherness and those shared adrenaline rushes didn't only exist at matches, but also in little pockets of suburbia.

Albion went into the final game of the season knowing a win would secure promotion straight back to the second tier of English football. I was as nervous as I'd been since the biliousness of starting secondary school a few months previously, but this was a better kind of nervous. It was a blazingly sunny day and the ground was awash with short sleeves and late-80s mullets. The crowd was initially quieter than usual as, despite having nothing to play for, opponents Bristol Rovers were defending stubbornly. Then, a floated cross from the left was met by the forehead of rough-and-tumble Albion forward Kevin Bremner. The ball flew into the net and the stadium exploded into life. Garry Nelson doubled the lead straight after half-time, signalling the start of the promotion party. I had never seen so many happy people. I didn't realise football could be like this, as the previous season had been nothing but hunched shoulders, grey faces, frowns and groans of dissatisfaction. It was quite something to experience these two opposing collective emotions in my first and second full seasons as a fan. Or rather, while writing these words many years later I would consider the juxtaposition for the first time and appreciate it retrospectively. At the time, I was too busy being 11 and standing atop an advertising hoarding waving my scarf over my head like I was king of the world.

A late Rovers goal temporarily turned the atmosphere from celebratory into apprehensive until three peeps of the referee's whistle led to a massive pitch invasion. 'Brighton are back!' the crowd sang as the players saluted them in a state of semi-undress from the directors' box.

Later, my family and I joined staff, players and their families for a celebration in the boardroom. It was the first and only time I ever set foot in there. The oblong room's brown decor was a throwback to an earlier decade but, whilst I presumed it was usually frequented by a handful of suited men, today it was filled with kids running amok and adults sinking bottles of beer. I have a vague memory of a player surreptitiously lowering one of the room's tall yucca plants out of the window to an accomplice on the street below. I can't recall who the culprit was and I have no idea why he did it. Exuberance? Drunkenness? A dare? Maybe he just really wanted a yucca plant. Whatever the reason, I'm sure it mirrored the tomfoolery that was occurring all over the county; the kind of non-malicious silliness that promotion and a few drinks can bring.

***

HIGH FIVES AND BIG STARS

The following season, rather than watching games from the terraces, I stood on the track as a ball boy. This meant I had the cacophonous noise from the North Stand behind me and got to throw the ball back to my heroes. It also meant that I wore a snazzy, two-tone blue tracksuit and hung around the changing room area before and after the game.

There were about ten ball boys and one ball girl (gender inequality in a nutshell, right there). Before games we would meet in the corridor outside the changing rooms. The head ball boy (much more about him later) would give us a kitbag of tracksuits and we would scramble to find one that fitted our frames of varying size. If we were lucky, they'd have been washed since the last game, but they usually gave off a musty whiff and had red stains on their backsides from the previous wearer sitting on the cinder track. When we'd found a tracksuit that vaguely fitted, we'd get changed right there in the corridor. Once kitted out, we would just loiter until kick-off. We were probably in everyone's way and were certainly louder than we should have been (I'm sure the match officials didn't appreciate a gaggle of kids talking loudly outside their door), but no one ever asked us to keep the noise down or found anywhere else for us to congregate.

We'd say hello to the players as they clip-clopped their way along the tiled corridor to warm up on the pitch, and we'd say hello to them again as they made their way back up the tunnel at 2.45pm. Our greetings garnered differing reactions. Some players grunted a barely audible reply. To them, we were annoyances, messing with their pre-match routine. Others were brilliant. Defender Gary Chivers always acted as though he was delighted to see us and would distribute enthusiastic high-fives as he passed. Little actions such as those meant a huge amount and proved that it doesn't take much to be a fan favourite. You either need to be a brilliant player, very enthusiastic on the pitch, or a character off it. For instance, you can be arrogant and lazy but supporters will likely forgive you if you regularly produce moments of unparalleled magic. Equally, fans will excuse a lack of talent if a player works incredibly hard for 90 minutes and always gives a hearty round of applause in the direction of the stands at the end of the game. The occasional badge-kiss never goes amiss either. Chivers was talented, enthusiastic and nice. He had the full set. There are usually a couple of players like this in every squad. They seem to take not just the club, but the community to their heart and immerse themselves in it.

Having greeted the Albion players on their way down and back up the tunnel before kick-off, sometimes we would engage with people even more famous than the likes of Chivers (imagine that!). One time, Chris Eubank Snr did some impromptu shadow boxing with us. He was at a game to show off his latest belt (by which I mean a boxing belt he'd just won, not his latest purchase from Marks & Spencer) and, while he waited at the top of the tunnel, he mucked around with us, pretending to give us cheeky jabs. This was long before his jodhpurs and monocle days and there was no sign of his meticulously constructed persona. He was just a bloke in a leather jacket who was really good at fighting, and he seemed happy to pretend to punch a bunch of excited kids.

Whilst meeting Eubank left me a little starstruck, my writing work as an adult has put me in contact with various celebrities. I've interviewed a plethora of musicians, movie directors, actors, models, artists, novelists and footballers. The famous people I encounter are invariably lovely, but I don't have any greater interest in spending time with them than I would in sharing a drink with your everyday football fan down the pub. Less interest, in fact. Celebrity for celebrity's sake is quite flimsy, and I rarely get excited when I speak to the people in magazines and on telly, because my heroes in adulthood are mostly obscure indie musicians. However, back in the late 80s, I was thrilled to meet any famous person and especially footballers. After each game, I would have to wait at least an hour for my mum and dad to finish work, so I loitered around the players' exit with a biro in my left hand and an autograph book in my right. I would then thrust these two items into the hands of any man that emerged from the dressing rooms with freshly washed hair and a bag of toiletries tucked under their arm.

To your hardened supporter, they were probably nothing more than second-tier has-beens/never-will-bes, and indeed looking back now it seems crazy that I was so excited to meet these away players, but I still have all these autograph books. They are basically a collection of pages containing illegible scribbles, with time long since having erased my memory of who these signatures belonged to. I collected the autographs of Albion's players too, over and over again. I got Garry Nelson's so many times that I could likely still replicate it now, over three decades on (legal note: I promise not to).

The visiting footballer whose autograph I was keenest to get was Paul Gascoigne, who played for Tottenham Hotspur at the Goldstone in a testimonial match. This was just before Italia 90, and Gazza's stock was rising to the extent that he had recently replaced Han Solo as my hero. Much like the *Millennium Falcon*'s pilot, he was a lovable maverick. I adored the way he played football with a smile on his face (Gascoigne, not Solo). He was like a grown-up version of the kid at school who was far better than anyone else and would run rings around everyone in the playground. When playing football in the local park, I pretended to be him (as much as I loved the Albion, pretending I was, for example, midfielder Mike Trusson didn't hold the same appeal).

After the match, I waited in the spot where I knew the Spurs players would pass on their journey from the dressing room to the coach. Unlike most weeks when this area was occupied by just me and a couple of sallow, anoraked, autograph-hunting men, there were loads of fans milling about on this April evening, all hoping to catch a glimpse of the new hero of English football. When Gascoigne appeared, it was like Beatlemania, had Beatles fans been teenage boys and adults who were old enough to know better. Everyone rushed towards him.

Gascoigne obliged every single request, laughing and joking with anyone in the vicinity before finally climbing on to the coach. He was the last player to board by some time, despite having been one of the first to emerge from the changing room. His arrival on the coach wasn't the end of his interaction with fans though. Once on board, he opened the sunroof and started throwing fruit through it to the cheering crowd. Why? Who knows? Why did Gazza do half the things he did? I caught a banana and kept it until it went bad.

Ever since his football career ended, Gascoigne's problems have risen to the surface. To be honest, it doesn't surprise me that some footballers haven't got the emotional stability to cope when the game eventually spits them out. I've heard ex-Brighton players from back in the day talk of how they didn't even know how to book an appointment with a doctor or what to do if their car broke down, because such things had always been sorted by their clubs. I assume and hope that, these days, the duty of care to players is much better than it was back in the 80s and 90s?

Gazza made another appearance in Hove around this time, when the Goldstone hosted England B's friendly with Italy. In the current era of super-stadiums, it seems remarkable that the tired old ground was considered a suitable venue for such a game. Something else that is hard to believe is that England ever had a B team. They've barely had an A team for much of my life. Back then though, there were some decent players on the fringes. Tony Adams, for one, marshalled the back four at the Goldstone and scored for the home side. These were in the days when we all thought he was a donkey. How wrong we were. Along with Adams and Gascoigne, Steve Bull, Paul Parker and David Batty also had a run out, as did Lee Dixon and Dennis Wise.

I got the late Italian striker Salvatore 'Toto' Schillaci's autograph that night. He went on to win the Golden

Boot at the 1990 World Cup. Admittedly, at the time, I wouldn't have known who Schillaci was had he walked up to me and written his name on a piece of paper. Which, of course, was exactly what he did. It was only after he started banging in goals the next summer that I dug out my match programme and noticed a scribble that clearly said his name. His autograph now sits up in my parents' loft with all the other squiggles, including Tucker from *Grange Hill*, who I saw outside the club shop before a West Ham United game. I didn't manage to get Phil Collins' signature when he surprisingly turned up at the Goldstone for an FA Cup match against Portsmouth, but that's just the way it is (a little Collins-related wordplay for you there). I also didn't get David Beckham's autograph when he made his Manchester United debut against Brighton at the Goldstone. He was just a skinny kid at the time. Who knew he would go on to become an international megastar?

***

BALL MAN

It won't surprise you to learn that ball boy duties were easy peasy lemon squeezy. We would form a guard of honour to clap the players on to the pitch, and then take our places around the pitch in order to chuck the ball back when it came near us. Our positions were decided for us by the leader of the ball boys, Keith Cuss. Keith was not a boy but in fact a fully grown man, maybe in his late 30s at least (remember how hard it was to judge adults' ages when you were a kid?). Oddly, as well as organising us, he was also a ball boy as well. Or ball man, I suppose. He was surely the oldest ball boy/ball man in the league, yet he seemed to really enjoy taking his place on the touchline each game. That is, until his status changed from old ball boy to dead-set Albion legend with just a flick of his balding pate.

Brighton were playing high-flying Manchester City at the Goldstone. Thousands of fans had travelled down from the North West, carrying with them those inflatable bananas that were de rigueur at the time. Their team were hot favourites to win against a struggling Brighton side, but they hadn't accounted for Albion's scrappy spirit and, with the game approaching its end, City found themselves 2-1 down. The visitors, desperate to carve an equaliser, attacked in ever-increasing waves and, as the action grew frenetic, Brighton's defence lumped the latest dangerous cross away. The clearance ballooned over the touchline and dropped towards ball man Keith. All he had to do was catch it and get it back to the City player who was racing towards him in order to take a quick throw-in. Albion's oldest ball boy did not catch it though. Oh no. Rather, he deftly flick-headed the ball into the crowd behind him. There was an audible gasp. This was unprecedented! A sharp intake of breath was followed by an uproarious reaction. Fans celebrated the ludicrous sight with a pantomime cheer while furious Manchester City players surrounded the offender. Presumably their rage was tempered by utter confusion: 'He just flick-headed the ball into the crowd! Wait. How old is that ball boy?'

This mad moment genuinely seemed to derail the visiting team and Albion went on to win by the odd goal in three. It would henceforth forever be remembered as 'the Keith Cuss match'. From memory, I think Cuss may have claimed that he merely ducked slightly so that the ball didn't hit his glasses and that his delightful flick-header was a complete accident. I also think that the club invited him to kindly pull the other one and, somewhat reluctantly I'm sure, relieved him of his ball boy duties. It was a real shame for Cuss, who was a nice guy and who loved the Albion. I think he continued to run a few errands behind the scenes, such as working behind the bar in one of the lounges for a while. Maybe I'm misremembering that, but, regardless, I'm fairly sure he disappeared from the inner workings of the club not long after the City game.

Cuss might have been the most high-profile ball boy departure during this era, but he wasn't the only one. A couple of years later, my friend Adam got the boot after a disappointing loss to Rotherham United at the Goldstone. The Seagulls, needing a win to keep their fading play-off hopes alive, succumbed to a 2-1 defeat, during which the referee's decisions didn't exactly endear him to the home fans. As the final whistle blew, Adam ran to another ball boy, asked to borrow his glasses, and then chased the referee. He handed these spectacles to the match official as a suggestion that his eyesight perhaps wasn't the best. The referee didn't understand Adam's intention and presumed he was being given an item of lost property. Adam, frustrated that his clever use of a prop hadn't got his message across, decided that the only way to proceed was to tell the referee in no uncertain terms what he thought of his decision-making. I believe there was swearing involved and that Adam got his point across with no confusion this time. That was the end of Adam as a ball boy, but he attends games with his family to this day. I'm sure from his position in the stand, he regularly advises referees that they need an optician's appointment.

There wasn't usually such drama on a matchday. The ball would go off the pitch and we'd go and get it. Simple. Having said that, we certainly tried our best to help the team out. We didn't go so far as to do 'a Keith Cuss' but if you looked closely, you'd notice a distinct difference in the speed with which we'd retrieve the ball depending on the score. If Albion were behind, we'd sprint as fast as we could in order to get the game going again. If we were winning, the ball boys and ball girl would all suffer from inertia. You know how slowly a substituted player leaves the pitch when his team are winning? They perform a jog which somehow manages to be even slower than walking? Well, that was how we'd 'run' to collect the ball. I remember the fans in the West Stand laughing and applauding the ridiculous slowness of my run as Albion hung on to a 1-0 lead in an FA Cup clash with Portsmouth (the Phil Collins game).

Some years later, long after my ball-boy days were over, Brighton boss Micky Adams seemed to take this gamesmanship to a new level. His multi-ball system at Withdean Stadium mysteriously switched to a mono-ball system when his team were narrowly winning matches.

After Cuss got the elbow, the remaining ball boys and ball girl (shall I just call us ball kids from now on?) looked after ourselves. We didn't really need managing, and we just decided between us who would be positioned where. I generally stood behind the north goal, but at various times I watched matches from in front of every stand. I hated sitting at the south end, largely because the view was horrible from there. I think the pitch must've sloped a little bit from the halfway line to the south goal line, because to sit on the ground at that end meant not being able to see the players' legs from the knees down when the action was towards the north. And if you're familiar with football, you'll know that the lower sections of a player's legs are quite important. So, whenever possible, I watched from the north end of the pitch. I loved it there. When a player scored at that end, I would give them a hearty slap on the back as they ran to the crowd, some of whom would spill through the gates as they celebrated. I shared a high-five with striker Mike Small on the pitch after a crucial 1-0 win over West Ham. I think that might have been the moment my life peaked.

Another one of the ball kids' roles was to replace the divots in the turf at half-time and full time. In those days, the groundsman was former player Frankie Howard (not that one). I'm too young to remember Frankie as a wing-wizard, but I spent plenty of time in his company when he was the club's long-serving groundsman. Frankie tended to the Goldstone's pitch with meticulous care, and many people have said that he treated it like his own back garden. While this is a pleasing analogy, it's more accurate to suggest that he actually saw it as his very own work of art. Frankie wasn't happy unless his canvas was an unblemished vision of green and white. Rain or shine, if you glanced across the Goldstone during the week, you would see him hobbling contentedly over the surface, his tired old knees barely keeping him upright as he worked hard to ensure the pitch reached his high standards.

Before each match, my ball-kid chums and I would get a mouthful from Frankie if we dared set foot on his white lines when we stood on the pitch to perform a guard of honour for the teams. Never mind that 22 burly sportsmen were just about to churn the ground with their football studs, if a 12-year-old in trainers tip-toed on to the touchline, they would receive a rollicking. His vitriol was only ever half-serious, but it was still enough to make us very careful where we placed our feet.

At half-time the ball kids walked across the lush and springy pitch, replacing dislodged chunks of turf under Frankie's watchful eye. I occasionally took a moment to stand in the centre circle and enjoy a panoramic view of the Goldstone, which was alive with activity. It was a magical sight and one I feel privileged to have experienced.

After midweek games in the winter, Frankie would enlist the ball kids to help place covers over the goalmouths to stop the ground from freezing overnight. He was insistent that we completed the task faultlessly. It didn't matter how cold or late it was (usually very cold and very late), or whether we had school in the morning (we almost always did); we were not allowed to go home until the covers were perfectly positioned. The result of his attention to detail? One of the best playing surfaces in the league. You would rarely see a balding pitch at the Goldstone; it was almost exclusively a blanket of beautiful green, even in the bleakest of winter months. I've heard people tell stories of him covering blemishes with green paint but I have no idea if this is true. What I do know is that the pitch was a testament to the love, dedication and professionalism shown by a man who continued to care greatly about football long after his playing days were behind him.

Although it was an honour to be a ball kid, the slight downside was that we also had to attend every home game involving the reserve team as well, who also played their matches at the Goldstone. For me, this meant coming over from Eastbourne on a school night to watch the stiffs play painfully dull matches against the likes of Watford or Reading. You have never experienced time standing still until you've stood in the rain watching Brighton's reserves play out a 0-0 draw with Charlton Athletic's reserves. Every now and again though, I would see a cracking match and it felt like being part of something secret and special. Just ask any of the few hundred people who watched Albion lose 4-3 to an Arsenal reserve team that had Ian Wright and Andrew Cole up front while Steve Bould and Colin Pates marshalled their defence.

Because all areas of the ground other than the West Stand seats were closed for reserve games, being positioned in front of an entirely empty North Stand was a lonely experience but also offered a strange sense of serenity. On rainy nights I would shelter halfway up the terrace and, as the players' shouts echoed around me, there was something oddly magical about being the only person in the entire stand while a game was taking place. I wish camera phones had existed back then because I could have taken some cracking pictures and videos of a near-empty, floodlit Goldstone. Unfortunately, those images are stored only in the deep pockets of my memory, ever diminishing with the passing of time.

***

NOTES IN THE REGISTER

When you are a football-mad kid, school is little more than an annoying distraction, only made bearable by the fact that you get to spend precious minutes kicking a ball with your mates in the playground before class and at lunchtime. At my school, these matches were full-scale battles played with rucksacks for goalposts on unforgiving tarmac which would rip holes in school trousers and leave stinging, bloody palms if you succumbed to a bad tackle and ended up crashing to the ground. During lessons, my friends and I would sneakily swap Panini stickers ('Got. Got. Got. NEED!'), discuss transfer gossip ('Paul Gascoigne to Lazio for £5m? No player is worth that!') and exchange interminable, tiresome banter about our respective clubs. There were plenty of Manchester United and Liverpool fans in my year, but I nestled myself in a friendship group forged by gathering the jetsam and flotsam. My mates all supported unfashionable teams that were the butt of everyone else's jokes. Among us there were fans of Southend United, Crystal Palace, Middlesbrough, Watford and Oxford United. An honorary member of our group was one of the school's PE teachers, Andy Sibson, who supported Leicester City.

A couple of times a year, my form tutor would call me to the front of the class and hand me a worryingly official-looking letter. What was it? A detention notice? No, it was from Mr Sibson, and it would simply say '1-0' or whatever the score was by which Leicester had just beaten Brighton. Preposterously, he also insisted that the school team wore the full Leicester City home kit, much to the confusion of opponents and to the annoyance of kids who supported the 'big' teams.

Teachers like Mr Sibson helped make school a little more enjoyable for introverted little nerds like me. Being talked to like an adult and engaging with grown-ups in conversations which were nothing to do with the curriculum really meant a lot to the kids who didn't necessarily fit in. Andy Sibson died aged 51 while playing football a few years ago. He never got to see his team win the Premier League but there is no doubt he made a difference to many young football fans, and every time I think of Leicester I think of him.

After a school day was over, my friends and I would head straight to the local park and play football until darkness prevented us from seeing the ball, when we'd reluctantly traipse to our homes and play Subbuteo on the living room floor or *Sensible Soccer* on the Nintendo. On days when my buddies were unable to go to the park, I'd play football on my own in my parents' back garden. I would construct all manner of scenarios, which almost exclusively involved me playing for Brighton and being the hero in a dramatic victory. While the cool kids spent their evenings smoking cigarettes and embroiling themselves in dangerous liaisons with girls, my nights involved a football and a vivid imagination.

***

AND AWAY

I started going to away games with my dad. We often travelled on the coach with the Junior Seagulls, which was the Albion fan club for under-16s, and I would stare out of the window in wonder at parts of England I had never before seen. We'd stop at service stations to stock up on sugary snacks and even sugarier drinks for the next leg of the journey, queuing at the checkout behind other clubs' fans as they ventured on their own away days. Service stations on Saturday mornings are brilliant places to be. It was like going on holiday for an afternoon every other week, if Stoke and Middlesbrough could be considered holiday destinations.

Upon arrival at a ground, we would circumnavigate the alien construction in search of the souvenir shop, where I would buy a pin badge or a pennant from a member of staff with an unusual accent. Then, we'd find the away entrance and I'd be swallowed by this unfamiliar structure.

My first away game was at West Bromwich Albion. It was a surreal experience. Everything was similar yet entirely different. The same green pitch but mowed with a different pattern. Fans sung the same Albion-related songs but with a West Midlands twang, and they wore scarves which were blue but a slightly darker shade than ours. Just as they did at the Goldstone, the players emerged from the tunnel in the middle of the main stand and the managers sat in dugouts either side of it; but the stand was bigger and the dugouts were of a different design. The layer of mist which hung over proceedings, coupled with the weird merging of the familiar and the new, made me feel as though I had entered the twilight zone.

I would eventually come to realise that this sense of altered familiarity is one of the most appealing things about football; an understanding of how things work and of being part of a world which has a specific order. Just as football fans find comfort in the routine of a matchday, they can step into a stadium anywhere on earth and, even if they don't understand a word anyone is saying, the metalanguage of football still makes perfect sense and offers a feeling of belonging. I went to a league game in Latvia a few years ago. I couldn't fathom what was being said over the tannoy, I didn't know who any of the players were, where either team stood in the league, what the supporters around me were talking about, or what their songs meant, and yet I felt entirely in my comfort zone.

A few weeks after the West Brom game, I went to Stoke City's ground. That was where I first saw Albion score an away goal. It was odd to be celebrating amongst a few hundred people as thousands stood in silence. I'd repeatedly heard the distant cheers of visiting supporters at the Goldstone, but had no idea of the pure exhilaration of being part of it; the joy of seeing something that we had woken early and travelled miles and miles for, in hope rather than expectation.

Travelling with the Junior Seagulls often included the added bonus of a game being arranged between ourselves and the junior team of Albion's opponents that matchday, usually at a school close to the stadium. We weren't really a proper team, as such. We never trained together, and the ability levels of the players varied wildly, but the important thing was that all were welcome. This might sound horribly trite, but the sense of inclusion was the best thing about it.

We were a mess of a team with vastly different heights, weights, fitness and skills, all playing in mismatched kit. We looked like the Bash Street Kids from *The Beano* and we often got spanked. We once lost 15-0 to Charlton and the kid I was marking scored a double hat-trick. I say 'kid' but he was massive and had a beard. Very occasionally though, we tasted glory, like when we hit an injury-time equaliser at Mansfield Town and celebrated as if we'd won the World Cup. Those moments remain as precious to me as anything the first team did during this time.

After we'd played, we'd mingle with our opponents, filling our faces with crisps and more fizzy pop before heading to the ground to watch the first team, usually still in our kits and covered in mud and grass stains. A day which involved a coach journey with my mates, service station stop-offs, playing a football match and then watching the Albion pretty much represented perfection. Sometimes things didn't go to plan though, such as the disastrous trip to Preston North End. The itinerary included leaving early to take on Preston's junior team at lunchtime, then a pie with our northern counterparts before heading to the stadium. The itinerary certainly did not include our coach breaking down on the motorway a few minutes from Preston and sitting in the middle lane for a couple of hours. We eventually arrived, aching and hungry, at 3.05pm. The game was already underway as we stepped into the stadium, where the home side were in the process of dismantling Albion on a plastic pitch which seemed incongruously space-age in comparison to the wooden stands that loomed over it. It wasn't a snazzy 4G pitch, but one of the hard, sandy, bouncy surfaces which gave the teams that adopted them (Preston, Oldham Athletic, Luton Town, QPR) an outrageous advantage. By 3.20pm, Preston were three goals to the good and our arduous journey had been rendered entirely pointless. Maybe my memory is deceiving me but I'm sure the Preston players wore tracksuit bottoms during the match so they didn't take all the skin off their legs when slide-tackling.

I would soon come to learn that this kind of doomed away defeat is part and parcel of supporting a football club. Further examples of this are consecutive trips I took to West Ham over two seasons. On my first visit to the Boleyn Ground, the Seagulls were 1-0 up and reasonably comfortable until defender Steve Gatting, under no pressure whatsoever, inexplicably lobbed the ball into his own goal. We went on to lose 3-1. If ever there was an example of how ridiculous and frustrating it was to support Brighton in those days, that was it. The following season, we were 1-0 up again when tricky Hammers winger Stuart Slater hit a screamer into the top corner and went on to score another to win the game. I was sitting in the home end, as our Junior Seagulls group often did on away trips, and as the fans opened their Cockney lungs to celebrate the winner, they startled a pigeon nesting in the roof, causing it to do a poo directly into my full cup of Diet Coke!

Most football fans have had a '3-0 defeat after a nightmare journey' experience. I'm not sure they will have had a 'finding a dead rat the size of a small dog in the toilets at Bournemouth's Dean Court on a freezing cold Tuesday night' experience, as I once did, but I'm certain that anyone who has watched a match from a terrace can empathise with what happened to me at Bristol Rovers. As a youngster, I saw Brighton play away at Rovers on two occasions. Both games were played in Bath (not in *the* bath, but in the very lovely city near Bristol). The first time I visited, Albion won 3-1. It was a sunny afternoon in a gorgeous part of the world and there was a huge contingent of Albion fans on the terrace behind the goal. If that sounds like a good day out, it was, but I somehow contrived to miss all of Brighton's goals.

Goals, especially away goals, can be rare creatures. As Oscar Wilde nearly said, 'To miss one may be regarded as a misfortune; to miss two looks like carelessness.' So how on earth did I manage to miss all three? Well, I was in the toilet for the first one. Too much of the aforementioned fizzy pop. It's the strangest sensation to realise you've missed a goal because you're in the loo. You can't rush back outside to see what is happening, so you have to just stand there and finish your business, half-happy that the team has scored and half-annoyed that you didn't see it. It's difficult to correlate the two emotions.

When the second goal went in, I was queuing for a burger. The burnt, gristly slab in a dry white bun didn't represent value for money and was certainly not worth missing another goal for. Looking back, I have no idea why I ever bothered buying food at football grounds during this time. It was exclusively horrible and I'm sure the grotesque meat that I forced through my system played a big part in me becoming a vegetarian in adult life.

Incidentally, whilst football stadium food has improved, vegetarianism doesn't seem to have stretched to some parts of the country. I was at Chesterfield's stadium a handful of years ago and I visited the food kiosk to ask what they had in terms of vegetarian delights. The slack-jawed teenage cashier looked at me blankly. There was one non-meat option on the menu that evening, a packet of Maltesers. And a criminally overpriced packet of Maltesers at that.

Anyway, back to sun-drenched Bath in the early 90s. Albion found themselves 2-1 ahead in the second half and were kicking towards the away fans. Having already missed both goals, I was determined not to blink. I'd already emptied my bladder and eaten some 'food', so I had no reason to go anywhere. Just as Brighton launched an attack, the world's tallest man positioned himself directly in front of me. So, while everyone else enjoyed watching blond bombshell Johnny Byrne secure the win, all I got was an eyeful of suede jacket.

Generally, I love standing on terraces, and I choose them over seats whenever the rare opportunity presents itself these days, but as a vertically challenged kid I often spent entire games craning my neck to get any kind of view at all. For instance, when Brighton played Manchester United at Old Trafford in the FA Cup in 1993, I saw virtually nothing for 90 minutes. I suppose it's akin to being a short person at a gig and seeing only the light show. On this anomalous occurrence in Bath, however, my view was almost entirely perfect and yet I still missed all the noteworthy moments. I felt like I was watching one of the censored movies in *Cinema Paradiso*, in which all the kissing scenes were removed by order of the local priest. Without witnessing a single goal, it was as though the win hadn't happened, and there was a slight emptiness to the experience.

The only remedy would be to return to the same stadium the following season and hope for better luck. A year on, I saw all of Bristol Rovers' goals, clear as crystal, in a 4-1 defeat. On the way home, the Junior Seagulls' coach broke down.

***

DENTIST'S CHAIR

When there was a midweek away fixture, my parents would invent a visit to the dentist so that I could secure the afternoon off school and travel to the game. Such was the frequency of my time in the 'dentist's chair', some of my teachers must have thought my teeth were in a woeful state. One time, however, I sheepishly handed my form tutor a note from my parents telling him I had a dental appointment and the giant of a woodwork teacher scanned it, signed it off and then, as I left the room, gave me a wink and said, 'Enjoy the game.' What a man.

Basically, I yearned to go to every Albion match possible because of a genuine fear of missing out. FOMO, if you will. I was certain that any game I skipped would be the one where something outrageous occurred. Indeed, capricious fortune dictated that this was often the case. Despite the frequency of my away journeys, I didn't go to Fulham when Brighton won 6-1 and I wasn't at Brentford to see a 2-0 FA Cup win in which Garry Nelson apparently scored one of Albion's greatest ever goals.

It has become one of those mythical strikes, about which people go all misty-eyed. There's no TV footage of it so if, like me, you weren't there ... hard luck. It's strange, in this age where nothing seems to be of any value unless it's shared online, to think that there were high-profile football matches played as recently as the late 80s that weren't filmed at all. They live as statistics and in the memories of the few thousand people who were in attendance. This, of course, means a 25-yard strike, over the course of being recounted through the years, becomes exaggerated to a 40-yard screamer, and so on.

When was the last time you went to a game and weren't then able to re-watch the action, either on TV or online? Eons ago, I suspect. Even as a kid I used to eagerly sit by the VCR during the local news and press 'record' when Brighton's goals were shown. I had dozens of homemade compilation videos of highlights. I've still got them, although of course I no longer have anything on which to play them.

Despite not witnessing Nelson's wondergoal, I was lucky enough to have plenty of amazing experiences obsessively following my team on the road when I was younger, such as having my photo taken on the pitch with Kevin Keegan before a 1-0 win at Newcastle United. I also won a bunch of money illegally playing the fruit machines at a service station as an underage kid on the way to a match at Blackpool, and I was there when winger Mark Barham curled a late beauty at Hull City to boost a stuttering play-off push.

Regarding that Barham goal at Hull's Boothferry Park in 1991, Albion had won just once in the previous seven Division Two (now Championship) games and hadn't scored in their last four, yet the team was somehow still occupying a top-six spot with a few matches remaining. The game had been awful and it felt as though a positive campaign was petering out. However, with a couple of minutes to go, Barham collected the ball just outside the box and curled it towards goal, where it nestled deliciously in the top corner. With that one moment of magic, the play-off dream was back on. There was delirium on the away terrace. Brighton's travelling support wasn't especially big that day, meaning there was an abundance of room for fans to celebrate. I ran aimlessly but jubilantly along the front of the terrace. Another young lad was charging in the opposite direction and we threw our arms around each other and jumped in circles. This kid was a total stranger, yet there we were, embracing like long-lost friends.

Any football fan who regularly travels to away games will know that these moments must be cherished due to their infrequency. Disappointment is far more commonplace. Not the kind of anomalous Preston experience I mentioned a few pages ago, but rather run-of-the-mill disappointment. A journey I took to Hartlepool United as a kid embodied this. Before I had even set off, I knew the day would likely be fruitless. It was a couple of years after the aforementioned Hull victory and Albion needed three points from the penultimate game of the season to stand a chance of making the play-offs (such was the club's trajectory at the time, we were now in the division below). However, in order to sneak into the end-of-season shake-up, we were also relying on a few of our rivals to slip up, which was unlikely. Regardless of the odds being stacked heavily against the Albion, I wasn't going to give up on the season until it was mathematically impossible for us to gain promotion (FOMO, remember), so I set off on my own at some horrific hour of the morning and headed forever north on the coach.

While I tried to bury a general sense of foreboding about the afternoon's outcome by playing on my Gameboy and filling my face with confectionery delights, I couldn't help feeling that it might have been a better idea to have stayed home and watched the telly instead. At the ground, I stood on an uncovered terrace with a few hundred other foolhardy souls at the mercy of a relentless, biting, gale-force wind which attacked us from the North Sea. To our left, just a fence and a couple of yards separated Brighton fans from a bunch of home-town louts yelling homophobic abuse in our direction from before kick-off for the duration of the afternoon. By the time the Albion players found themselves a couple of goals behind and playing like they were already on their summer holidays, I was dreaming of being at home with *Noel's House Party* on the telly and dinner in the oven. As the wind continued to batter my face into numbness, Hartlepool seemed like the worst place in the world. The final whistle blew on a lifeless 2-0 defeat and I trudged back to the coach with the same feeling I have felt on too many other occasions: the desire to click my heels together three times and be instantly transported home, rather than having to endure a seven-hour coach journey, the batteries of my Gameboy long since dead.

Confusingly, my FOMO was counterbalanced by a growing concern that my presence was a jinx on the team. I'm not the kind of person that normally believes in hocus-pocus, but it seemed that results were broadly better when I didn't attend away games than when I did. Take my first ever trip to Wolverhampton Wanderers as a perfect example. Brighton had never lost to Wolves in their entire league history and had won every single time they had faced them at their Molineux stadium. Playing them away meant a guaranteed three points, so I ventured to the West Midlands with high hopes. By the time I took my seat slightly after kick-off (traffic jams), Albion were already

1-0 behind and we chased shadows for the remainder of a timid 2-0 loss. I still blame myself for that defeat. To offer further evidence of being jinxed, I was at Selhurst Park when arch-rivals Crystal Palace humiliated Brighton 5-0 (more on this later), but I didn't attend a few years later to see a legendary 1-0 victory there, and I wasn't there when Anthony Knockaert won a Premier League fixture with an absolute beauty into the top corner.

Of course, I'm not jinxed. There is no such thing. But the fact that a normally sensible person like me would even consider this to be a possibility illustrates how rational thought goes out of the window when it comes to football. It is replaced by ridiculous superstition. Fans can trace most superstitions back to their origins. They wear a certain item of clothing to a game and the team wins, so they wear it again the following week. The team wins again and it becomes a ritual. A supporter takes a slightly different route to the ground one day, the team wins, so they start taking that same route every match. These strange quirks continue for weeks, months, years. When a fan's team is victorious, it's all because they were wearing their lucky underpants. If they forget to pull on said pants and their team loses, they'll see it as their own fault.

These superstitions take one of two directions. They either run their course and are abandoned once supporters realise that their ritualistic actions have absolutely no bearing on how their team plays, or they remain an integral part of a matchday routine, ad infinitum. When the team achieves a good result, it's thanks to these superstitions, and when they lose it's in spite of the lucky underpants, not because of them. We tell ourselves that, without the power of our supernatural undies, the defeat would have been even worse.

Why do we entertain these illogical beliefs? Maybe it's to feel less helpless. When the players step on to the pitch on a Saturday afternoon, there isn't much we can do to assist them in achieving our common goal. We shout and sing to create a good atmosphere, but considering how invested we are, it's frustrating to have no other way of contributing to a team's success; so we invent these odd rituals to feel as though we are, through some mystical power, helping the players. Or maybe pure desperation for success leads to these superstitions. We'll try anything and we're happy to throw rational thought out of the window in the vain hope that there is some supernatural, universal link between a pair of pants and a football club's fortunes.

It's not just fans though. Players put on their kit in a particular order or insist on listening to a certain selection of songs before a match. Managers, too, can be susceptible to such things. An example of this is how one of the best kits in Albion's history was almost canned after just a few uses. When, in 2000, the team suffered a couple of bad results while wearing their new Centenary strip, manager Micky Adams apparently swore that if they lost when they next wore it, it would never be seen again. Thankfully, considering how the club shop had already received a mass order of replica Centenary shirts, Albion won that match and the kit went on to be synonymous with one of the most successful spells in the club's history.

Back in the 80s, as well as our lucky mix tape, the Townsend family had a superstition which, rather than being proactive, was entirely reactive. Our ritual didn't occur pre-match but was instead put into action while the game was taking place. We saw it very much as a troubleshooting measure. If Albion went 1-0 down, it was up to the Townsends to put out that particular fire. Here's what happened: every time Brighton fell behind, each member of the Townsend family would remove their left sock. Oddly, I have no idea how or why this bizarre ritual came about. There must have been a reason for it but I can't for the life of me remember what it was. I do know that it initially occurred exclusively while we were listening to away games on the radio, but we soon started doing it at matches we were attending. This is how things panned out:

1. The opposing team would take the lead.
2. All Townsends would peel off their left sock.
3. Albion would, at some point, equalise and often go on to win.

It was that simple. We were doing a great job in assisting the players' success. Never mind that this all started during the 1987/88 season, when the team was brilliant. No, it was all down to the exposure of our left feet.

The left sock removal gradually fizzled out. To take off a shoe, then a sock, then replace said shoe on a football terrace was, quite frankly, the behaviour of lunatics. Also, it led to one very cold ankle in the winter.

***

MY FAVOURITE GAME

Everyone has an all-time favourite football match, don't they? Well, Brighton's 1990/91 season featured mine.

Nowadays, I can barely recall what I did last week, but time will never erase my recollection of one cold January in 1991 when, as a 14-year-old, I made my way north to the home of The Beatles, of Brookside, of the best football team in the land.

I didn't know it at the time, but the 1990/91 campaign would be the last period of genuine positivity at Brighton for some years. Against a backdrop of growing financial uncertainty and modest attendances, Albion manager Barry Lloyd had built a decent side. Lloyd took some stick from fans at times, which I feel was unfair. He was undoubtedly astute and wily, and repeatedly pulled together a hotchpotch of players that nobody else wanted and turned them into an impressive football team. The first half of the season went well enough and we really began to go through the gears in the new year. Newcastle United were smashed 4-2 at home with one of Lloyd's unknowns, Bryan Wade, scoring all four goals. Wolves were dispatched and West Ham United were beaten at the Goldstone. However, the thing that really left fans to think that maybe, just maybe, we were good enough to be promoted to the top flight was an FA Cup fourth-round tie against Liverpool.

I watched the cup draw on good old Ceefax and jumped around my parents' lounge in delight when Albion were paired with the giants of English football. The Brighton directors were probably doing the same thing in their own houses. Talk was rife about how perilous the financial situation had become, so this game would provide a payday which could help keep the bailiffs from the door, at least for the time being. I'm not sure Lloyd and his staff would have been so excited, though. In the early 90s, Liverpool were a seemingly unstoppable football force. The likes of John Barnes, Ian Rush, Peter Beardsley, Steve McMahon and Jan Molby played attractive, expansive football under the guidance of player/manager, Kenny Dalglish. Teams would go to Anfield and freeze; Crystal Palace were famously stuffed 9-0 there the previous season. Albion's coaching team must have been wondering how on earth they were going to keep the score down.

I was one of over 5,000 Albion fans who made the journey to Merseyside, and the first stop upon arriving at the famous old stadium was the Hillsborough memorial, just outside the ground. The footballing landscape has changed a lot since the tragedy, and in the 21st century we are lucky to be able to witness football in a broadly safe environment. But those of us who went to games in the old days know that stadiums were potentially dangerous places. Many of us will have felt less than fully safe in a football ground at some point, but we put our faith in the authorities on the assumption that they were in control of the situation. Hillsborough proved we were foolhardy to do so. The fact that what occurred at Hillsborough didn't happen to you or me at a different stadium was as much down to pure luck as anything. We could easily have gone to a game and not come back. I cannot suitably put into words how much respect I have for the families of the victims of the Hillsborough disaster. They were slandered, lied to and treated with utter contempt by figures of authority, but they kept fighting for justice for decades with dignity and fortitude, no matter how weary they became and how hopeless things seemed.

Having paid tribute to the Liverpool supporters who lost their lives, Albion fans filed into Anfield and occupied the multi-coloured blocks of seats behind the goal, excited yet fearing a thrashing. This was the first time I had been in such a cathedral of football, and I spent most of the first half in awe of my surroundings. The legendary Kop, at the far end of the ground, was a vast terrace upon which thousands of supporters, their heads as small as full stops, were making an imposing din.

Pleasingly and somewhat surprisingly, it was 0-0 at half-time and the consensus in the away end was that we were playing rather well. Full-back John Crumplin, whose slightly tongue-in-cheek nickname was 'Football Genius', was keeping actual football genius John Barnes in his back pocket. Almost immediately after the restart, however, moustachioed goal machine Ian Rush snuck behind our defence and scored in front of the Kop. Soon after, he did it again. The noise at Anfield increased further. Red flags were raised, scarves were held aloft and home supporters hailed a certain victory. At 2-0 down, we were surely cooked.

What happened next took everyone by surprise. Brighton's Paul McCarthy, a strong, galloping Irish centre-back, was knocked off balance in the area, directly in front of the away end. All eyes turned to the referee, who hesitated briefly before blowing on his whistle and pointing to the penalty spot. Penalties for the away side were a rare thing at Anfield back then. Mike Small slammed the ball home, meaning we had seen our team score against these megastars. That was enough to qualify this as a great day. So, when Johnny Byrne headed an equaliser a few minutes later, it led to such chaos in the away end that you'd have thought we'd won the FA Cup, rather than scoring an equaliser in the fourth round. Liverpool were visibly rattled. This wasn't how things usually happened here. What's more, if there was going to be a winner, it looked like being scored by this bunch of chancers from the south coast. Albion's heroes had their tails up and were going for unlikely glory. They almost got it too, but for a good save from goalkeeper Bruce Grobbelaar towards the conclusion of the match.

What a game. The Liverpool fans, despite their disappointment, magnanimously clapped the Brighton players off the pitch while the away end gave a rousing chorus of the club anthem, 'Sussex by the Sea'. If I close my eyes, I'm there now, standing on my plastic seat, holding my scarf aloft and yelling the words at the top of my voice. Whilst the fact that my all-time favourite match didn't even result in a win succinctly illustrates what it's like to be a supporter of Brighton, or indeed, of any number of teams; there is something invigorating about being in an away end with thousands of fellow fans at the conclusion of a successful match. Everyone sings louder than they do at their home ground, the sense of achievement is that bit stronger, the camaraderie intensified.

The best thing about the Liverpool game ending all square was that it meant we got to do it all over again a few days later and, if anything, the replay at the Goldstone was even more breathless. It played out over 120 floodlit minutes. Albion went behind before unthinkably turning the match around to lead 2-1 in extra time while also having a perfectly good goal disallowed. Liverpool equalised and then showed the extra bit of quality required in these situations. They won by the odd goal in five, but it was thrilling to have pushed the best team in Britain to their limit over 210 minutes. There was a taut intensity to the cup tie that simply cannot be replicated away from the sporting arena.

The Liverpool double-header spurred Albion on in the league. They built up a head of steam and, on the final day of the season, found themselves one win away from a place in the play-offs. This was despite having a negative goal difference. Generally, teams don't get promoted with a minus goal difference, but then Brighton have never done things the easy way.

***

BORDERING ON UNBELIEVABLE

On an overcast May day, Ipswich Town, resplendent in a bright orange away strip, stood between Albion and a first-ever appearance in the play-offs. Brighton took an early lead and Ipswich looked uninterested in doing much about equalising until, in the second half, a clumsy tackle led to the away side winning a penalty. Town's Chris Kiwomya stepped up. His shot was firm but Player of the Season and magnificently named goalkeeper Perry Digweed guessed correctly and flung himself to his left. At full stretch, he planted both palms flatly behind the ball and deflected it to safety. The crowd went berserk and, directly behind the goal in my ill-fitting ball kid tracksuit, I did the same.

We'd survived this potential derailment of our promotion push; the play-offs were a certainty now. Only, they weren't. Shortly afterwards, Kiwomya scored from open play. Our party had been well and truly pooped and the season was set to fizzle out on its final day. How typical of Brighton. The clock ticked insistently towards full time. Ipswich supporters sang songs which mocked Albion's apparent near miss, while Brighton fans in the North Stand behind me pressed their ears to portable radios. If Albion's rivals for sixth place, Barnsley, failed to win, then a 1-1 draw at the Goldstone would still be good enough. All we had to do was match their result. To increase the sense of disappointment though, news filtered through of a Barnsley victory. They had leapfrogged the Seagulls into sixth place, the final play-off spot. Their fans were apparently already on the pitch celebrating. The clock ticked past the 90-minute mark at the Goldstone. The season was in stoppage time.

Needing to score, Albion attempted one last attack down the slope toward the south goal. Johnny Byrne was fouled on the edge of the box, a free kick was awarded and the physiotherapist scurried across the pitch to tend to the wounded player. Treatment took an eternity as Byrne lay crumpled on the turf. It was as though someone had pressed pause during a movie's final scene to go and make a cup of tea.

Eventually, Byrne rose gingerly to his feet. The Ipswich wall was in place. Silence descended. Captain Dean Wilkins stood over the ball. He was a magician from a set piece and, like all great sporting moments, what came next seemed to happen in slow motion. The ball cleared the wall and curled towards the right-hand post. The Ipswich goalkeeper flung his body across goal. There was no sound from the crowd, as sharp intakes of breath were held within lungs. Then, something magnificent happened. The ball's trajectory was suddenly halted. Not by the goalkeeper or by the post, but by the net. It bulged in the beautiful way that it does, before the ball feathered down the side netting and settled on the ground.

There was a brief, pregnant pause as the realisation of what had just happened went from eyes to brains to hearts, and then ... pandemonium. If this had been a film, it would have been criticised for being too far-fetched; the team captain curling a brilliant free kick into the top corner in injury time at the end of the season to ensure a play-off place. Being a Brighton fan at that time was rarely so good that it bordered on unbelievable. It had happened, though. It had actually happened.

There are few greater feelings in life than a crucial injury-time winner, and the fact that moments like these are so rare make them even more special. The pure, unshackled joy of it. Nothing else in the world matters or, indeed, even exists for a few seconds as you share the same release of delight and relief with thousands of like-minded people. In these instances, we are all lottery winners. Moments earlier, every one of us had assumed our hopes of victory were to be dashed and then, in an instant, our hearts are pounding and we are yelling with joy. Unexpected, unscripted, unbridled.

The sense of delight was such that it provoked a pitch invasion from the North Stand. Supporters danced on to the playing surface as Wilkins wheeled away in celebration. He slid on to his back and was immediately piled on by his team-mates. Fans who had momentarily lost themselves suddenly remembered they were on the playing field while a game was taking place and quickly vacated via the nearest touchline. Nobody bothered heading back on to the terraces; instead they stood at the edge of the pitch as if they were watching a Sunday League game down the local park. Their trainers kissed the white touchlines, ready to run straight back on to the pitch at the final peep of the referee's whistle.

They didn't have to wait long. The game was concluded with no further drama and, as players and officials sprinted to the safety of the tunnel, thousands of people flooded back on to the pitch. Nothing had been won yet but our season had just been extended in the most marvellous way. This was worth celebrating. Goodness knows how Barnsley fans felt as news of Brighton's late winner reached them while they were dancing on their pitch. Not great, I imagine.

It was the perfect afternoon for everyone related to the Albion, not least for the skipper. Wilkins had a few critics among Brighton fans, but he was a beautiful player and was capable of doing things others simply could not manage. Several years later, I played in a beach football match with him and his skilfulness was stunning. While we were warming up, I crossed balls for him and, barefooted, he effortlessly volleyed every single one of my erratic deliveries into the top corner. I'm sure every football fan has harboured daydreams of turning professional, or wondered what might have been had they trained harder as a kid, but playing alongside Wilkins in that beach football match demonstrated the chasm between nobodies like me and those that make it.

Another indisputable fact about Wilkins was that he really cared about Brighton & Hove Albion. Immediately after his final game for the club in the mid-90s, I watched as he shed a tear in the Goldstone tunnel. He wasn't to know that he would come back to manage the team some years down the line and would do so with distinction, coaching a bunch of youngsters to play attractive, winning football. He was a popular figure at the club and is still greeted warmly whenever he returns. I doubt there has ever been a time, upon visiting, that someone hasn't talked to him about that late winner against Ipswich. I'm sure he doesn't mind. After all, there are worse things for which to be remembered.

***

NO ONE LIKES THEM

Victory over Ipswich Town set up a two-legged play-off semi-final against Millwall. I didn't hold out much hope of victory, as I'd been at Millwall's ground, The Den, earlier in the season when the home side tore Brighton apart. What a terrifying place that stadium was, especially for an away fan in the home end. As I mentioned earlier, on Junior Seagulls trips we often found ourselves sitting with our opposition's equivalents in the home areas of the ground. This was never as enjoyable as being with the rest of the Albion supporters, but the fans that surrounded us were usually friendly enough and, for the most part, we were able to cheer our team without inhibition. Not so at Millwall. Just the icy stares from the hardened faces in the seats near ours were enough to ensure that Albion's junior contingent and their parents sat in absolute silence from first whistle until last during that 3-0 loss. It was very thoughtful of the Brighton players to help us remain quiet on that day, by giving us literally nothing to shout about. It would be accurate to say that Brighton fans weren't exactly relishing the prospect of going there again for the play-off match.

Before that though, the first leg at the Goldstone saw a young English prospect called Teddy Sheringham impress early on as the Lions attacked the south goal. The Londoners soon took a 1-0 lead and remained in complete control throughout the first half, with the large away contingent in good voice. I was standing on the track in front of the away terrace during the first half and I had a whole lot of colourful language directed at me throughout the 45 minutes. Being positioned there was most certainly a case of drawing the short straw when we were choosing ball kid positions that day.

Albion equalised before half-time and really seized the tie in the second period. Mike Small put the Seagulls in front and, two minutes later, he deftly headed the ball on for winger Clive Walker to run through and make it three. Small, the undoubted star of the show, then produced a beautiful assist for Robert Codner, who calmly slotted home to make the score 4-1.

Nothing gets the blood pumping as hard and fast as when your team scores goals in quick succession. You've barely caught your breath from celebrating when, bang, the ball hits the net again. It's thrilling to see two goals within a couple of minutes of each other, so when three goals are scored in seven minutes in a play-off semi-final, well, little compares to that.

Millwall were punch drunk and clinging to the ropes, and the remaining half-hour played out with almost no incident. If you watch the highlights on YouTube, it's remarkable to see how much time Albion ate up by passing the ball back to the goalkeeper. Total Football it was not, but it ensured that Albion would take a three-goal advantage to London. It wasn't long before the backpass rule would be brought in, and there was a lot of fuss about how it would ruin the game. It didn't, of course.

Despite a healthy lead, no Brighton supporter was assuming they were safely through to a Wembley final. Football fans never underestimate their team's ability to let them down, and if you wanted an intimidating place to host a play-off second leg, then you couldn't choose a better venue than The Den. It was located on Cold Blow Lane, for heaven's sake. In spite of the less than enjoyable experience on my previous visit, I was in attendance. The Den? Aged 14? On a school night? What were my parents thinking? Well, like me, they were thinking, 'I really hope the Albion back line doesn't buckle under this intense Millwall pressure.' I know this because they were at the game too, watching Millwall throw everything at Brighton from the first whistle. It was no surprise when the home side took the lead after a few minutes, signalling that it was going to be a long, nervy night. Albion kept the score at 1-0 until the second half and, as Millwall's attacks grew increasingly desperate and greater in personnel, the Seagulls picked them off with two smartly taken counter-attacking goals. We were going to Wembley.

After the final whistle, a big bunch of Millwall fans, furious at the defeat, refused to leave the ground and instead engaged in a running battle with the authorities on the terrace. A police officer's helmet was set alight at one point (it wasn't on the police officer's head at the time).

Brighton achieved this impressive 2-1 victory wearing a pink away kit. These were seemingly unenlightened times in that particular corner of London and the players were roundly whistled by home supporters throughout. Their thinking, presumably, was that pink equals gay and homosexuality deserved to be mocked. Sadly, even though decades have passed since that night, some football followers still consider casual homophobia as 'banter'. As we all know, it's not. It's abhorrent and there is no place for it in society. Should marginalised supporters be subjected to such abuse when they attend a football game? Of course not. Should residents of Brighton and Hove accept such mockery of their cosmopolitan city and its vibrant culture? No. Football has spent too long in the dark ages. It is supposed to be an all-encompassing 'beautiful game', and yet it is being held back by those who think it's funny to sing homophobic songs, to shout furious abuse or to send racist messages online. The way that rivalry and banter can so quickly turn to racism and homophobia is indicative of how far we still have to go to combat prejudice and hatred in football and in society at large. The fact that many people still think it's okay to write something horrific on social media from the safety of their anonymous account is an example of why the anti-racism movements and the Pride supporters' clubs are so important.

Talking of fans behaving reprehensibly, later that year I'd be back at The Den for another midweek game between Millwall and Brighton. My third trip to Cold Blow Lane in a few months? I really knew how to enjoy myself. In the second half, Millwall's Chris Armstrong scythed down Albion's John Robinson, causing an almighty ruckus between the two teams. Pantomime oohs and aahs echoed from the half-empty stands when, from nowhere, a teenage fan jumped the barrier and drop-kicked Robinson squarely in his back. It was an implausible occurrence and caused all hell to break loose. Albion goalkeeper Mark Beeney sprinted from his area to grab the offender, literally by the scruff of his neck, while a group of Phil Mitchells in the Millwall end attempted to climb into the Brighton enclosure to dish out a few beatings. It was as frightening a sight as this skinny, teenage wimp from sleepy Eastbourne had ever seen. Before the Millwall supporters could pull themselves over the fence and cause havoc on the away terrace though, the local constabulary intervened.

Many years later I'd end up living in south London and I'd see that Millwall FC works hard to improve the lives of those in the community, and that their fanbase is – like most clubs – mostly made up of thoroughly decent humans, but on this particular early 90s evening I can't deny that I breathed a sigh of relief when I made it back to the safety of Eastbourne in one piece.

The previous, pink-kitted victory at Millwall in the play-offs set up a final against Notts County at Wembley, with the winner earning a place at the top table of English football. Having performed so well in pink in the semi-final second leg, I expected to see Brighton's players walk out at Wembley pink and proud. I was not expecting the team to step on to the hallowed turf dressed like giant red and white Chewits wrappers. Large red swirls on a white base. The shorts had the same pattern. Sartorial suicide. The home equivalent was an infamous deck chair effort with stripy shorts. I recall Albion's shop manager at the time crying when she first saw them.

The play-off final in 1991 was only the club's third appearance at the famous old stadium, meaning it should have been one of the defining moments of any Brighton fan's life. The day, though, was entirely deflating. By the time Dean Wilkins scored a late goal, Notts County were already 3-0 up. The carnival atmosphere before kick-off, all face paint and flag waving, dissipated as soon as County took an early stranglehold on the game, and Brighton's supporters were forced to watch a season of hard work amount to precisely nothing over the course of 90 miserable minutes. It wasn't a remotely enjoyable game. The play-off final never is for the loser. There is too much at stake. At least with other cup finals you can treat the occasion as a one-off bonus. If your team wins, great! If they lose then, sure, it's disappointing, but it doesn't have much bearing on the following season. A loss in the play-off final brings nine months of toil to a heartbreaking conclusion and it's difficult to garner any positives from such an experience.

I left the stadium with slumped shoulders, frustrated that the players hadn't really given a true representation of themselves. I sat on the coach back to Brighton, my red and white face paint now nothing more than an annoyance and my souvenir flag an unwanted reminder of just how football can let you down.

It is widely accepted that a play-off final defeat is one of the hardest footballing blows from which to recover. Anyone who doubts this theory need only look at Brighton's performance the following season. The Wembley hangover was such that, rather than the team challenging at the top of the table again, they were relegated. As hangovers go, that's pretty huge.

***

LET THE HARD TIMES ROLL

Failure to reach England's top division resulted in several miserable years for Brighton & Hove Albion and culminated in the darkest days in the club's history. The early to mid-90s was an era when local newspaper *The Argus* seemed to always prefix the club's name with the words 'cash-strapped'.

By now, I had outgrown my ball kid tracksuit and, rather than going down the Keith Cuss route and becoming a ball man, I instead took on a part-time job in the souvenir shop, where my mother still worked. This counter service store was in a large cabin at the Goldstone, and I worked matchdays and the occasional weekday afternoon around my A-level studies. The tough economic climate at the club was obvious. Sizeable weeds climbed through the cracks in the terracing, the toilets smelled horrific and a big brown rat took residence in the shop's stock room. Staffing levels across the club were skeletal. It was clear that a large injection of funds was desperately needed, and there were frequent whispers about some potential takeover or other. I remember a rumour that a courier was due to arrive one lunchtime with documents from an unnamed foreign businessman who was going to save the club from financial ruin. Part of the deal was that the trim on the team's socks would be changed to his home country's colours. I can't remember the country. The courier never came, we weren't saved, the socks remained unaltered. This anecdote's vagueness gives a good impression of what it's like to be a fan or an employee of a club on the brink of going out of business. There is so much hearsay and so many rumours which offer hope and excitement but that usually result in precisely nothing.

Brighton & Hove Albion were in a real mess at this time. Full-time staff sometimes went without pay at the end of the month and, rather than getting a wage slip, were essentially sent an IOU in the form of an apologetic letter. Like many clubs struggling for cash, Albion survived because of very sizeable chunks of goodwill from their employees and the continued generosity of their fans. A 'Save Our Seagulls' auction was held on a local radio station. Supporter groups held fundraisers. Every penny counted. One afternoon, several members of staff sat around a portable radio in the club shop at the Goldstone, nervously waiting to hear the result of a High Court winding-up order. There was due to be a match that evening, but if the news was bad then there would be no game that night and maybe no club by the end of the week. For the full-timers sitting around me, their entire livelihoods were at stake. Brows were wrinkled as news from the High Court began to filter through. The outcome was favourable. The game that night could go ahead. There were no celebrations though, no whooping and cheering, just a few sighs of relief and the softening of jaws and shoulders. Everyone was of the understanding that it was nothing more than a stay of execution. Not long after this, keeper Mark Beeney was sold to Leeds United. This wasn't your everyday transfer either. Beeney's sale facilitated the payment of a tax bill, which kept Brighton & Hove Albion in business. Although he was one of the best goalkeepers many Albion fans had ever seen play for the club, it felt like a simple choice: no Beeney or no Brighton. Whilst, these days, some top-end players are earning hundreds of thousands of pounds a week, this is the kind of trade-off that many teams' supporters have to accept on a regular basis; lose your best players or risk losing your entire club. It seems inequitable.

Before this period, Brighton's financial problems had never been anywhere near the forefront of my mind. When I was a kid, all I cared about was how the team performed. By the time I was an awkward teenager with long, lank hair and acne-ridden cheeks, I had a much clearer understanding that the situation was perilous. I was, however, still far more interested in Albion's fortunes on the pitch and Nirvana's musical output than I was about what went on in the corridors of power. Then a politician called David Bellotti was appointed chief executive and everything would change forever. Soon, like every Albion fan, I would take an unprecedented interest in what was going on behind the scenes of the football club I loved.

When Bellotti first joined, he was given a hero's welcome. I think he even walked around the perimeter of the pitch shaking hands with fans before one home game. He had previously achieved unlikely success as a Liberal candidate in Conservative-leaning Eastbourne, and hopes were high that he could turn things around at the Albion. One of the first major actions after his arrival was the removal of manager Barry Lloyd. The team wasn't performing well and the mood on the terraces had been teetering towards toxicity. Lloyd had grown unpopular with some fans and it was obvious that a change was required, but it was still a sad day for backroom staff when he left. I liked Lloyd as a person and I saw first-hand just how hard he worked, not just on the playing side of things but also with the day-to-day running of the club. However, his replacement, Arsenal and Republic of Ireland legend Liam Brady, was the kind of heavyweight appointment that suggested the club meant business.

Soon after showing Lloyd the door, Bellotti was culling members of the backroom staff as well. One of them was my mother, who had been splitting her time between the club shop and the main office. Within a week of giving her the elbow, he asked her to come back because the club was struggling to function without her. That's entirely true, by the way; I'm not just lavishing undue praise on my mum. Making people redundant to cut costs is a standard measure, but when a business is running on a skeleton staff anyway and when those employees have years of knowledge and experience, removing them is like pulling cogs from a machine. Take out what seems to be a small, dispensable piece and the entire thing stops working. Despite smarting from being given the boot in the first place, my mother still loved the club and therefore accepted Bellotti's U-turn and went back to work. She barely missed a day for the next 20 years.

Although Bellotti had failed to ingratiate himself with the staff, who watched helplessly as several colleagues boxed up their possessions, he seemed to be maintaining a positive façade when dealing with fans and press. His talk of relocating the club to a snazzy new stadium meant that, on the surface, things were looking up. Then the bombshell.

In the summer of 1995, *The Argus* broke the news that Albion's bosses were selling the Goldstone to pay off debts and were moving the club to Fratton Park in Portsmouth. There was no consultation with supporters' groups. They didn't even put out a press release informing fans of this decision. The next day, the same newspaper revealed that plans to eventually return to a stadium in Brighton had already been rejected by the local council. It also transpired that a no-profit clause had been removed from the club's constitution, meaning that directors could now profit if the ground was sold. Two years of relentless supporter protest against chairman Bill Archer, shareholder and former chairman Greg Stanley and chief executive David Bellotti followed. We gave the rat in the shop stockroom a name. We called him David.

***

BELLOTTI

A lot has been written about this tumultuous time in Brighton's history and I don't claim to have expert knowledge of everything that went on. I was just a dumb teenager at the time. For a thorough account of what happened, track down a copy of the excellent book, *Build a Bonfire*. What I can do instead is offer an insight into what it was like to be a peripheral staff member behind the scenes during this period.

Working in the shop on matchdays meant I was part of the front line at the club. When the 1995/96 season started, all supporters wanted to talk to us about was the Portsmouth move. Alas, we had no insights to offer. I'm pretty sure that Bellotti, Archer and Stanley hadn't even bothered to advise senior members of staff what was going on, so plebs like us were never going to be in the loop. Indeed, throughout the entire period of conflict between fans and club owners, the only information any staff gained came via *The Argus* and rumours we heard from supporters. So, there we were on a sunny August day, fielding questions about Portsmouth from understandably angry fans, but we were unable to do anything other than look blankly back at them. I made a large, hand-written sign to display above the counter. It read, 'Please don't ask us about the P Word. We know nothing'.

Chairman Bill Archer was a phantom. I never once met him or even saw him. Nor did many other staff at the Goldstone. While Archer remained at a safe distance in his home in the north of England, Bellotti was his mouthpiece. And, my goodness, he liked the sound of his own voice. The antagonism between supporters and Bellotti grew, and he alienated the core of Brighton's fanbase by banning some senior members of supporters' groups from the Goldstone. This didn't stop the protests, though; rather, they were organised almost weekly, the first one of note being a pitch invasion which held up a televised match at Bournemouth. All the while, the team slumped to the wrong end of the league. It felt as though the club was being eaten from the inside out. At one match, a banner was raised which read, 'Homeless, broke, the board's a joke'. If it was a joke, it wasn't a very funny one.

The Bellotti era was a relentless, ongoing nightmare, and the employees who had to be at the ground every day suffered as much as anyone. Most members of staff at this time were genuine Albion fans and, as well as having the same concerns about their club as supporters did, they also had the displeasure of having to go to work in a depressing atmosphere every day. Bellotti, though, breezed around the offices as if life was peachy, while many employees wished he was literally anywhere but there. As fan protests increased in intensity and regularity, he would repeat two phrases. 'Bill [Archer] and I are going nowhere' was his favourite. He used this when people asked if the chairman would sell the club to any potentially interested party, or whenever his role was questioned. Another one of his verbal crutches was, 'Bill and I, we did laugh.' He'd say this when referring to a piece of press coverage about the club that he considered to be fake news. In all honesty, it felt as though he was rather enjoying his ongoing battle with the fans, like it was a fun game for him. The more supporters wanted him gone, the deeper he dug his heels.

As one might expect from a politician, Bellotti talked a good game even if he wasn't providing much substance. When opposition directors visited, he would bend their ears about the vision he and Archer had for the club. I know this because after a midweek home defeat, I was subjected to some suit from the away club (possibly Darlington, I can't remember) telling me just how impressed he was by the Albion's apparent blueprint. To the rest of us, the 'blueprint' to build a stadium on the outskirts of town amounted to nothing more than a couple of colourful drawings. Indeed, the plans were 'pie in the sky' according to the leader of Brighton Council. This visiting official, though, was convinced. Never mind that he was only standing alongside me inside the West Stand because he didn't want to exit the ground while there was an angry mob of protesting Albion fans outside. The message from Bellotti to representatives of other clubs appeared to be that everything was going to plan and that there definitely was a plan and that the plan was great and that they shouldn't listen to any of these silly supporters. As objects were hurled at the West Stand windows and as fans banged their fists on the locked wooden doors, the away director, whoever he was, turned to me and said, 'Stick with Archer and Bellotti son, they know what they're doing.' At the end of a long day and another home defeat, I was too tired to argue. A few minutes later, my family and I walked through the same protest to get to our car. We certainly didn't fear the crowd of furious fans. Heck, we'd have been protesting with them but for the fact it would have cost us our jobs. Although Brighton supporters hated the regime, they were still sympathetic towards the staff who were forced to work in this poisoned environment. Anyone who had followed the Albion for any length of time (and let's face it, how many new supporters were the club attracting during this period of pure hell?) knew how much the employees cared. Why else would people work there, considering there wasn't even a guaranteed wage slip at the end of each month?

Essentially then, it wasn't a dispute between the supporters and the club, but rather between the supporters and the board. They tirelessly fought the regime, yet at the same time would sneak snippets of information to staff regarding possible takeovers to keep our spirits up. And so, as we made our way through groups of fans protesting outside the Goldstone after most home matches during the Bellotti era, several people would stop chanting to say hello and to have a chat, their anger temporarily dissipating. The national media sometimes presented Brighton's dissenting masses negatively, but anyone who took the time to study them more closely would see everyday people, often entire families, who had been driven to protest, to become activists, completely against their nature.

When Brighton's final game of the 1995/96 season, against York City, potentially the last ever at the Goldstone, had to be abandoned in the 16th minute as thousands of fans charged on to the pitch in the biggest protest to date, news outlets spoke of hooliganism rearing its ugly head again. Most people who were in attendance, however, would likely offer a different story. Whilst a few were there solely for a fix of anarchy, the majority of malcontents who stepped on to the playing surface during the match were law-abiding citizens who wouldn't normally dream of breaking the rules. They were reluctantly making their way on to the pitch because they felt they had no other option than to deliver this bold statement. While fans snapped the crossbars to ensure the game couldn't continue, I spotted a couple of old grannies having a sit down in the sunshine on the turf. Just like everyone else, they wanted to show their dismay at what was happening at the club. They hoped to bring it to the nation's attention so that someone, anyone, of authority might step in to act.

Fans who were praying for an intervention, for someone to take a thorough look at what was happening at the club, were to be disappointed. All the Football Association did was give the Albion a suspended three-point deduction in response to the protest. With the season ending in relegation to the league's basement division, with the Goldstone having been sold to developers, with nowhere for the team to seemingly play for the 1996/97 season, and with the same men still in power ('Bill and I are going nowhere'), Brighton's long-suffering supporters went into the summer break feeling more helpless and lost than ever. The close-season would not serve to reset outlooks or heighten optimism on this occasion.

With no practicable alternative available (the Portsmouth ground-share had been dead for ages), the board were obligated to pay the site's new owners to allow the Albion to spend a further season at the Goldstone. Unthinkably, performances on the pitch got even worse in the 1996/97 season, and the protests continued to increase in size, regularity and intensity, despite the FA's suspended sentence hanging over the club. The actual football matches were practically a sideshow by now, as each home game became another opportunity for fans to try something new. There were walkouts and boycotts, while another smaller pitch invasion against Lincoln City delayed a game and saw the FA further punish the fans by deducting two points from the team, who slumped to the bottom of the entire league.

The Goldstone was in lockdown. An exclusion zone was formed around the directors' box in the West Stand to prevent fans getting close to Bellotti. This didn't stop him being verbally barraged at every game and it failed to prevent a group of supporters sprinting from the North Stand, across the playing surface and into the exclusion zone to chase him out of the directors' box within 30 seconds of kick-off on one occasion.

Hundreds of fans travelled to Archer's house in the sleepy village of Mellor, Lancashire, one Saturday afternoon to voice their concerns. He wasn't home. He remained a ghost. Thousands of supporters marched through London. Anything and everything was attempted in the hope of rescuing this once proud club, which was now on its knees, seemingly gasping its final breaths.

Liam Brady's frustration with the situation was such that he had resigned as manager some time ago. His replacement, Albion hero Jimmy Case, was sacked before Christmas. Former Charlton Athletic boss Steve Gritt was announced as the new manager. His arrival was greeted with abusive, misspelt graffiti about him on the West Stand wall. The general assumption by now was that anyone newly employed by Archer and Bellotti would merely be their puppet, and that they could not be trusted. The Seagulls were 12 points adrift at the bottom of the entire league with no money, no home to call their own and no ground-share agreement in place for the following season. Simply, the club was rapidly spiralling towards oblivion.

Gritt's first game was at home to Hull City, where fans would attempt another new protest. They distributed hundreds of whistles in the hope of causing aural chaos. The thinking, I presume, was that the referee's whistle wouldn't be heard, meaning the game would have to be abandoned. The game wasn't called off though, and the whistles actually created a carnival atmosphere which helped the team romp to a surprise 3-0 win. A fan handcuffed himself to one of the goal frames at half-time and remained there for the duration of the interval while maintenance staff found some bolt-cutters. This kind of occurrence felt entirely normal by now.

Far from being the board's puppet, Gritt became popular with supporters and staff alike. He was a measured, decent man who always spoke highly of the fans and tried his best to distance himself from whatever inflammatory statement was coming from the boardroom. Under his calm influence, the team started to improve, particularly at home. Off the pitch though, things grew worse. A consortium led by local businessman and Albion fan Dick Knight was repeatedly knocked back by Archer.

Time moved forward. There was to be no further extension to the stay at the Goldstone, meaning bulldozers would be ripping down nearly 100 years of history at the end of the season. To add insult to injury, whilst the club seemed as though it was going out of business, the company that bought the Goldstone for £7.4m sold the land less than a year later for £23.86m.

***

FANS UNITED

When a teenage Plymouth Argyle fan shared an idea in an Albion forum on the embryonic internet, he couldn't have imagined what his lightbulb moment would become. He made the simple suggestion that supporters of all clubs should attend Brighton's match against Hartlepool United wearing their own team's colours as a show of support to Seagulls fans and to add their voices to the protests. It would, appropriately, be called Fans United.

The idea had spread like wildfire by the day of the Hartlepool match. Thanks to the hard work of supporters' groups and with help from radio shows such as Danny Baker's *606*, thousands of fans from other clubs had promised to turn up to Brighton to show solidarity. By the time I opened the doors to the club shop at 10am on a misty February morning, people sporting unfamiliar replica shirts were already milling around outside the Goldstone. Usually at lunchtime on a matchday, the ground was pretty quiet but, on this day, our shop was bustling with football lovers from all over the world, buying badges and programmes, and sharing stories with strangers. As kick-off approached, the crowds outside the turnstiles were vast, swarming across pavements and spilling into the road, illustrating how fans had descended on Sussex from all over the country and, wonderfully, from across Europe as well. Amongst supporters of hundreds of clubs, there were busloads from Charlton Athletic, fans from Germany, from our rivals Crystal Palace, from Liverpool, the Netherlands and, of course, Plymouth. For so long, Seagulls supporters had felt entirely alone, like no one was even looking or listening. The FA didn't care, much of the media didn't care; it seemed that nobody gave a damn. But here was visible proof that football fans really did give a damn. They had travelled many hours and miles at their own expense to stand shoulder to shoulder with their downtrodden brothers and sisters.

The atmosphere during the game was magnificent and, amid comically foggy conditions, Albion destroyed Hartlepool 5-0, with striker Craig Maskell scoring a hat-trick and then throwing the ball into the crowd after the final whistle. It was a nice touch, and it gave a clear indication that the players were on the fans' side too. As Brighton supporters left the stadium, they did so having made new friends and happy in the knowledge that things were maybe, just maybe, looking up. Sure, we were still marooned at the foot of the table, but at least we were winning games and word was spreading about our plight.

On a broader note, the kaleidoscope of football shirts displayed on the terraces that day made me realise that supporters have far more in common with followers of their biggest rival than with most other people in the world. They share similar goals, have equal passion, and enjoy the same recreational activities. The only difference is the colour of their scarves. In keeping with this, the modest Hartlepool contingent took the defeat in their stride, especially considering how far they'd travelled only for their team to get battered. They even started their own chorus of 'We Want Archer Out', to the applause of the rest of the stadium. Many visiting teams during the latter stages of the season did the same.

As supporters bounced towards Brighton and Hove's various boozers with their new-found buddies, I felt humbled by what I'd just experienced. From that day, Albion fans' attitudes towards other clubs shifted. Even nearly three decades on, football fans know they can rely on Brighton supporters to give them their backing whenever the going gets tough and, since Fans United in 1997, I've never been able to truly say that I hate any other team. Hate is such a horrible word at the best of times.

If Fans United taught me to be generous of spirit towards supporters of all teams, then working at a football club diminished any sense of traditional rivalry. Ask any

Albion staff member which clubs they like and dislike and you'll probably be surprised at the answers you receive. Each individual football club employee has their own favourites and antagonists. They enjoy dealing with the friendly clubs and grow to dislike those where their equivalents are rude, officious or obstructive. During my time working in the ticket office at Brighton & Hove Albion, I made friends in box offices at Bristol City and Wolves and I enjoyed chatting to the ticket office manager at Leeds United, whose name was Katie Holmes. I'm fairly sure she wasn't Tom Cruise's ex-wife.

As an aside, in the ticket office we would sometimes find fans who shared celebrity names and deliberately sit them in adjacent seats. So, you'd have Paul Weller next to Liam Gallagher, who in turn would be next to Paul Daniels. We hoped that they would learn of each other's names and consider it an amazing coincidence.

Back to 1997 and, as the February mist turned to rain, we locked up the club shop and walked away from the Goldstone with the feeling that there just might be some light at the end of the tunnel.

***

GOODBYE GOLDSTONE

Whilst the team couldn't buy a win on the road, their home form continued to be excellent, allowing them to gradually chip away at the gap between themselves and the rest of the league. They had the full backing of the fans, who were embracing the dichotomy of continuing to rally against the board while vocally supporting the players. Crowds were growing in size every game and, although the future still looked very grim, the Football Association had finally, finally, stepped in and were arbitrating between the club owners and the consortium led by Dick Knight. Despite this positive occurrence, sometimes the sheer weight of the situation threatened to collapse everything beneath it. A heart-stopping 4-4 draw against Leyton Orient was an example of this. Firstly, Orient's Scott McGleish almost caused a riot by turning to the North Stand and pretending to shoot them with a make-believe gun when he scored. To a crowd of supporters at the end of their collective tether, this felt like a cruel and inflammatory action. During the same game, someone ran on to the field from the Brighton end and tried to give Orient's Ray Wilkins (brother of Brighton legend Dean) a firm kick up the backside. It felt like the Wild West.

By the time Albion played the last ever evening game at the Goldstone, the chance of catching one of the handful of relegation-threatened teams above them was genuine. The floodlights on each corner showered the stadium in yellow illumination one last time as Albion won by a single goal against Barnet. Next, high-flying Wigan Athletic played the penultimate match at the Goldstone and succumbed to a 1-0 defeat. A couple of hours after the final whistle, my dad and I went for a kickabout on the pitch, taking it in turns to ping shots at each other in the north goal. I think it was the first time we had kicked a ball together on the hallowed turf, and we knew it would be the last chance we'd get. As the ball nestled in the net or, more often, bounced around the empty terrace behind the goal, we told ourselves to remember and cherish the moment.

Every goal Albion scored in the run-in to the 1996/97 season was greeted with greater fervour. Each game grew in importance. We all understood just how much was at stake. Every win or draw made that shard of light at the end of the tunnel seem slightly brighter. A 1-1 stalemate at Cambridge United meant that Brighton were just three points behind their closest relegation rivals, Hereford United, with two games remaining. Only one team was relegated into non-league each season in those days. Albion's final match? Hereford United away. The fixtures computer had outdone itself.

Before that showdown though, Brighton & Hove Albion would play their last ever match at the Goldstone Ground. Within a couple of weeks, the bulldozers would be moving in and the historic, worn-out old stadium would cease to exist anywhere but within our sepia-tinted memories. There would be no protests like there had been a year ago though. In fact, the mood on the day was the opposite of that sun-kissed afternoon of turmoil 12 months previously, because the club's owners had, at long last, succumbed to pressure and reached an agreement with Dick Knight. The sense of optimism was palpable. Archer and Bellotti were still there for the time being, but they no longer had full control. The board had been reshaped. Essentially, the cavalry had arrived. It felt like a rock had been lifted from everybody's backs.

As much as this was a day for saying goodbye to the Goldstone, the game against Doncaster Rovers was crucial. A win here coupled with a defeat for Hereford in their match at Leyton Orient would see the Seagulls haul themselves off the foot of the table for the first time in months. However, if Hereford avoided defeat and Brighton lost, the Seagulls would be relegated, which would be the worst possible way to bid farewell to our home.

I arrived for work in the club shop before 9am. It was raining. A dull drizzle. The store smelt even mustier than usual. A shutter which protected one of the two small front windows refused to open. It never opened. My mother, who had been the shop manager for a while by now, spent the previous couple of weeks stocking up on Goldstone-related memorabilia. Bellotti had long since forbidden her from ordering any new merchandise, but she simply ignored him. Secretly doing the opposite of what Bellotti demanded had become the norm for most of the club's employees by this time. In our hearts, everybody at the club was already working for Dick Knight.

A few weeks earlier, my mum and I had walked around the Goldstone, taking pictures of the stands. I took the film to Boots for processing and we had badges made up from the photos. We also put one of the images on a T-shirt. It was all very DIY. I hand-drew another T-shirt design of a fan forlornly holding a blue and white scarf by his side. We spent the Friday before the Doncaster game making the shop as pretty as a cabin with a broken shutter and a resident rat could be.

On the day of the final match at our beloved old stadium, people were literally ripping display items off the walls and putting an arbitrary amount of money in our hands by way of payment. It was chaos, but it was thrilling chaos. Fans were buoyed by the news of the takeover, and it showed in their demeanour. For so long we had witnessed only furrowed brows and frowns, and heard hushed rumours about takeovers, spoken more in desperation than expectation. Now, even though we were still being forced to leave our home and faced the prospect of being relegated out of the league in just a few hours, we had that one thing that had been absent for so long. We had genuine hope.

Because everyone was keen to get in the ground as early as possible, by 2.45pm, usually our busiest time, the shop was dead. It was as if a micro-tornado had ripped through it. There was hardly anything left to sell. No more T-shirts, no more programmes, no more VHS tapes, no more scarves. Just an empty counter, bare walls, and some exhausted staff. With no customers left to serve, we closed ten minutes early. This meant that, for the first time since I was a ball boy four years previously, and for the last time ever, I got to see a kick-off at the Goldstone. Usually, by the time we'd served the final customer and locked up, the game was at least five minutes old. Today though, I was in my West Stand seat to see incoming chairman Dick Knight take his position in the directors' box to a roar which intersected relief and gratitude. Moments later, the teams took to the field, and the very clear sense of an era ending caused me to shed a tear. That might sound melodramatic to non-football fans, but I'm sure everyone else in the stadium felt the same at that moment. Countless memories and emotions, not flashing before our eyes, but gently embracing us.

This was the place where I had done the majority of my growing up. I knew every cranny of the place. I had watched from every vantage point. I'd sat on the track in front of a heaving North Stand, stood completely on my own on the East Terrace during reserve games, wedged myself between two strangers at the front of the West Terrace back in 1986. I'd spent hours in the car with my family travelling to and from matches, listening to that lucky compilation tape. I'd kicked cans around with other kids outside the players' entrance while waiting to collect autographs. Some of those kids would go on to be lifelong friends. Around me were fans that had been coming to games for 30, 40, 50 years, each with their own stories to tell, each with their own matchday routine. By 4.45pm, that routine would cease to exist. It was difficult to fully comprehend.

The ambience around the stadium wasn't entirely melancholic though. As I mentioned, people had been generally upbeat in the build-up to the match. Now, as the finality of it all took hold, the mood had become sombre, but it changed again as soon as the referee signalled the start of the match. Focus immediately shifted to the importance of the game. Although it was sad to say goodbye to the Goldstone, if the team didn't avoid relegation, there was a good chance we'd be saying goodbye to the entire club. Voices were raised, pulses quickened.

I recall practically nothing of the 1-0 win. I think the pressure of the situation caused my brain to short-circuit, because all other aspects of the day aside from the game are crystal clear in my mind. All I really remember of the 90 minutes is the North Stand singing regular updates of how our relegation rivals, Hereford, were faring in their match. They were losing.

Incidentally, I think I have watched video footage of the winning goal approximately a gazillion times since that day. Even all these years later, it gives me goosebumps to see Stuart Storer ram the ball home and to hear the commentator yelling his name.

Because there was no merchandise left to sell, we didn't open the club shop after the match. Instead, just like everyone else, I made my way on to the pitch. Fans had flowed across the playing surface as soon as the referee blew the final whistle, and thousands more were now strolling down the terraces on to the sodden grass, some of them perhaps for the first time, everybody for the last. The rain was coming down but nobody cared. The final score from the Hereford match filtered through. They had lost, meaning that we had been elevated from the bottom of the league, having done the unthinkable in clawing back a 12-point deficit. A draw against Hereford next week, in the final game of this long, tumultuous campaign, would ensure our remarkable survival and send them out of the league instead.

Conflicting emotions fought for prevalence over the next few minutes, creating a bizarre cocktail of mournfulness and joyousness. It was so sad to be leaving our home, but the overwhelming feeling was one of optimism. It's a word I have used more than once in this chapter, and I make no apology for it. We'd been bereft of even a semblance of optimism for months, years even, yet now it lived in the smiles and the shining eyes of fellow supporters. Optimism was all around.

It was almost time for fans to leave this familiar stomping ground. People dug their fingers into the turf and gently, almost reverentially, pulled up as much as they could carry. Others took advertising boards, seats, parts of the goal net, anything they could get their hands on by way of a memento. With soil under their fingernails and hearts heavy yet pounding with pride and excitement, people reluctantly, oh so reluctantly, shuffled away, their minds skipping through Goldstone memories and thinking ahead to the do-or-die game at Hereford next week.

'Do-or-die' was the only way to describe it. To reiterate, if Albion avoided defeat, they would remain in the Football League against all the odds. If they lost, Hereford would leapfrog them and send the Seagulls tumbling into the non-league abyss. With no stadium to call their own, it was generally accepted that this would signal the end of Brighton & Hove Albion Football Club despite the consortium's involvement. Whilst the win over Doncaster had given everyone a tremendous boost, the importance of the next match could not be overstated. Simply, it was the most important game that the club would ever play.

Leaving the Goldstone on that soggy afternoon didn't represent the same finality for staff members as it did for most. Whilst the ground had hosted its final game, the club would still operate from there for a little while, meaning I would be back in the rat-infested shop on Monday to help prepare to move everything across to our new offices and merchandise store in Brighton's city centre. So, it was strangely painless to walk out of the car park at around 7pm after the Doncaster game and join the rest of the staff and players at the club's end-of-season party in a hotel on the seafront. Thinking back, this seems like an absurd idea. Firstly, what kind of party would it have been had results gone against us earlier that day? Equally, having an end-of-season shindig a few days before the biggest game in the club's history surely represented utter madness. In actuality though, it proved to be just the tonic. For two years, you could have cut the atmosphere at the club with a knife but, as the booze flowed that night, there was a mood of merriment and of hope. Late in the evening, I asked left-back Stuart Tuck if he was confident that we'd get the result we needed. 'Yeah, we're going to do it,' he replied with the utmost assuredness, as if the result wasn't in any doubt whatsoever.

The following week, I watched the players train on the pitch, tiptoeing around the gaping holes. My dad drove over one day with a spade and liberated a big square of turf, which he then re-laid in our back garden. On the Wednesday, I said my own goodbye to the Goldstone.

Whilst my first game was in 1986, I'd been to the Goldstone Ground once before that, with my dad on a non-matchday sometime at the end of the 1970s. I don't remember this and have no idea of the reason for our visit. Indeed, I would have no idea it had ever happened were there not photographic evidence of me on the North West Terrace wearing a snazzy pair of dungarees and with a shock of blond hair. All these years later in 1997, I made one last journey along the long, snaking corridor that ran the length of the West Stand, running my fingers along the walls on either side as I went. I had one last glance into the Seagull Lounge and then took a final stroll through the tunnel that I had run up and down on countless occasions as a ball kid. I stood on the turf for a few moments and breathed it all in just once more. All the ghosts were still there.

I stepped off the pitch, back up the tunnel, past the dressing rooms, out of the main exit, on to the street and made my way to the train station. I didn't look back and I have never since returned to that part of Hove.

***

THE MOST IMPORTANT GAME

It all came down to this. In the last few days the club had welcomed Dick Knight, hauled themselves off the bottom of the league and said goodbye to their home of nearly 100 years. Now there was one more obstacle to negotiate, the last game of the season at Hereford United, who were propping up the table. After nine gruelling months of football, Hereford had exactly the same number of points as Brighton. The only reason that they were bottom was because they had scored fewer goals. Football truly is bonkers sometimes.

When tickets went on sale for this match some weeks previously, Hereford seemed clear of relegation danger, so the home club allocated Albion fans over 3,000 tickets. This was just under half of the stadium's capacity. An horrific run of results for them, coupled with Brighton's unlikely upsurge, had led to this game being infinitely more significant than anyone could have imagined. Having so many fans from the south coast in attendance would be a huge boost to the Seagulls.

I didn't go to the match. Despite the newly upbeat feeling around the club, Albion's away form had been awful, meaning that Hereford were probably still favourites. I couldn't handle the thought of watching the home fans celebrating their survival as my club died a terrible death, so I made the cowardly decision that I didn't want to be anywhere near Herefordshire on that May afternoon. My parents also chose not to attend the game, so we found ourselves at home together, tense, nervous and irritable to the point that none of us could bear to be in each other's company. We hardly uttered a word all morning and, upon kick-off at 3pm, my mother and father went out for long walks through the same woodland that my mum and I strolled through on FA Cup Final day in 1983. They set off in opposite directions. My dad took a radio, my mum didn't. She just wanted to be alone with her thoughts, oblivious to what was occurring. I sat in my bedroom and listened to the game on the radio.

I coped well enough with the drama at first, despite the crackly commentary being relentlessly fraught. When Albion's Kerry Mayo sliced the ball into his own net to give Hereford the lead, I resigned myself to defeat with a level of composure that took me slightly by surprise. As Hereford continued to bombard the Albion goal, I just laid on my bed, underneath my Nirvana and Carter USM posters, and waited for the inevitable second goal which would put an end to my football club. I suppose I'd felt so downtrodden for such a long time that I had simply accepted Albion's fate. There was nothing I could do to help. But wait. I suddenly realised there *was* one action I could take. Partly as a nod to happier times and partly through sheer desperation, I removed my left sock.

In the second half, Hereford got edgy. Having been dominant in the first period, they now didn't know whether to stick or twist. Did they go for the killer second goal that had eluded them before the break, or simply defend their lead? Stuck in no man's land between the two mindsets, they ultimately did neither. On 62 minutes, Craig Maskell's shot hit the post and substitute Robbie Reinelt was on hand to fire in the rebound in front of the Albion fans behind the goal. The partisan radio commentators yelped ecstatic words through the airwaves and I completely lost the plot. I didn't for a moment expect us to equalise, so when we did I could barely cope with the emotions stirring in me. I leapt from my bed and ran around the empty house, arms pointing directly outwards, aeroplane style, before performing an ill-judged and painful knee slide across the carpeted living room floor. My head was pounding. My heart felt as though it was going to burst through my ribcage. The team had given me hope and, as we all know, it's the hope that kills you. Entirely coincidentally, my mum came into the house at that exact moment. She saw me on my knees.

'What's going on? What's the score?' She paused, and then said, 'Why are you green?'

The third question didn't really register with me at the time but when I later asked her about it she told me that the colour had drained from my face and my complexion had a sickly green tint.

'We've just equalised. 1-1. Robbie Reinelt. Half an hour to go,' I told her, the words tumbling from my mouth in something like the correct order. She processed these facts, the strain instantly showing on her face.

'I'm going out again,' she said with a frown. And with that, she performed a sharp about-turn, walked back up the garden and disappeared into the woods. Back into the unknown.

I immediately realised that, like her, I was too stressed to listen to the rest of the match. I'd been kidding myself that I had come to terms with relegation and everything that came with it. The equalising goal had defibrillated me, and now I just felt sick. I ran up the stairs, switched off my radio and pulled on my trainers. I was still wearing just one sock. I had no idea where to go or what to do but I knew that I couldn't bear listening to the commentary anymore. It's not like watching a game on television or being at the ground, where you can see the action unfolding in front of your eyes. On the radio, all you get is a cacophony of noise with each home attack, making it sound as though a goal is certain every time the opposition crosses the half-way line. I pulled on my coat, left the house, and went to the local park, where I sat in the drizzle, radio-free and clueless of what was going on in deepest Herefordshire. I sucked in the damp air, trying to turn my short, sharp breaths into deeper, calmer inhalations. I didn't have a mobile phone back then (did anyone?), nor did I own a watch, so before I left the house I picked up my battery-powered bedside alarm clock in order to keep an eye on the time. I sat on the swings in an otherwise completely empty recreation ground, watching the seconds tick over. Goodness knows what I must have looked like. A six-foot-tall 20-year-old with weird hair and ripped jeans, sitting on the swings in the rain, only wearing one sock and holding an alarm clock.

As the minute hand ticked past 4.45pm, I accepted that the match was likely over, so I took myself home. My mum arrived at the house at the same time and was equally unaware of the score. We turned on the radio in the living room, and learned that the game hadn't yet finished, but was in injury time. We quickly ascertained that the score was still 1-1 and it seemed that the home side was piling on the pressure. The commentators sounded exhausted, as though they had played the match themselves. I thought they were genuinely about to cry as a home striker escaped Albion's defence and had the chance to score the most important goal in Hereford's history. When he put the ball straight into the Brighton goalkeeper's hands, the commentators let out a sigh of relief, as did my mother and I.

'Switch it off,' my mum exclaimed. 'I can't listen to it.' I turned the dial until, with a click, the commentators fell silent. We instead put the television on and referred to our old friend Ceefax. We both stood there, transfixed by the blocky text. At least now we were sheltered from the tenseness of the commentary. If we were to concede a late goal, Ceefax would inform us entirely emotionlessly. A swift bullet to the temple. The page ticked over, seemingly interminably.

> Hereford 1-1 Brighton
> Hereford 1-1 Brighton
> Hereford 1-1 Brighton

Then, something happened. The screen changed very subtly. But it changed magnificently.

> Hereford 1-1 Brighton FT

It was full time! I leapt into the air and started lapping the house, aeroplane arms deployed. My mum got straight on the phone to share words of delight with colleagues, and my dad came running down the garden, still with his radio earplugs in, arms aloft like Ronnie Radford. Just as we did all those years ago in Gerry Armstrong's living room, we held our own impromptu celebration on a square of carpet in sleepy Eastbourne and it felt wonderful.

Albion had survived against all the odds. I needed a pint. Like the rest of Sussex, I went straight to the pub.

PART TWO: PRIESTFIELD

THE COMEDOWN

ALBION WERE saved. Against all odds they had retained their place in the Football League and the board had been restructured to accommodate Dick Knight's consortium. Meanwhile, Tony Blair had just been elected as Prime Minister and Britpop dominated the charts. It felt like everything was finally going to be alright. No wonder Brighton fans boozily celebrated for days. Two years of hurt, anxiety and protest had concluded with Albion's thrilling Great Escape, both on and off the pitch. Every pint tasted delicious, every embrace was emotional and triumphant. The unwinnable war was won.

However, if you'd have walked into Brighton & Hove Albion's administration offices the week after the Hereford game, you would have assumed the club had been relegated. Although David Bellotti would eventually leave the club and Bill Archer's shares would, in the future, be bought out, very little changed in the short term for Albion's employees. After the joy of avoiding relegation on Saturday, staff returned to work at the beginning of a new week to be greeted by Bellotti, who despite the takeover, was still present, and likely still pig-headedly insisting, 'Bill and I are going nowhere.'

The players trained at Sussex University and the new club offices were based in a dreary, five-storey building in the middle of Brighton. It had brown, tiled carpets (the kind that trapped rogue staples like a spider's web), strip lighting and a lift that spent more time out of order than it did carrying people to their desired floors.

I continued to be employed part-time while at college, splitting my days between working in the shop and in ticket sales. There was no physical ticket office. We accepted season ticket applications by post and allocated them using large paper maps of the stands, created by sellotaping photocopied sheets of A3 together. When we allocated a season ticket, we put a small coloured sticker on the corresponding seat on the map and hand-wrote seat details on the front of the season ticket booklet. There wasn't a computer in sight, just sticky fluorescent dots on a massive piece of white paper, which sat on the boardroom table.

Down the street, equidistant between Brighton station and the beach, was the merchandise store. The stockroom was damp, and diesel fumes from passing buses secreted a layer of black gunk atop all surfaces. The Goldstone was a relic, but at least from the back of the club shop you could look out across the pitch and daydream of past glories. From the new club shop the vista was nothing more than a busy road, a convenience store and a Boots.

Once supporters had finished celebrating the Hereford result, they too were left to contemplate the detritus of war. Their home ground was already being bulldozed, and the club ended up having to share with Gillingham at their Priestfield stadium. This meant a 140-mile round trip to Kent every other week. Due to a delay in the takeover being fully completed, sitting in the directors' box at the first 'home' league game in August, flanked by stewards, was a certain David Bellotti. Needless to say, it made for a hostile atmosphere as the 2,000 home fans who had made their debut journey to Gillingham vented their anger and frustration that this loathed figure had not yet left the club.

Bellotti's visible presence in the main stand was a fittingly depressing way to start the season. During the 1996/97 campaign, everyone had fought so hard to save the club, the players had sweated blood to secure an astonishing survival and the football played over the final few months was thrilling. In the 1997/98 season, the team's performances were woeful and had Doncaster Rovers not been even more hopeless we'd have faced another relegation scrap. Because Doncaster were always doomed to finish at the foot of the league though, Albion's players simply limped through the season knowing they wouldn't be relegated, no matter how badly they performed. The results didn't matter. Games were played in front of small clusters of fans, who attended for reasons of loyalty and obligation rather than the expectation of entertainment. For the second season running, Brighton finished one place off the foot of the league.

Priestfield was only accessible to Albion on matchdays and even then it seemed to be handed over reluctantly. Nobody wanted us there, especially the Gillingham staff who, while pleasant people, were understandably annoyed that they were obligated to come in on their Saturdays off and babysit us. Because we weren't permitted to make use of Gillingham's club shop, I sold merchandise from two trestle tables outside the ground. Every game that I worked during our first season there, a police officer would try to move me on. We'd have the same conversation. They'd tell me that street trading wasn't permitted and would try to usher me away under the vague threat of taking further action against me. I'd explain that I was standing on Gillingham FC's property and that everything was legitimate. It was true, the tables weren't positioned on the pavement but on the concrete which made up the very edge of the entrance to the car park. That was the concession Gillingham had made, a small patch of concrete on the edge of their car park. So, rain or shine, I would stand behind wallpaper paste tables and sell replica shirts, programmes, scarves and other bits and bobs. At 3.10pm, once all the supporters were in the stadium, I'd load the tables and the remaining merchandise into my dad's boot, ready to take them back to Brighton. I would then walk down the empty street and into the stadium, through the belly of the main stand, just as I used to back at the Goldstone. The game would invariably be about 20 minutes old by now and I usually missed absolutely nothing of note. Upon taking the stairs up to the stand, I had rows and rows of empty seats from which to choose.

Squeezed between streets of terraced houses, Priestfield was a typical lower league stadium. Behind both goals were terraces, one covered, one not, and on either side were seated stands. At the top of the main stand were some executive boxes. They were probably once considered plush but, by the end of the 20th century, 'executive' seemed a bold word to describe these tiny rooms with worn-out furniture and televisions from a different decade. A few of the boxes sat empty during Brighton's games, so during the winter months I figured I'd make use of the facilities, because the view was good and the window offered welcome protection from the cold. One evening, I found a box which was occupied by a few of the injured and unselected players, so I joined them, sitting on the spare seat at the end of the row. The match was typically scrappy and lacking quality to the point that my attention was increasingly drawn towards a nature programme on the old TV in the corner. Soon, everyone in the room was more focused on watching the documentary about crocodiles than on the game in front of us. Half a dozen professional footballers and a club employee had our backs to a football match and were instead glued to a small, fuzzy television. I think this serves as a suitable illustration of how travelling to Gillingham every other week sucked the enthusiasm out of everyone. The crocodile documentary was great, but I can't recall what the score was in the match or who Albion were playing that night.

I think Knight's takeover was completed reasonably early during the first season at Priestfield, and although Archer kept his shares for a few years, it meant Bellotti was finally gone. Oddly, I don't remember the former politician actually leaving. You'd have thought that champagne corks would have been popping in the office, but they weren't. I have a feeling he just packed up his things one night and that was it; the next day there was an empty space. I never saw him again. I don't think anyone related to the club did. He died in 2015, aged 71.

***

ARSENAL

While working part-time at the Albion, I was also offered some seasonal hours at Arsenal Football Club. My sister was working at Highbury and she wangled me a Christmas job in the merchandising warehouse, just around the corner from the ground. The work was easy but the shifts were long. I spent 11 hours a day parcelling things like scarves, replica shirts, pens and badges, breaking only at lunchtime to pop into Highbury to say hello to my sister. After work, I'd doze to the rhythmical rattle of the underground en route to my friends' flat in Stratford, east London, where I slept on a paper-thin sofa-bed in the living room each night. My pals were art students and would stay up until the early morning, meaning I only slept for a handful of hours each night. At 7am I'd wake to the insistent beep of my alarm clock and make my way through the snowy Stratford streets to the underground station, where I would squeeze myself on to a tube filled with downbeat commuters, miserably going about their mornings while their body language suggested they'd rather be doing absolutely anything else. One morning, after my friends had been up particularly late, I was so tired when I got dressed that I forgot to change out of the top in which I'd slept. It was an Albion home shirt. Going to work at Arsenal wearing the colours of another club probably wasn't the best idea, yet there was no antagonism, no banter. All I received from my colleagues were sympathetic looks. It was as though they were thinking, 'Oh dear. Brighton fan? Poor chap.'

The Arsenal job only lasted a few months over the Christmas period but, because my sister occasionally had complimentary tickets at her disposal, I attended a few matches at Highbury over the next couple of years, and I also went to an FA Cup Final. I was even at Highbury on the day they won the Premier League. I didn't have a ticket but had arranged to meet my sister afterwards for some drinks. As full time approached, I stood on the street outside the ground as the roars from inside drifted through the air. It's an eerie feeling being on the outside of such an event, so close to the action but entirely detached. I knocked on the wooden exit door and asked the steward if I could come inside and wait for my sister. Amazingly, the orange-jacketed custodian obliged and let me in on the understanding that I would wait on the concourse and not, under any circumstances, head up into the stand. I agreed. Obviously as soon as the steward went back to his post I dashed straight up the stairs. As I reached the top, Tony Adams put the icing on Arsenal's cake with a cracking half-volley.

As Adams and his team-mates paraded the Premier League trophy around the pitch after the final whistle, I couldn't help but feel as detached as I had when standing on the street outside a few minutes earlier. Arsenal had been good employers, I'd made friends at the club and the team had offered exotic excitement while Albion were in the doldrums but, simply, they weren't mine. Around me, fans were crying with delight, hugging, singing and waving flags. An old man in a flat cap in front of me shook my hand and offered a smile full of gaps and delight. I was an imposter. I hated Priestfield and the woeful football on offer, but at least I belonged there. I had earned my right to watch my awful team play terribly. Here though,

I was aboard a bandwagon that I hadn't even intentionally jumped upon. It had picked me up through a combination of a temporary job, a bunch of free tickets and my own team being useless.

A few hours after the game, I somehow found myself trapped and alone in the pitch-black stockroom of the Arsenal merchandise store. Some staff had been having celebratory drinks in the small space at the back of the club shop once it had closed for the day and I'd tagged along. I went to the toilet at the back of the stockroom and, when I came back, I found that they had turned off the lights, locked up and moved on to a local pub, completely forgetting that I was in the loo. I still didn't have a mobile phone, so I had no choice but to sit and wait until someone realised I was no longer with the party. There I was, a Brighton fan sitting alone in a windowless room at Highbury while, on the streets outside, thousands of Arsenal supporters celebrated. It was a fitting metaphor for my relationship with the club. When, about 20 minutes later, someone noticed I was missing and came back to let me out, I headed home to Eastbourne rather than continuing the pub crawl with them. It wasn't my celebration.

Before the following season kicked off, my sister gave me a ticket to see Arsenal play Manchester United in the Charity Shield at Wembley. Jaap Stam made his debut for United and Arsenal won 3-0. In the pub afterwards, while fans tunelessly sang Arsenal songs, I found myself walking the sticky carpet with a 'Bring home the Albion' petition in my hand, asking punters if they would kindly sign it. The petition was aimed at supporting the Seagulls' planning application to play future home matches at Withdean Stadium, back in Brighton. Withdean was a tiny local athletics ground. The Goldstone it wasn't, but anything was better than Priestfield. To their credit, the Arsenal fans took a few seconds out of their boozy Sunday evening to read the blurb at the top of the page and sign their names, but it struck me that they would never really understand what it was like to support a club fighting for its very survival. Probably unfairly, I assumed each person I approached to be thinking, 'How sweet. Little Brighton and their cute petition.' I was half-surprised that none of them ruffled my hair (not that they'd have managed to, I was sporting a very regrettable, gel-heavy, Peter Andre look at the time).

However, rather than being jealous of Arsenal's success, I actually left the pub feeling prouder of my club than ever before. Sure, Arsenal were a far better team than Brighton, and their fans were unquestionably loyal and passionate, but they'd never had to petition to have a home stadium, or march through London to Downing Street in a bid to keep their club afloat. The 'Wenger Out' protests a couple of decades later represented as tough a time as many of their fans had ever experienced. This isn't a dig at Arsenal or their supporters, by the way. I enjoyed being around the club, and their fans are mostly a good bunch. It's not Arsenal supporters' fault that they don't know what it's like to have been in the kind of serious crisis suffered by the likes of Brighton, Bolton, Plymouth, Blackpool, Orient, Coventry, Bury, Macclesfield, Southend and Reading to name just a few. But what I will say is that, during the tough times at the Albion, it felt like being part of an important movement, and now I look back on those troubled years with a surprising amount of fondness.

***

THREE LIONS ON MY CHEST

It's a good job Albion fans were able to focus their energy on trying to bring the club home, because the more traditionally rewarding aspects of supporting a football team continued to be absent. We remained a poor team in a rented stadium in a broken town, miles from home and, like everyone else, I attended games out of duty and sought my entertainment elsewhere. So, when the opportunity arose for me to attend an England international game against Bulgaria, I jumped at the chance to spend an afternoon at a packed Wembley, watching the country's footballing elite.

The day before the match, I headed to the sports shop in Eastbourne's unintentionally retro shopping mall and bought a red England shirt. It was on offer as part of a closing down sale. Incidentally, the shop had the same 'closing down' sale for about 20 years. They even moved premises during that time. With three lions on my shirt, I took a train to London Victoria on matchday, and sang 'Eng-er-land' with my pals on the tube while tourists and shoppers eyed us nervously. Now that I am in my middle age, the idea of belting out football chants on public transport makes me more than a little uneasy. Sure, there's nothing wrong with a sing-song on a train which is packed exclusively with supporters of your team, but the memory of doing so on a carriage filled with parents and old ladies heading home from Sainsbury's makes me cringe as much as I do when I recall my Peter Andre haircut.

The walk along Wembley Way from the station was beguiling, as the majestic grey structure with its iconic floodlights grew closer. Even though it was past its best and would soon be razed to the ground and rebuilt, it was still an imposing sight. I made sure to take it in. As a Brighton fan, I didn't know when I would next visit. My seat was in the gods, directly in front of the England band. The drummer stood approximately two feet from my right ear. Boom. Boom. Boom. Maybe they were generating a good atmosphere which reverberated around the rest of the half-full stadium, but it was impossible for me to tell, as the incessant pounding of the drum was all I could hear. Still, at least a thrilling game awaited me.

The match ended 0-0 and was almost entirely without incident, aside from the crowd booing manager Glenn Hoddle as he made his way to the dressing room at half-time and at the final whistle. I had nothing against Hoddle (this was before he aired his views on reincarnation); he had been a wonderful player and seemed to be a good manager, but there was literally nothing to shout about during the game and his team were playing awfully, so at least booing him brought a few moments of animation from the crowd. To be honest though, I'm not usually much of a booer. Firstly, booing is a weird thing for a fully grown adult to do. Secondly, how much does it achieve? Think about it, as those England players disappeared down the tunnel at half-time, did they do so with a sense that the fans were behind them, resulting in them feeling incentivised to go out and give them a second half to remember? Not likely. Imagine if the players had instead been roared off the pitch by a vociferous Wembley as a show of unity. They wouldn't have thought they were being cheered to the dressing room because they had played well, but rather would understand that the fans were trying to give them a much-needed boost.

The boos were entirely justified at full time though. It was a pathetic performance and one which had cost tens of thousands of people a lot of money to experience. With my ears ringing and my head aching, I made my way back to Eastbourne, cursing myself for thinking I could get an exciting football fix from watching England.

The Bulgaria match is one of six international men's games that I have attended, and they have all taught me that international football outside of the finals of major tournaments is nowhere near as good as its domestic counterpart. Sure, the players are the best from their respective countries, and I enjoy seeing fans of all clubs come together, but these matches sometimes lack the intensity and edge of league football. Perhaps it's because the fans and players are all day-trippers, attending/playing once in a blue moon, whereas we religiously sing and sweat for our own clubs every week through thick and thin. I suppose I got the same feeling watching England as I did Arsenal. There was just no connection. Brighton and I had been through so much together. I belonged to them and they belonged to me, regardless of what division or stadium they were playing in.

I almost attended one other England game in the 90s. I was offered a chance to be at that breathless Euro 96 semi-final between England and Germany, but I turned down the ticket. If that seems like a wasted opportunity, allow me to explain. Albion had been allocated a few tickets for the big game, and all but one got snapped up. There weren't many employees at the club then, so it wasn't long before my point in the pecking order was reached, and I was asked if I wanted to buy the ticket. I discovered that my seat would have been situated directly next to a certain David Bellotti, so I politely declined and watched it on telly instead.

Nowadays I barely bother with England men's games at all, even on TV, aside from the big summer tournaments. Does it make me a bad football fan to admit that I missed the first half of a World Cup qualifier because I was watching *The Great British Bake Off*? Probably, but in my defence it was the *Bake Off* semi-final. Besides, for so long the England team was made up of some difficult characters. It's hard enough to get behind a national team which perpetually fails, so to pepper it with misbehaving millionaires makes it even less appealing.

Far from being an anomaly, the 0-0 draw with Bulgaria at Wembley was a carbon copy of several other England games. Each match was a microcosmic example of English football in general at that time and, to some extent, English culture. Desperately trying to cling to the glory days of yesteryear, Eng-er-land was weighed down by arrogance and a deluded sense of grandeur to the extent that it was a sinking ship, water seeping through rotten wood while the band played on pig-headedly and its passengers drunk themselves into oblivion to a chorus of 'vindaloo, vindaloo, la la'. Depressingly, rather than rethinking English football's infrastructure, the FA and the big clubs just carried on regardless, papering over the cracks by forever yelling at us that the Premier League is the best competition in the world, as if that was the answer to everything.

Things have broadly improved on the pitch over recent years, but a small section of England fans continue to embarrass the country on the world stage. If you or I had a spare day in a beautiful city like Amsterdam before going to watch England play the Netherlands, what would we do? Visit the Van Gogh Museum? Anne Frank House? A bike trip around the city, taking in a few cafes and bars? Surely what we wouldn't do is set up camp outside one pub, drape St George crosses all over it, intimidate locals and tourists with xenophobic football chants, throw bikes into the canals and then start fights with the police. And yes, I know there are countries with fans far worse than England's, but that doesn't stop me being embarrassed by the small minds and big mouths of a minority of supporters of our national team. I suppose every country and every domestic team has their share of idiots, but it's just a shame that they are generally the ones that leave a lasting impression. Think about the Euro Final in 2021 between England and Italy. All those people causing trouble on Wembley Way and breaking into the stadium ticketless. In contrast, I went to the final of the Women's Euros between the Lionesses and Germany in 2022 and it remains one of my favourite football matches of all time. The atmosphere was magnificent, yet entirely safe and friendly, and the game was a cracker without a toxic undercurrent threatening to ruin it for everyone. No infuriated, beetroot-faced men, but rather people passionately supporting their team while showing respect for their opponents. And England actually won a trophy! It was a day I will never forget.

Similarly, I have enjoyed attending Albion's women's games in recent years. I went to the Palace away match in 2024 at Sutton United's stadium and, while the rivalry was at the forefront of the atmosphere among the decent-sized crowd, Jayne and I never felt anything other than entirely safe throughout. There was a mixed fanzone before the game, and we even had to walk through the home stands to get to the away end. Imagine that happening in a men's game! Sure, we got called 'Seaweeds' a few times as we passed the Palace fans, but it was said with a cheeky smile and a laugh each time. After Albion's 1-0 win, we took the train home with zero concerns, despite being surrounded by Eagles supporters. Later the same season, we went to Leyton Orient's Brisbane Road to see another 1-0 Albion win, this time against Tottenham Hotspur Women, and found the environment to be similar. The atmosphere and competition is intense for 90 minutes, but on either side of the game and at half-time it simply feels like a shared community of people keen to help the sport continue to grow, regardless of which team you support. Because of this, Jayne and I get to as many of the Albion Women's London games as we can. If you have yet to attend a women's match, you're missing out on a really enjoyable experience.

***

PROGRAMMES

Have you ever felt like you don't need more *things*? Moving house a couple of times inspired me to declutter, so something I consequently stopped buying was football programmes. When I was younger, I collected one from every Brighton game I attended. Every single one. I still have them, chronologically ordered in binders (yes, I'm a nerd), from my first game in 1986 until the last ever game at the Goldstone in 1997. Despite my decluttering, I haven't been able to part with them. It would be like putting my childhood on eBay. Besides, there is something rather nice about having tangible proof of all the games I went to as a youngster, especially as my memories from childhood grow ever blurrier with age. It remains a space-consuming collection in my parents' loft though (sorry, mum and dad), especially considering I have barely ever revisited any of the programmes from the moment I placed them in their binders. I haven't looked at them once in the last two decades. I guess it might be interesting to dig them out and have a leaf through them at some point. There's one in 1989 in which I was the 'featured ball boy' with a photo of me and a little interview, and there were a few in about 1996 in which, ridiculously, I was modelling some of the official leisurewear as a fresh-faced teenager. But I doubt I would find much of interest in any of the rest. Still, if you ever want to know what Garry Nelson's favourite TV show was in 1988, then I can rifle through the archives for his interview and let you know.

During the Gillingham years, there was a printing error in a programme, which became part of the lexicon at the club offices. After a few matches of the first season, the production of the programme changed hands, with the publishers responsible for creating them under Bellotti's command having been replaced. On page three of the next programme, the incoming editor proudly announced an exciting new era of quality content. They told us that we could expect a much better read and that gone were the days when each programme contained a 'number of mistakes'. However, they'd seemingly forgotten to proofread the editorial and what went to print was that we would no longer see a 'nukber of mistakes'. This most ironic of misspellings caused much hilarity around the Albion's administration offices (which demonstrates that there wasn't much to laugh about during this period of the club's history) and, from then on, the word 'nukber' was used to refer to any mistake or mix-up.

It's fair to say that Albion's entire spell at Priestfield could be suitably described as a 'nukber'.

* * *

GOOD RIDDANCE

If you check the attendance records for Albion's second season at Gillingham, you'll notice that the exact same number of people were at two consecutive league matches. There were 2,703 supporters there for both the Chester City and Torquay United games, which, as well as being quite the coincidence, is an example of how the crowds had remained pretty small during the sophomore season at Priestfield. To be honest though, it was impressive that any fans bothered turning up at all. The people who travelled up to Kent and back on buses, trains or in their cars continued to do so because they were blindly loyal to the Albion. They had fought tooth and nail to rescue their club from oblivion and they certainly weren't going to give up now. Fans signed petitions, arranged marches and lobbied anyone necessary in a bid to enable a permanent return to Brighton. At the conclusion of each game, the PA system belted out 'We Gotta Get Out of This Place' by The Animals.

After an unimaginable amount of red tape and heavy opposition from local residents, Albion were eventually granted permission to play at Withdean Stadium in Brighton from the start of the 1999/2000 season. Things were looking up, and there was even a spell during the second campaign in Gillingham when results were decent. Former captain Brian Horton had taken over as manager from Steve Gritt by now. Gritt was and remains a hero at Brighton & Hove Albion, but things hadn't worked out the season after he masterminded the Great Escape, resulting in his departure. Horton, a legend during his playing days, injected new-found energy to the side and the mood around the club was as good as it had been for some time.

The new boss was a delight to work with. Some afternoons after training had finished he'd pop into the office in the middle of Brighton and sit at the reception desk, chatting away to staff and answering the phone when it rang. If you called the club around 1998/99 and spoke to a northern man who had no idea how to transfer your call but was disarmingly jolly, it's more than likely you were talking directly to Albion's manager.

Disappointingly, Horton left during that season to manage one of his other former clubs, Port Vale, and the wheels immediately came off Albion's wagon. Assistant boss Jeff Wood took over but was relieved of his duties before the campaign was done as his team dropped towards the wrong end of the table. Micky Adams was appointed as the next manager. He would help the club achieve a level of success that we hadn't experienced for a very long time. Adams took charge for the final few games of Albion's two-year stay at Priestfield. Whilst he would soon bring the good times back to the club, these early matches were largely unmemorable and therefore in keeping with the rest of our time in Kent. I must have attended about three-quarters of Brighton's games at this temporary home and I can't think of any abiding highlights. If pushed, I suppose the Fans United Two day was fun. In a similar vein to the seminal Hartlepool match at the Goldstone, it brought together supporters from all over the country in a show of unity. Visitors Doncaster were in a terrible state, so over 6,000 fans turned up to bring their cause, as well as Albion's continuing homelessness, to the broader consciousness. The fact that they were treated to possibly the worst professional football match I have ever seen, a 0-0 draw bereft of skill or guile, didn't seem to bother anyone as they mingled and made friends in the afternoon sunshine.

The generally accepted highlight from Brighton's two years in Kent was a Boxing Day clash with Colchester United, which saw the Seagulls fight back from 3-0 down at half-time to draw 4-4 in a frantic second half. I wasn't there to witness the excitement, as I had chosen to instead stay home and paint the radiators in my flat. I was listening to commentary on the radio and I dropped a dollop of paint on the carpet when the fourth Albion goal went in. I suppose the resultant stain would have been avoided had I gone to the game, but choosing to paint a radiator instead of attending a match is a solid example of how arduous it was to support a poor, bottom-tier club who played 70 miles from home.

Apparently, Kent Police were concerned that Brighton fans might smash up the ground at the conclusion of the club's last game as tenants at Priestfield, but no one did. In stark contrast to the tearful Goldstone farewell two years previously, everyone simply made their way to the exit without so much as a glance back at the place they had been forced to call home for too long. No furious tearing apart of the grandstand, no emotional goodbyes, just good riddance.

PART THREE: WITHDEAN

BACK HOME

BRIGHTON'S RAILWAY station hummed with activity on a short-sleeve summer's afternoon, as thousands of people, bedecked in blue and white, boarded trains. It was a glorious sight. One stop and approximately three minutes later, fans spilled from the open carriage doors at Preston Park station and snaked their way down residential streets. Their destination was a tiny athletics venue by the name of Withdean Stadium. This was Albion's new temporary home, while planning permission was sought for a permanent ground. The stadium was shadowed by lush green woods, earning it the nickname 'The Theatre of Trees'. On one side of the pitch, a roofed stand held 1,500 people, while uncovered seating accommodated 4,500 on the other side. There was a sandpit next to one of the touchlines, an eight-lane running track circled the pitch and there was nothing behind either goal, other than a hammer-throwing net at one end and some hospitality cabins at the other. The changing rooms were also cabins, the club shop was a van in the car park and there was no ticket office, just a dusty little window for ticket collections. It certainly wasn't like any other ground in the league. Midweek games had to be arranged around local athletics meetings and no matches could be played on Saturdays in

December as they would interfere with the park-and-ride Christmas shopping buses. Seriously.

None of these logistical considerations created problems on the Seagulls' first ever game at Withdean though. It was a celebratory day from start to finish. The sun warmed fans' necks as they tightly clasped their tickets at the turnstile queues, ready to enter their new home for a pre-season knockabout with Nottingham Forest. No more journeys to Kent, no more swathes of empty seats. Whilst fair-weather followers of Premier League clubs might have snorted in derision at a set-up that was decidedly non-league, Albion fans who had spent countless hours on double-decker buses to Gillingham for two years, wiping condensation from the windows and wishing for a nicer view, were in heaven. They could now watch their team in a sold-out stadium and be back in a pub in the centre of Brighton not long after 5pm.

The campaigning would continue. Of course it would. Albion's tireless supporters had spent over five years protesting and campaigning and they remained intensely focused on helping the club to secure a permanent stadium on the outskirts of town at Falmer. Several more years of hard work were required if the club were to ever have a place to truly call home again. For one afternoon though, that could all be put on hold. Brighton were back.

Albion's debut appearance at Withdean passed with no major logistical problems and a few days later it was time for the club's first ever competitive game at their new home, against Mansfield Town. Again, it was the kind of sunny day which made jumpers superfluous as fans squeezed on to trains at Brighton and then made their way towards the novel little stadium. As they did so, they passed residents, who stepped into their gardens to watch the flow of people passing by. When Albion were going through the rigmarole of submitting a planning application to play at Withdean, the Not In My Back Yard brigade spent months and years scaremongering locals into believing that Brighton fans would cause chaos in the area, fighting in the streets, weeing in gardens, parking across driveways and leaving mountains of rubbish in the pretty neighbourhood. Representatives from the club worked hard to allay these fears.

They created a huge no-parking zone and included free travel on buses, trains and park-and-ride with each match ticket. Meanwhile, supporters' groups arranged for litter pickers to patrol the local area after matches, making sure all the rogue Mars Bar wrappers and Coke cans were removed. Now, on this summer's day, residents were seeing with their own eyes that any concerns they had were largely unfounded. Walking past their houses were a high proportion of families, seniors and kids, not the gangs of louts they were expecting.

And so, rather than boarding up their windows and cowering behind their sofas, the people who lived around Withdean Stadium would look out every couple of weeks on to streets transformed into something vibrant and actually rather lovely. Fans would offer a wave, sometimes stop for a chat and, in general, treat the area with absolute respect. The lesson here, of course, is that just because someone pulls on a football shirt, it doesn't mean they instantly become a yob, and if you treat people respectfully, they will likely reciprocate.

The atmosphere at Withdean was especially upbeat on this first league match. As the teams took to the field there was the distinct sense that we were finally able to put the dark days behind us and look to the future. The positivity in the stands translated on to the pitch, as Albion set about walloping Mansfield. New signing and local lad Darren Freeman had the definitive dream debut, smashing in a hat-trick, his shoulder-length mess of hair flowing behind him as he tore through the visitors' defence. The game ended 6-0 and remains one of the all-time iconic Albion matches.

As the stands emptied and delighted fans filtered away from the leafy suburb, litter pickers set about their task and Withdean residents must have wondered why they had spent the previous few months protesting and stressing about the impact Brighton & Hove Albion would have on their lives. Indeed, from then on, the relationship between the club and most local residents was amiable. One local would gleefully let off fireworks from their back garden whenever the team scored, and I think that some of the people who were originally the most vocal in their protests went on to become season ticket holders. That might only be a very small example of how a football club positively impacts an area, but given the opposition that the club initially faced, it feels significant.

I can probably talk with more authority than most about the views from the stands at Withdean, as I saw the vista from every single seat. I was one of the people who reapplied numbered stickers to seats every August, only for them to peel off at the first hint of morning dew. Considering the stadium was as ramshackle as anything the league had ever seen, the views weren't too bad in many of the home areas, and anybody who complained about the outlook from their seat needed to spare a thought for the away fans in the latter seasons at Withdean. Initially housed under cover in the North Stand and then given a reasonable spot when more temporary stands were erected behind a goal, they were finally relocated in a new West Stand behind the other goal line, miles from the pitch to the point that they were almost in a different postcode. So distant was the action that, when London teams visited, some of their fans would probably have seen more if they'd stayed home and looked in a southerly direction out of their bedroom windows.

The club's administration offices weren't based at Withdean. They remained in central Brighton and, while they were now in a slightly less grim building than before, the entire operation continued to operate on a shoestring. An average working day at a football club is often just one big problem-solving session. When coaching staff decide on a whim to, for instance, give a Hungarian left-back 45 minutes in a reserve game so that they can have a look at him, it isn't as simple as giving him the address of the ground and reminding him not to forget his boots. The hours that Albion's long-serving former club secretary, Derek Allan, spent hovering around the fax machine waiting for incomprehensible documents from various Eastern European football associations are testament to that. The anachronistic and bureaucratic way in which the governing bodies ran the game in those days meant that Derek always seemed to engage in a ridiculous amount of paperwork when performing a seemingly simple operation. There was so much red tape involved with the administrative side of not just the first team, but the reserves and youths as well. I'm sure things are easier now that most correspondence is done online, but if you were ever at the club's offices at the start of the 21st century and happened to see someone standing frustratedly over the fax machine, that was likely Derek, who was club secretary for well over two decades.

The reason it was particularly hard for Albion staff to deal with flies in their ointment was because there was a continuing lack of resources and people power. Down in the ticket office, where I was now working full-time, the server crashed every morning. Every single morning. Not even the geekiest of computer geeks was able to work out why, and there was no money to replace it. So, at the start of each working day when we should have been answering calls and selling tickets, we'd instead be repeatedly rebooting the server until it decided to whir into life. It was a frustrating waste of time. On matchdays, we'd have to physically carry everything we needed up to Withdean, as we didn't have enough hardware to store any there between games. We'd literally unplug a ticket printer from the office in town, carry it up to Withdean and link it up to a laptop there. On cold days, the printer refused to work unless it was warmed up with a hairdryer. That isn't an exaggeration; a hairdryer was a vital piece of kit on matchdays. After a few gusts of hot air, the printer would reluctantly start coughing out tickets. Running an entire ticketing operation on a matchday from one slow laptop and an even slower server sums up how challenging Withdean's setup was. There were no ticket sales permitted at the stadium (all tickets had to be sold in advance), but there were still plenty of collections, enquiries and reprints. The ticket collection point at Withdean was situated nowhere near the laptop. That would have been too easy. There was no electricity in the small gatehouse from which we dealt with enquiries, so a seemingly simple action of, for instance, reprinting a lost ticket would go thus:

A supporter would approach the ticket collection point and explain they needed a reprint. Julie, the ticket office staff member who operated the gatehouse, would write their details on a piece of paper and hand said paper to one of her two young children. They would then run to the office cabin and hand the supporter's details to whoever was operating the laptop. This was usually my mum. She would type in the details and wait ages for the slow server to locate them on the system. If everything about the supporter's request was legitimate (and in this time of sold-out matches, it often wasn't), she would reprint the ticket. Assuming the printer didn't need another blast from the hairdryer, it would spit out the ticket. Julie's offspring would then run back down to the ticket collection point, hand the ticket to Julie and she would pass it on to the waiting fan. That was how one relatively simple enquiry was dealt with. This process would be repeated dozens of times each game. The queue would grow larger as kick-off approached and people became increasingly impatient. Because there was only one laptop, if a complicated query emerged, it would take longer, and the queue would consequently increase in length. So, if you ever wondered why you had to wait an age to collect your ticket at Withdean, it's likely because the fastest way to print it involved two adults, two locations, a young child, a slow laptop and a printer which would only work in a warm climate.

It was clear within a few weeks of the move to Withdean that the team's popularity had outgrown staffing levels and facilities, but there was never really an option to employ more people or improve technology. The stadium's small capacity and the cost of matchday operations meant, I think, that the club was haemorrhaging money. So, whilst absolutely nothing was simple about the day-to-day running of Brighton & Hove Albion at this point, staff just had to roll up their sleeves and get on with it. Surprisingly enough, working in these conditions was kinda fun. There was a certain Dunkirk spirit to being part of a small group of dedicated employees who were doing a decent job despite our nomadic existence. The fans were happy that the team was back in Brighton and performing well, and Micky Adams was well respected by the players and popular around the office. There was a sense of togetherness and a feelgood factor that had been missing for some years.

***

WHEN THE BALL HITS THE NET

Sometimes a player comes along who turns all fans, regardless of their age, into star-struck schoolkids. For Brighton supporters older than me, it was Peter Ward. With corkscrew curls and a hip-shaking swagger, his goals at the end of the 1970s helped elevate Albion to the top division for the first time. As far as cult heroes go, the ultimate icon was Russian international Sergei Gotsmanov, who lit up the Goldstone for a short spell in the late 1980s.

He was quick and silky and the fact that he didn't speak a word of English made him exhilaratingly enigmatic to a teenage boy like me. He played up front and scored a bunch of goals, including an extraordinary one against Hull City on a misty Friday night at the Goldstone. Gotsmanov picked up the ball and seemed to dribble around the entire visiting team, leaving a ragged collection of limbs in his wake. It was like a badly choreographed scene from a football film, with defenders conveniently falling out of the attacker's way as he skipped towards goal. The remarkable thing, though, was that as Gotsmanov shimmied past the goalkeeper, he cheekily raised both arms into the air *before* nonchalantly slotting the ball into an empty net. It would be something I'd unsuccessfully attempt to re-enact on the school playing field in the following weeks and months. When Ross Barkley celebrated in a similar fashion before scoring for Everton in 2017, Brighton fans of a certain age were transported back to that Friday night in Hove, when a Russian loanee elevated an otherwise unremarkable occasion into something unforgettable, merely by raising his arms a couple of seconds early. Football really doesn't need to do much to spark happiness and create memories, does it?

I'm not sure how apocryphal this is, but I heard a story that Gotsmanov used to deliberately park his Lada on double yellow lines around Brighton, picking up dozens of parking tickets in the process. Somehow the purpose of double yellows got lost in translation and he thought that they were areas where you were supposed to leave your car. Presumably he thought the tickets on his windscreen were notes of commendation for his excellent parking skills.

Sergei wasn't around for long enough to be the next Peter Ward, but during the first season at Withdean a genuine contender to Ward's throne would emerge. By the latter stages of the campaign, optimism was eroding. Micky Adams' team had stagnated and promotion hopes had faded to nothing, so the Seagulls moved into the transfer market in the hope of re-energising their season by recruiting a loan striker from Bristol Rovers. He was a tall, gangly teenager with the gait of a foal, and he had been struggling to get game-time at Rovers, who were then managed by Ian Holloway. It's fair to say that Brighton fans weren't expecting a great deal from a player who couldn't make the Rovers first team. His name was Bobby Zamora.

Zamora's impact was immediate. He headed a goal on his debut at Withdean and went on to score five more in the remaining five matches of his loan spell. It didn't quite propel the team back into the play-offs, but he showed enough promise for Albion to scrape together £100,000 to sign him permanently. For the next three years, Zamora's performances would repay that transfer fee several times over. It would be unfair to say that Brighton became a one-man team but there is no doubt that Zamora would terrify opponents. He was strong, confident, good in the air and had a deadly left foot. He got the crowd on their feet and brought the best out of his team-mates, including left-footed right-back Paul Watson, with whom he seemed to share a telepathic relationship. When Albion won a free kick in opposition territory, Watson would quickly dink the ball towards Zamora, who had a knack of timing his run to perfection to break the offside trap, leaving him completely alone in the penalty area to head past a stranded goalkeeper while defenders stood on their heels, blaming each other for not picking up the run. This happened with remarkable regularity and is an example of football being a very simple game when it's done right.

On a winter's afternoon on a sandy Withdean pitch, Zamora scored a goal against Halifax Town that was greeted not with cheers, but with gasps of astonishment. A high, spinning ball dropped from the clouds into the box. Zamora positioned himself underneath it and blasted a first-time volley into the far corner of the net from a tight angle. Imagine a lower league version of that famous Van Basten strike and you'd be close. Not many goals make you involuntarily shout, 'oh my god', but that's exactly what I did as it almost took the net off.

There were so many other moments of magic at which to marvel. Away at Bury, he chipped one past the goalkeeper with such deft skill that there was no doubt in anyone's mind this kid would be playing in the Premier League before too long. And at Chesterfield one night, he noticed the goalkeeper was only holding the ball in one hand, so he kicked it loose and tapped it into the empty goal. A few minutes later, he outpaced two defenders and hit a screamer to secure the win.

Incidentally, Zamora's cheeky first goal at Chesterfield emulated a classic Brighton moment from the 1990s, when George Parris did a similar thing against Bristol Rovers. After an attack broke down and the Rovers goalkeeper picked up the ball, Parris literally hid behind the goalpost. As the goalkeeper dropped the ball and began to run forward with it, Albion's midfielder dashed out, tackled him and stroked it into an empty net. The goal earned

Parris the nickname of 'Sneaky George' and, if you ever wanted proof that football is really just pantomime with more cardio, Rovers fans were even shouting 'he's behind you!' to no avail.

On the pitch, Zamora was a superhero; every kid wanted his name on the back of their shirt. Off the field, he was affable, humble and a great ambassador for Brighton & Hove Albion. He was obviously so much better than the level at which he found himself though, meaning Seagulls fans were forever in fear that he was going to be sold. I think this was before there were designated transfer windows, so there was always a nagging worry that a Premier League club was going to snatch him from us at any time. Scouts and managers turned up to every home game. Southampton's Gordon Strachan and Glenn Hoddle (boooo!) from Spurs seemed to be permanently present. This is a fear that grips all fans of lower league clubs. You want your players to be good, but you don't want your best players to be *too* good, or they won't be yours for much longer. It's a strange tightrope to walk.

The financial constraints of playing at Withdean coupled with the cost of trying to move to a permanent stadium meant it was only a matter of time before an offer came in that was too juicy to turn down. A £1.5m bid came from Tottenham Hotspur in July 2003 and, with that, Zamora became a Spurs player. It seems like pocket change in today's market but to a club playing at a rented athletics track it was huge. The sense of sadness was undeniable though. We'd seen him grow from a lanky teenager into an England U21 international and now a rich club had just plucked him away from us by waving a few quid in our direction. I was at a Super Furry Animals gig in London when I found out Zamora had finally gone. A friend texted me to tell me the news. The fact that I can still remember exactly what I was doing when his departure was announced shows just what a seismic event it was.

Before he left the club, Zamora had three incredibly successful seasons as a Brighton player. He signed permanently before the start of the 2000/01 campaign, and his arrival made Albion one of the favourites to be promoted from the league's bottom division. The fans were certainly confident. So much so that, before kick-off at the first game away to Southend United, they chanted 'bring on the champions'. This level of arrogance was unusual amongst Albion fans, who had grown used to their team being largely useless over many years. It also seemed misplaced, at least initially. The chants acted as a rallying cry for Southend's players, who promptly dispatched Brighton 2-0. Micky Adams' men would go on to lose three of their first four league games. If they were to be champions, they would have to buck their ideas up. Fortunately, they did. The club hadn't won promotion since 1988, meaning it was hard to remember how it felt to experience glory, and I don't think I was the only supporter who was nervously waiting for things to go wrong, but with each passing week throughout the season the prospect of going up, and perhaps even winning the league, became increasingly likely. All home games sold out in minutes as each one took on an increased level of significance. In February, Cardiff City visited. They had money to burn and were one of Albion's promotion rivals. Victory in that game would be huge.

On any matchday during the Withdean years, there were few more depressing sights for a fan upon opening the curtains in the morning than being greeted by rain. In the spring sunshine or on a crisp, clear autumn night under floodlights, the silly little stadium was an oddly pleasant place to watch football, but in messy drizzle or a downpour, it was hideous. The annoying thing about playing in a stadium that was open to the elements was that it seemed to rain almost every game. Sussex could have been enjoying a heatwave from Monday to Friday but, if the Seagulls were at home on the weekend, the weather would inevitably be awful. Aside from a few outdoorsy types who owned a full set of waterproofs, most supporters would arrive hopelessly unequipped for such conditions. Despite taking shelter until the last possible moment, many fans found themselves sitting in wet jeans and sodden trainers by the time the referee blew his whistle to signal the start of the match. The club sold plastic ponchos from the mobile shop for a quid, but they were almost as ineffective as Albion's defence had been during the Priestfield years. Sometimes though, the games were so engaging that the rain didn't matter at all. For instance, it was only upon getting home from the match against Cardiff and watching the highlights on TV that I realised just how heavy the downpour had been. It was a magnificent encounter. Zamora gave Albion an early lead, after which they desperately hung on for the remaining 75 minutes while the visitors, whose players were technically better than Brighton's, threw everything forward. Albion players were out on their feet by the final moments of the game, the heavy surface sapping what remained of their energy. The home fans recognised this and played their part, defying the stadium's poor acoustics to create a din. The team reacted, chasing every ball as if they were Tom Hanks trying to recover Wilson from the sea in *Castaway* and Albion held on for a vital win. Rain? What rain?

Brighton wouldn't lose another home game for the remainder of the season. Withdean wasn't usually a cauldron of noise and the pitch was a bog in the early years, but home advantage was gained via the fact that opponents were so weirded out by the surroundings. The experience was surreal enough to knock them out of their stride. Even for the lower leagues, it was an odd place, with its temporary stands and running track in the shadow of a nature reserve. By the time our opponents had got to grips with Withdean's oddness, Albion had invariably stolen a march on them.

***

BROWN ENVELOPES

Brighton won promotion with games to spare, away at Plymouth Argyle, and many fans were taken by surprise by the timing of Albion's triumph. To gain promotion that day, the Seagulls needed to win and rely on quite a few other results going their way, certainly too many to realistically expect promotion to be secured down in Devon. However, one by one the scores fell the way Albion needed, and a 2-0 win over Argyle meant that we were up. Those of us who didn't make the long journey to Plymouth grew more and more incredulous that every other result was going in our favour. When the final whistle blew, I cracked open some booze. I was 11 years old when we had last won promotion and, having waited over a decade to experience such success again, it felt somewhat anticlimactic that it tasted of cheap lager and that I was experiencing it alone in the living room of my small flat in the centre of Eastbourne. Still, the bonus for people like me who regretted deciding against an arduous trip to Plymouth was that, soon after, we had the chance to win the title in a match against Chesterfield.

Chesterfield had led the way for most of the campaign but, hampered by an inquiry into illegal payments to their players, their form tailed off to the point that Albion had whittled away their lead and eventually overtaken them. When the two teams faced each other in Sussex on the first day of May, Brighton knew that victory would secure the Division Three championship, the club's first silverware since the 1960s. As the teams took to the field, Albion supporters waved brown envelopes of various sizes at their opponents in reference to the aforementioned illegal payments. Stationery banter.

The game was tight and uninspiring and, with no sign of a breakthrough well into the second half, I started talking to a God in which I didn't believe, in a 'I know you're not there, but just in case you are' kind of way, pleading with the omnipresent one to see his/her way to letting Albion score a goal. Soon, I was suggesting a trade.

'Okay God, if you let us score, I will actually start believing in you.'

Still no goal.

'Okay God, if you let us score, I will even start going to church.'

Still no goal.

'Okay God, if you let us score, I will ...'

My train of thought was interrupted by an Albion corner. It was met by the shiny head of centre-back Danny Cullip. The ball ricocheted into the roof of the net, directly in front of the travelling supporters. Cue delight on the other two sides of the stadium. Albion were minutes away from winning the league, something that hardly anyone in the ground had ever previously witnessed. History was being made in front of our eyes. Chesterfield weren't especially bothered with trying to force an equaliser because results elsewhere meant that, despite losing, they were about to be promoted. As the referee blew the final whistle, I felt an unusual sensation. My team was successful. Aside from one glorious season in 1988, the Brighton players I had watched for years were always nearly-men or, more often, nowhere-near-men. So, it was new and unusual to finally experience what it was like to win something. A few minutes later, under a navy night sky, Albion's players held aloft the Division Three trophy to a strobe of camera flashes and a mighty roar from the crowd. The team then performed a lap of honour before disappearing down the tunnel. In this pre-smartphone era, my dad managed to get some amazing camcorder footage of the players celebrating in the changing room. Beer and champagne flying everywhere, shirtless hugs and tuneless singalongs.

As the stands eventually cleared, I went to the hospitality lounge for a drink. It was twice as busy as normal, twice as noisy. Micky Adams soon appeared, suited, smiling and carrying the trophy. He eventually and reluctantly let it go so it could be passed around the room. People kissed it, held it aloft and posed for photos with it, before handing it to the next eager recipient. When it reached me, I did the same. My mum, dad and sister were there with me, so we grabbed a quick family photograph. It was the first time we'd stood together in a photo in years. In it, we are red-cheeked and beaming. After sinking several bottles of beer, I made my way on to the now empty streets outside the ground, still giddy with excitement. I paused, remembering my nervous, very one-sided conversation with God from earlier in the night. Had it really had an impact, or was the victory simply down to the granite forehead of Danny Cullip? Either way, I'm afraid to say that I reneged on the deal I had made. Sorry God.

***

WHAT DO I KNOW?

Doesn't there always seem to be a supporter sitting close to you, either in the pub or in the stands, who believes themselves to be a football oracle? They spend 90 minutes making loud proclamations about how the forwards need to 'play between the lines', with the sole purpose of letting everyone know just how knowledgeable they are. They seem entirely oblivious to the fact that anyone within earshot would prefer it if they kept their dazzling insights to themselves, thank you very much. However, whilst most of us limit our verbal output to shouts of encouragement or despair, or to having a sing-song, if we're being completely honest there is something of this person in all of us. Simply, football fans think they know as much as the experts. We post on our socials about how the manager made the wrong substitutions or how so-and-so should have passed instead of shooting, and we do so with the assuredness of a *Match of the Day* pundit and on the assumption that anyone gives a hoot about our opinions.

Peter Taylor, who took over as Brighton boss after Micky Adams departed for Leicester City, proved in no uncertain terms that when it comes to football knowledge there is a reason why some people are managers and others pay money to sit in the stands. Brighton had continued their fantastic form after Taylor took over from Adams. Adapting with ease to the higher division, the team were pushing for back-to-back promotions, yet the cynics amongst Brighton's sell-out crowds suggested that Taylor had simply inherited a squad on an unstoppable upward trajectory and that anyone could have successfully managed them. This was nonsense. The proof, for those who needed it, that Taylor knew what he was doing came when Albion faced Alan Pardew's Reading at home in the second half of the season. It was an important game between the division's top two sides. When a colleague put a teamsheet in my hand 45 minutes before kick-off, I studied it and quickly concluded that Taylor had gone quite mad. He'd picked a starting eleven that no one could have second-guessed. I reread the A4 piece of paper in the hope it would make more sense a second time. Maybe it was some kind of Da Vinci code that required deciphering. But no, even after a few minutes I still couldn't fathom what shape the team would take, and it seemed as though Taylor had randomly picked eleven names out of a hat. The teamsheet was passed around the office at Withdean and raised many eyebrows and even a few chuckles. I was convinced we were going to get slaughtered. A terrible night in the pouring rain (surprise, surprise) awaited. What actually happened was that Brighton absolutely smashed Reading that night. And that is one of many reasons why Taylor has managed England and I have not.

Not only was he a good manager, but also a genuinely top man. The first thing he did when he became Albion boss was to take all the staff out to dinner. Not just the training staff. Everyone. All the people who worked in the administration offices, the shop and the ticket office joined Taylor and his coaching team in a small restaurant in Hove for a meal and some drinks. It was a nice gesture, especially considering there were some managers who I never once met while I was employed by the club. Taylor, though, was clearly keen to bring as much unity as possible to a club fragmented by the fact that its small team of staff worked across three separate locations. To him, it was probably just a nice way to meet and greet his new colleagues, but to the rest of us it was a surreal experience. This was, after all, the man who had handed David Beckham the England captaincy.

Taylor has drifted into semi-obscurity in recent years, making it easy to forget how famous he was at the time. A month or so after he'd taken us all out to dinner, my mum and I went with him to a pub in Eastbourne, where he had promised to draw a charity raffle. He didn't know the area and asked if, as locals, we'd accompany him. It was then that I saw first-hand how people acted differently around him than with Joe Nobodies like me. When we stopped for petrol on the way, the bloke behind the counter went all shy and giggly when he served him. When we arrived in the pub, Taylor walked through the door and the music stopped, pool balls halted mid-roll and every punter in the packed establishment stared in awe. He chatted and signed autographs for much longer than he would have liked, I'm sure, but his demeanour didn't betray any desire to go home.

That evening gave me a glance through the looking glass at what an annoyance fame must sometimes be. Not Peter Taylor's level, but mega-fame. Sure, there are upsides (the money, the lifestyle) but imagine being a superstar and wanting to go to the supermarket without having to pose for a billion selfies. Imagine being papped and having the unflattering images shared online. Imagine being Amy Winehouse, whose entire unravelling was played out through a never-ending flurry of flashlights. All she wanted was to be left alone and to exorcise her demons through her music. But the press wanted the smeared make-up, barely conscious Winehouse for their front pages, so that we could all have a jolly good laugh. If that's what fame can entail, then I'm very happy to be nobody.

Brighton and Reading met again less than a month after Taylor's tactical masterclass at Withdean. This time, they played out a draw in Berkshire, which was notable for two reasons. Firstly, ensuring our rivals didn't beat us was another important step towards winning a second successive title. Secondly, it was at this match that my mate Mark gave himself whiplash while celebrating a last-minute goal. Actual whiplash, diagnosed by a doctor. The fact that the goal was immediately disallowed made his injury even more comical.

Mark experiences the spectrum of football emotions more acutely than me. Sometimes, when reminiscing about the old days, he will still lament a defeat so passionately and animatedly that you'd be forgiven for thinking he was talking about a game that had just happened, rather than a humdrum match at Priestfield which the rest of us had long since forgotten. We all know a Mark, don't we? Sometimes we are Mark. Although I doubt many of us have given themselves whiplash celebrating a disallowed goal. I guess everyone reacts differently to their team scoring. Some people, usually blokey blokes, are super-aggressive; all fists, beetroot faces and bulging eyes. Others stand relatively still with arms outstretched and chest puffed, a la Eric Cantona, in the direction of the away fans. Some hug the nearest person, while a small number of strange individuals react by merely giving a somewhat gentle golf clap. I personally enjoy seeing, as a group of players celebrate, a rogue fan trying not to drop his burger as he scuttles to the front of the stand in their direction. Then, of course, there is the lone pitch-invader who can't resist treading the turf to cuddle his heroes. My favourite thing about them is that, almost as soon as they've placed a foot on the turf, you can tell from their body language that they know they've crossed a line. Indeed, that's literally what they've done. They don't quite know what to do next and, as they desperately try to retain their footing on the watered surface, you can see them thinking, 'I'm getting banned for this, aren't I?'

During my childhood, I made the trip to Swindon Town's County Ground on the Junior Seagulls coach and, as usual, sat in the home end. The game ebbed and flowed and I even shared my bag of Revels with the young Swindon fan next to me, secretly hoping that he'd pick all the disgusting coffee ones. Surprisingly, during an era when Brighton were awful on the road, we went a goal ahead. Entirely unsurprisingly, the home side equalised and, soon after, grabbed a winner. This prompted the Swindon fan, who had barely made a sound all game, to celebrate wildly, directing his emotions solely in my direction, pointing in my face and then laughing like a cartoon villain. He performed a solo chorus of 'you're not singing anymore', again, entirely for my benefit. I considered mentioning to him that I hadn't been singing in the first place, but, as his eyes grew increasingly maniacal and he began to jump even more furiously on the spot, I realised it would have perhaps only served to stoke his fire. After celebrating, he just sat down calmly and continued watching the game as if nothing had happened.

It's curious how some people feel the need to immediately rub opposing fans' faces in their own misery. I understand that there is an important place for *Schadenfreude* in football, and that the game would be dull without a healthy dose of rivalry, but I've never really wanted to take a moment as pure and magical as a goal and turn it into something spiteful. I think there is enough cynicism in the world already, and certainly not enough undiluted joy to waste it in such a manner. I suppose goals make us lose all cognitive thought and instead provoke visceral and raw emotions, causing involuntary actions. At least that's what another one of my friends, Andy, will have you believe if you ask him about his reaction to a late goal against Bristol City at the climax of the 2001/02 season.

Albion knew that a win in the Easter Monday match at Withdean would put them on the brink of promotion to English football's second tier. With the game level deep into injury time, a hopeful inswinging cross was fired into the box. Striker Lee Steele, who seemed to be so far offside that he was practically leaning on the goalpost, flicked a header into the net to secure the three points. While City's players complained to the referee's assistant about Steele being approximately ten yards offside, I turned to celebrate with my buddy Andy, who had been sitting next to me in the front row of the South Stand. But Andy was nowhere to be seen. Where on earth had he gone? Amid a sea of limbs, I spotted him. He was literally skipping with joy along the running track. Skipping! Arms aloft, he pranced towards the end of the stadium where Steele had essentially sealed promotion.

When was the last time you skipped anywhere? Andy's unscripted delight remains one of my all-time favourite football memories. It shows just how much happiness the game can bring and how it has the power to regress adults to childlike glee.

***

POST, NOT VERY MODERN

By the time the 2002/03 season kicked off, I was the ticket office manager at Brighton & Hove Albion. Because there were only a small number of matchday tickets on sale for each home game, they were sold via a somewhat convoluted and old-fashioned postal ballot, dreamed up by the club's then safety officer as being the fairest way to distribute them. For every match, we invited people to provide a postal application by a certain date, after which we would literally perform a lucky dip. The successful applicants got tickets in the post, while the unsuccessful ones got an apology letter. It wasn't an ideal arrangement and most people, understandably, couldn't be bothered with the effort involved, meaning we didn't receive very many requests. So, despite the generally accepted assumption that it was impossible to see matches at Withdean, the truth is that very few people who applied were unsuccessful.

The club was now entering the fourth year at Withdean and there was no sign of a move to our own stadium at Falmer happening any time soon. We'd marched, lobbied and signed countless petitions, yet the club still faced seemingly immovable opposition at every turn. Crystal Palace legend Steve Coppell had become our manager, despite having been the protagonist in one of the Albion fans' anti-Palace chants for years. We lost his first match 4-2 having led 2-0. The next week, as fate would have it, we went to Selhurst Park for a match against Palace, our first meeting in years. Despite the miserable run of results, there was palpable excitement about the upcoming fixture and we'd sold about 6,000 tickets, meaning there would be almost as many Seagulls supporters at Selhurst Park as there usually were at Withdean. My ticket office colleagues and I headed to the match on the train, and our entourage included my friend and workmate Gary who, rather than taking a seat alongside us in the away stand, instead headed to the home end. Gary, you see, was the same ardent Palace fan that was in my small cluster of misfit chums back in school. Although he worked diligently in the Albion ticket office and attended several Brighton games, Gary's only love was the team in the red and blue. We didn't keep this a secret either. Regular visitors to the ticket office would often tease him about his favourite team and, to his ultimate credit, he took the banter in good spirit. This, in my opinion, is the very definition of how a rivalry should be. Give me light-hearted teasing over abuse or fisticuffs any day.

Once in the stadium, we waved to Gary from our position at the side of the pitch as he took his seat behind the goal. The pre-match atmosphere was fantastic. Brighton fans were in good voice and there was a strange sense that this would be the day that Albion finally got a much-needed win. It was written in the stars.

Only it wasn't. I think it is the worst I have ever seen an Albion team perform, which, considering how we spent a lot of time at the foot of the entire league, is really saying something. The goals flew in with painful regularity and, out of the corner of my eye, I could see Gary jumping up and down jubilantly. By the time Palace went five goals ahead with a worryingly large chunk of the game still to go, Palace fans were even singing Coppell's name. It was a horror show. It finished 5-0, with striker Andy Johnson bagging a hat-trick. We could have lost by ten. As I left the stadium with a handful of Albion staff members and 6,000 thoroughly miserable souls, we were greeted by a line of police officers blocking the road, ready to keep us there until the home supporters had dispersed. I found myself right in front of the police line and the mood behind me quickly turned nasty. Having been humiliated by our main rivals, we all just wanted to go home, and a surge of bodies from behind me attempted to break through the human barricade. The police pushed back. Scuffles broke out. As the situation grew uglier, one of my party flashed his Albion staff pass to a member of the local police and explained untruthfully that our car was in the stadium's car park. We were permitted to slip through the cordon.

Happy to be out of the melee and with none of us wearing Brighton colours, we wandered past the ground towards the train station. After a few minutes, a group of Palace fans ran down the street, swinging fists at the few other Albion fans that had managed to somehow break through the police line and who were looking for some aggro. Like anyone with half a brain, I do my best to stay away from violence, so battling Palace oiks was the last thing I wanted. My friends felt the same, so we ducked into the nearest newsagent, as did a handful of bemused local shoppers. The shopkeeper hurriedly locked the door behind us, before peering through the window at what was unfolding outside, just as they would in a zombie movie. It turned out though that, while these Palace and Brighton hoodlums were faster than your average zombie, they were certainly less of a threat.

Exclusively in their teens, they were soon chased off by police, and resorted to taking out their aggression on bus shelters and bins as they ran. Realising that we weren't dealing with a violent firm of hooligans but rather a bunch of kids buzzing on cheap lager, we excused ourselves from the shop and made our way back out on to the south London streets, keen to get back to Sussex and forget all about the dismal afternoon we'd just experienced. On the train home, we met up with Gary, who was mercifully humble in victory. Humble that is, until he got a few beers inside him in one of Eastbourne's dingier nightclubs that evening. Then, for my benefit, he requested that the DJ gave a shoutout to 'Andy' in congratulation of his hat-trick earlier that day. Considering the amount of stick he got about his chosen team when working in the ticket office, and bearing in mind the drubbing that they'd just given Brighton, his 'banter via the medium of DJ' seemed entirely justified.

The only positive from the Palace game was that it was Albion's nadir, and Coppell soon got the team playing really rather well. Apparently his preparation for games was incredibly meticulous, and his players knew, to the finest detail, exactly what to expect from their opponents. Micky Adams always used to say that failing to prepare meant preparing to fail and Coppell obviously also adhered to this notion. Along with the manager's fine work, the Withdean factor continued to work to Albion's advantage, with pampered second-tier players being susceptible to the oddness of their surroundings. I remember Italian striker Fabrizio Ravanelli warming up as a substitute for Derby County and surveying the scene with a look of bewilderment in his eyes. His facial expression suggested he was thinking, 'How has it come to this?' as his Derby side lost 1-0. Similarly, Wolves didn't cope very well with playing at Withdean for the first time and were blitzed 4-1, while Watford were spanked 4-0.

For other teams though, the stadium was an enjoyable novelty rather than a hurdle. Norwich City supporters, for instance, had a great time on their first visit. Not only did they see their team stroll to a comfortable 2-0 victory, but they were lucky enough to be present for something of a landmark occasion. A few minutes before kick-off, Albion's stadium announcer, with the pride of a father revealing the arrival of his firstborn, guided everyone's attention to a new stadium clock. Joy of joys! A clock. It wasn't even a very nice clock. It looked like it had been stolen from a train station concourse. The Norwich fans took the opportunity to give it a wonderfully sarcastic standing ovation. There were many times when the limitations of Withdean drew unfair ridicule from opposition fans, yet on this occasion their mockery was entirely justified. If our status as the division's poor relations hadn't already been cemented, then this certainly did the trick. It was professional football's equivalent of a schoolkid turning up on a non-uniform day in his supermarket trainers while everyone else was wearing the latest Nikes.

Despite Brighton performing well under Coppell, the team never fully recovered from the slow start to the season and the campaign ended in relegation at the appropriately named Grimsby on the final day. I was on a three-month sabbatical in Australia at the time, and I can confirm that there are few weirder ways to endure your team getting relegated than by following the score on a communal computer in a hostel in Alice Springs. I don't think it was possible to stream games online in 2003 (if it was then I certainly didn't know about it), so I had to settle for constantly refreshing the BBC's webpage for 90 minutes. It was a dry and emotionless way of watching Albion fail to avoid the drop. At the conclusion of the match, I logged off, walked into the hostel garden, opened a beer and gazed up at a crystal clear night sky. I felt as though I could reach up and grab a handful of stars. However, even though my surroundings were preferable to being in Grimsby, I still felt a twinge of guilt and detachment at not being at the game to cheer on the team. I finished my drink and went to bed, the snores of the nine other people in the dormitory and the grumbling disappointment of relegation keeping me awake.

***

MOUNTAIN OF TICKETS

Albion's 2003/04 season was a strange one. In keeping with the trend of short-term managerial stints, Steve Coppell departed, to be replaced by Mark McGhee. The Scot was popular around the club and put together a solid team. Despite not always looking like promotion material, we nonetheless found ourselves nestled in the play-off positions after 46 games.

With Albion bringing home a rather fortunate 1-0 win from the first leg of the play-off semi-final against Swindon Town, the Withdean weather outdid itself for the return fixture. Fans turned up in shorts and T-shirts only for blue skies to give way to the mother of all storms. Thunderbolt and lightning, very, very frightening. Everyone got soaked. The supporters who travelled down from Swindon saw their team completely outplay Brighton. They led 1-0 after 90 minutes, meaning the match went to extra time, during which the visitors doubled their advantage. It seemed that they were going to the final, and deservedly so.

I'm not proud of this but with the aggregate score at 2-1 to Swindon, I remember thinking that, as disappointing as the imminent defeat was, at least I wouldn't have to deal with the logistical nightmare of trying to shift 30,000 tickets for the final. Whilst I wanted Albion to go to the Millennium Stadium (now named the Principality Stadium) in Cardiff and achieve promotion, I was absolutely terrified of the prospect of having to allocate all those tickets. Our set-up was barely sufficient to fulfil our everyday duties, let alone an actual cup final. I understand that this reaction will seem appalling to anyone that hasn't worked at a football club, but if you say the words 'play-offs' or 'cup run' to a member of staff at any ticket office in the country, you'll likely witness a Pavlovian look of dismay on their faces. Any such supplementary matches strike terror into the heart of your average ticket office worker. I'll talk more about this later, when I delve into an FA Cup ticketing debacle of which I was at the epicentre, but the fact was that we had four members of staff, three computers, three phone lines, no internet, and printers which broke if you so much as looked at them the wrong way. So, as awful as it sounds, part of me was relieved that I would no longer have to worry about the play-off final, and I started to think about my summer break.

It soon became apparent that I was lying to myself. I wasn't relieved, I was just trying to put a positive spin on a wasted opportunity. How did my self-deceit become apparent? Well, when centre-back Adam Virgo popped up with a last-minute header to level the tie, I went absolutely nuts, hugging anyone close to me, yelling and doing some kind of celebratory jig. We'd equalised in the last minute of a play-off semi-final! I was over the moon. Sure, somewhere in my mind was the nagging worry that this goal might result in a queue of thousands of people outside my office but, to hell with that, we'd equalised in the last minute of a play-off semi-final! I imagine my facial expression at the time perfectly combined happiness and utter panic.

I've never felt confident about a penalty shoot-out involving Brighton, except on this occasion. There was no doubt in my mind that Albion would win it. Swindon's body language was enough to convince me of that. They were seconds from the final, only to have it snatched from them, while the Brighton players had been resigned to their season being over but had earned an unlikely second chance. Swindon's heads had dropped. This was only going to end one way.

It did. Albion won the shoot-out and booked a place in the final against Bristol City. The Withdean pitch was invaded by joyous fans. What a night it had been. The Seagulls were one game from promotion.

A couple of days after Albion overcame Swindon, I stood at the end of the long table in the club's boardroom with club secretary Derek Allan, looking at a mountain of play-off final tickets that had just been delivered by motorbike courier. They would go on sale the very next morning, in what would be the biggest ticketing operation that the club had overseen since the 1991 play-off final. It was a daunting prospect, but the sales day actually turned out to be a fantastic occasion. Fans lined around the block for hours and hours and hours at Withdean Stadium and at our town centre ticket office, and the atmosphere was one of merriment and anticipation. The queues snaked for what felt like miles. We opened at 9am and were still selling tickets at 10pm. At no point was there a time when we weren't serving. We had cardboard boxes under the counter filled with thousands and thousands of pounds in bank notes (another indicator of how low-tech our operation was). As night fell, queuing supporters utilised the off-licence across the street and, with bellies full of beer, treated bemused Saturday night party-goers to uproarious choruses of 'Sussex by the Sea'.

It was an almost indescribable feeling when my ticket office pals and I stepped into the Millennium Stadium on a boiling hot May day and witnessed a sea of blue and white. Just over a week previously, this had all been nothing more than an ominously large pile of tickets on the boardroom table. Now, here we were, in a beautiful arena which made Withdean look like my back garden. The past month of play-off madness had been worth it. The hours of overtime from staff with aching backs and tired eyes, and the patient, good-natured queuing from fans, many of whom were inconvenienced by having to journey into the centre of Brighton from all over the country to buy their tickets, had created this magnificent scene.

The game, played under the harsh stare of the sun, produced the kind of tension typical of a cup final. Albion's defence was strong and McGhee's industrial gameplan for the players to disrupt the flow and stop Bristol City from getting into a rhythm was working to perfection. Extra time seemed likely until Brighton striker Chris Iwelumo was felled like an old oak tree in the area. Penalty!

Leon Knight stepped up to take the spot kick with seven minutes to go. There was a slight pause in his approach and then he arrowed the ball into the bottom left corner. The blue and white half of the stadium erupted with noise as Knight threw off his shirt and ran to the corner flag. 'We're actually going to win this,' I remember thinking, almost in disbelief. And we did. We were up.

It was a perfect occasion. I cringed then, as I do now, to think that I was almost pleased when it seemed like we were going to lose in the semi-final. Whilst working at a football club can gradually ebb away at the supporter in you, days such as these remind you of why you fell in love with the game in the first place.

***

MARIE

The ticket office shared a space with the merchandising team. I worked behind the ticket counter with my Eastbourne pals Phil and the aforementioned Gary the Palace fan, and there was always some form of japery going on. Like the time we conspired with club shop manager Ian to persuade sales assistant (and future kit man) Chris that he was entitled to free Coca-Cola from any shop in Brighton due to a sponsorship deal with the Football League. Completely unaware that Ian had surreptitiously created this 'free Coke' card using Microsoft Word and a laminator, Chris presented it to some very confused newsagents all over the city. None of them gave him a free fizzy drink and it took him ages to notice that the Coca-Cola executive who had signed his card was a certain Mr A. Conn. Admittedly, it doesn't sound all that funny now but it had us in stitches at the time.

We were a close-knit gang, and an integral part of the team was Julie, who also ran the ticket collection booth at Withdean. Her mother, Marie, came in part-time to answer the phone and deal with administrative tasks.

One afternoon in September 2004, Marie was randomly murdered by a complete stranger on her way home. All these years on, I still can't bring myself to write about her death and the harrowing emotional and mental impact it had on all of us. I must have written this chapter about a dozen times before deleting it all and starting again. So, rather than going into any of the details, I have decided to settle on a few simple paragraphs by which to pay tribute to Marie, and also to Julie, who overcame unimaginable grief to eventually return to work after the death of her mum.

As well as being a loyal and long-standing Albion fan, Marie was an important member of the ticket office team. Being of pensionable age, Marie was available to come in whenever we needed her, often at short notice, and would undertake the dullest of tasks with enthusiasm. Putting tickets in envelopes, filing paperwork; there was no task too small. She was good company and a genuinely lovely person, always with a kind word. She loved spending time with the lads in the ticket office and club shop, and she encouraged us to spread our wings. It was at Marie's insistence that Gary the Palace fan took the recording of a song he had written to the BBC Radio Sussex offices up the road. They played it later that week and Gary has gone on to record albums and he has performed countless times live as a solo artist and in bands. He now presents his own radio show on Hailsham FM. Marie also told me I should pursue my writing. Within two years I had my own newspaper column. I doubt that would have happened had she not encouraged me.

It took a very long time for us to recover from what happened to Marie. In truth, things were never the same again. Our office had always reverberated with laughter and silliness, but it became desolate for months. Going to work felt flat and pointless and sometimes almost impossible. I can't speak for my former colleagues, but I felt like an empty shell. For the sake of our collective mental health though, during the grieving process, feelings of shock and mourning were gradually pushed to the backs of our minds, replaced by fond, happy memories. We used to call Marie 'the old lady in the attic' because she was advancing in years and worked quietly in the upstairs office. When this was referenced in her funeral service, we chuckled through our tears.

The wake played a big part in helping to shift our collective mindset as well. It was held in the sponsors' lounge at Withdean, which was the perfect location to pay tribute to someone who cared so passionately about the Albion. We drank big glasses of red wine and shared stories as the afternoon sun lowered behind the trees, casting long shadows over the pitch.

The Albion lost a loyal member of their family in September 2004. Over two decades later, Marie Harding lives on in the memories of everyone who knew her. She should be honoured by all Albion fans for the unassuming contribution she made to the club in her own small way.

***

THE TIME I RUINED EVERYONE'S CHRISTMAS

In December of 2004, Albion were drawn away to Tottenham Hotspur in the FA Cup. A January trip to a Premier League stadium represented an appealing day out for fans who were used to watching their football in what was essentially a glorified school playing field, so demand for tickets was massive. We had at least four times the number of members for the size of the away end at Spurs. Four into one doesn't go.

Everyone was feeling the strain. Supporters were understandably frustrated at the annoyingly slow and convoluted postal application process (away tickets weren't allocated by ballot, but rather in date order of receipt), while we struggled to deal with the sheer volume of requests, and we were still reeling from losing our friend and colleague Marie. Our energy and spirits were as low as they had ever been, as postal sacks filled with applications were dumped on our doorstep every morning.

Inevitably and predictably, our allocation of tickets was exhausted with thousands of unprocessed applications remaining. I recall looking through the piles of unsuccessful requests and grimacing at names I recognised; there were plenty of loyal fans who were unlucky, and informing these unsuccessful supporters turned out to be a PR disaster … caused by me. On the afternoon of 23 December, we sent apology letters to supporters who missed out, assuming they would land on doormats a few days after Christmas.

You know how anything you post in December takes an eternity to arrive at its destination? Well, I can tell you with absolute certainty that the postal service was on top of its game on 23 December 2004, because the letters arrived with supporters the very next day. On Christmas Eve! This meant two things: firstly the advertised 'last post day for Christmas' doesn't seem to mean much (which is good to know if you ever forget to send your auntie a timely gift).

Secondly, it meant that we had just ruined Christmas for thousands of Albion fans. The letter from the club was the equivalent of Santa Claus arriving on Christmas Eve without any presents and instead doing a poo on the living room carpet. This was entirely my fault, and I suppose I should have had more faith in the postal system.

How do I know that we ruined Christmas? Because people told us so in their hundreds. One man even went to the trouble of bringing his young son into the ticket office on Christmas Eve just so we could see how sad he was. He stood in front of us, absolutely fuming, pointing at his son. 'Look at his face,' he instructed us. I can confirm that his son did indeed look very upset. I fully understood everyone's frustration. Supporters had adhered to the application process and waited patiently, yet a large percentage of them had missed out on an attractive fixture. No wonder they wanted to vent on someone. We'd been skipping lunch breaks for weeks and working into the dead of night with no overtime, meaning we were exhausted, and I really don't think we deserved the amount of stick we were getting but, equally, I absolutely understood why people were angry at us.

Incidentally, this was the second time I had spoiled at least one child's Christmas at the Albion. Several years earlier when I was a teenager, I had agreed to fill in as Gully, the club's mascot, at the Junior Seagulls' festive party as the person who usually undertook the role was otherwise engaged. I arrived at some community centre or other and pulled on the costume, which included yellow leggings, flippers, a big feathery torso and seagull head (this wasn't the current day Gully costume, but an earlier, more basic incarnation). It was suffocatingly, swelteringly hot, and I could barely see a thing because the two eye-holes immediately steamed up. When I entered the party I was mobbed by excited kids before fulfilling all manner of duties, including doing the 'Gully Cokey' whereby I put my left foot in, my left foot out, and so on. As the party drew to a close, several kids came up to ask for Gully's autograph. However, I could only just about see directly in front of me. I couldn't look left or right, and if I tried to tilt my giant head down it would have fallen off. This meant that I couldn't see the pens or the autograph books that were being held in front of me. Gully doesn't speak and there were no assistants to help me out, so I ended up signing precisely zero autographs and giving no explanation as to why. Whilst this was simply because I couldn't see anything, as far as the kids were aware their favourite mascot was arrogantly snubbing them point-blank by refusing to give them his autograph. What a diva! I have no doubt they went home sad and confused.

Back to the Spurs game in January 2025, and I decided to give up my ticket. This wasn't a philanthropic gesture. In truth, I'd had enough of the match before a ball had been kicked. I didn't want to be anywhere near White Hart Lane when the game took place and, when the Seagulls lost the match 2-1, not a hint of sadness could be found within my emotions. The idea of having to sell tickets to a replay made me anxious to the point of feeling physically sick. Unlike the Swindon play-off semi-final, when I was lying to myself that defeat would be a blessing, this time I was truly relieved.

If it makes you angry that an employee of a football club can have such a reaction, think how terrible it made me feel, and consider it an illustration of how working for a club can have such a dramatic impact on a person's relationship with it. It's an honour and a privilege to have been involved with the Albion throughout my life, but it is also inevitable that the dynamic between a person and their club shifts when the line between support and employment is blurred. As I mentioned when talking about the David Bellotti years, fans put their hearts and souls into supporting the team, but their jobs outside of football allow them to focus at least some of their energy elsewhere from Monday to Friday. When you work at your club, you're a supporter on a Saturday but you also live it all day, every day. No sooner have you finished dealing with the fallout from one match than another comes along. Every conversation, every telephone call, every email, every meeting is about your beloved club. This is great when things are going well, but the lack of respite can genuinely damage your mental wellbeing and your relationship with the club when things go awry.

Whenever a match sold out, people who didn't get tickets would tell us that the system was unfair and would label us as unhelpful and officious. I'm a big boy, I can take my share of stick and I know that often the complaints were at least semi-justified but, considering the amount of effort and thought we put into our work, it really did hurt to be sworn at or told we were bad at our jobs. I think if supporters had spent a day in the ticket office alongside us during that era, they would have witnessed just how many obstacles were in our way and how we were honestly trying our best, and they might have altered their judgement. As an example of this, when we were allocating season tickets at Priestfield, a handful of fans came into the office together to complain about an error we had made during the process. They were right, we had made a mistake, but it was fixable and I tried to field their questions as politely as I could. However, when one of them criticised our team for a lack of efficiency, things grew heated. I flounced from my desk like Kevin the Teenager and told the group to follow me. I led them into the boardroom and, gesticulating like a magician's assistant, showed them the high-tech system we were using to complete the task in hand: the big paper map and coloured stickers on the table. The disgruntled fans surveyed the scene, then eyed my downbeat expression and shot me a look that said, 'rather you than me'. The correct thing for me to have done, of course, would have been to take their criticism on the chin rather than confronting them about it, but if anyone had a right to moan about how terrible the ticketing facilities were it was surely us, the people who had to wrestle with them every single day. I still see those particular fans at games from time to time, and whenever I do my cheeks redden at how badly I handled the situation all those years ago.

A few weeks before the Spurs tickets went on sale, we played West Ham United away. In terms of preparing supporters and staff for the maelstrom of misery that we were set to encounter with Tottenham, it was a helpful warm-up. Tickets sold out in a heartbeat and lots of fans were very annoyed to have missed out. One fellow got particularly cross when he tried to buy one a couple of days before the game. Think of the two rudest words in your vocabulary. That's what he called me when I told him he couldn't have a ticket. Another time, someone threw a phone at my head when they didn't get what they wanted. This actually happened.

Incidents like this led to me feeling increasingly detached from other Albion supporters. It was the strong sense of affinity with my fellow fans which had initially appealed to me about attending games. Take that away, and what is left? Just 22 men kicking a ball around in front of a bunch of strangers. I generally finished work at the ticket office in town at 2pm on a Saturday and would walk to the station. Once there I would jump on a train to Withdean, where I would continue my duties in the build-up to kick-off. Sometimes, when arriving at Brighton station, I'd get the overwhelming urge to go straight home to Eastbourne, rather than spend another afternoon surrounded by Albion fans. As I type these words now, they sound ridiculous … as though they are someone else's thoughts, yet this was undeniably how I felt at the time. I know plenty of people who have worked for other clubs and who have all gone through the same emotions. The football industry can be a joyless place at times. I started to think that maybe it was time for a change.

***

RETURN TO OZ

After avoiding relegation on the last day of the 2004/05 season, Albion finished the following campaign bottom of the table, recording just seven wins along the way. For the first time, there were often rows of empty seats at Withdean, and there had been no real progress on the move to a permanent stadium. It was all getting a bit stagnant.

One lunch break, I walked past a travel agent in Brighton's city centre. On a whim, I went in. A month later, I had quit my job and was on my way to Heathrow airport, ready to spend the next year in Australia. This was entirely against my nature. Anxiety is never far from my surface and I usually meticulously plan my life to the finest detail (just like a Steve Coppell team talk), so the idea of dropping everything and disappearing to the other side of the world terrified me. I'd fallen in love with Australia on my previous visit though, and I felt like a little fear might shake me from my funk. My flight coincided with my 30th birthday. I celebrated alone on the plane with a couple of those tiny bottles of wine and some movies on the seatback screen.

A few weeks later, I watched my first Albion match of the season on TV. Or rather, I didn't. I had every intention of catching the game against Blackpool which had surprisingly been chosen for broadcast on one of the Australian satellite channels, and was really excited about it as it was the first time in my adult life I'd be watching the Seagulls entirely as a fan, rather than as a member of staff. The drop to League One meant that there was the possibility of a promotion push and I was looking forward to being a supporter again, albeit a faraway one, rather than a beleaguered and perpetually irritable ticket office manager.

The plan was to find a pub in Sydney and watch the game with my new flatmate, Vicky, who was also a former Albion employee and who had left for Australia a few months previously. She had worked in the Albion's administration offices for several years and the two of us were good pals during that time, turning any simple task into a two-person job just so that we could hang out and be silly. There was a spit and sawdust 24-hour boozer two minutes from our apartment in Sydney, which seemed as good a place as any to cheer on the team. Our plan, however, went awry. Firstly, Vicky couldn't make it after all, which meant I was flying solo. Secondly, I was disappointed to discover that my chosen pub was showing all manner of other sports on its multitude of screens, but not the Brighton game. My request to switch channels was flatly refused by the surly bartender, and this wasn't the kind of establishment where a whinging Pom should start an argument. The barman's demeanour suggested he was less hipster and more borderline lunatic, so I about-turned and trawled the rainswept Sydney pavements with no clue as to where I was going. On each new street, I hoped I would chance upon a bar showing the game. If there happened to be some fellow Albion fans with whom I could enjoy it, that would be a bonus. I found neither.

Nearly a decade on from this moment I would watch a Brighton match on a big screen in Sydney with over 100 Seagulls supporters (I'll talk more about this later on) but in 2006, when networking tools like Facebook, Twitter/X and smartphones weren't a thing, I forlornly and blindly zigzagged through the unfamiliar city in the knowledge that I probably wouldn't get to see the game. Dejectedly, I settled on finding an internet cafe (remember them?) and, just as I had the previous time I was in Australia, I logged on to the live vidiprinter on the BBC website. Upon doing so I discovered that Albion were losing by one goal, two goals and then three. I headed back to my apartment and crawled into bed. I wasn't sure if I felt dejected because the team had lost, or because I had thought that watching the game would make me feel connected to Sussex. This was the first time that I had spent a prolonged amount of time away from the club. I'd barely missed a home match in two decades, yet here I was, unable to watch my beloved side, even on the telly. I would become accustomed to missing games over the next few years, but it is not something that ever gets any easier. As a football fan, you can distract yourself with other activities, but there is simply nothing like being in your home stadium.

Across the next decade, I split my time between England and Australia. Taking a left turn from my life in the football industry, I started writing for the music press in Sydney. I also did some DJing, both in Australia and in the UK. Being involved in music meant that, even when living in England, my whereabouts often left me unable to attend Albion games, and I'd regularly have to rely on radio commentary, stuttering internet streams or social media to find out how the Albion were doing. When living in Oz, the time difference meant that I would often spend my late-night Saturday DJ sets paying far more attention to score updates on my phone than on mixing songs. Belated apologies to Sydney's weekend revellers.

I'm sure you know how it feels to try to keep tabs on your team's fortunes in tricky circumstances. We've all been at a wedding on a matchday and had to find inventive ways of keeping up with the football scores, haven't we? When Jayne and I were planning our wedding for August of 2020, one of my first concerns was whether the date we picked would clash with a home match. As it turned out, Covid caused us to reschedule the wedding for June 2021 anyway, which meant the only football we would potentially miss would be the European Championship. In the end, the pandemic meant we had to move it again, to July 2022. Joyfully, that year's World Cup was scheduled for December!

There have been several times, however, where my friends' nuptials have clashed with Albion fixtures. I was asked to DJ at a reception in Sussex one hot August day, which meant I was unable to head to Brighton's game at Birmingham. Thankfully, I don't think anyone noticed that I was checking the scores during the speeches as Albion slipped to a 1-0 defeat. To be honest, it was probably good for my ongoing friendship with the happy couple that Brighton didn't score. It wouldn't have gone down too well had I jumped up and celebrated an equaliser mid-speech. I know this to be true because that's pretty much what I did when my cousin got married a few years earlier. Albion were playing Carlisle United away and I was sneakily listening to radio commentary through an earpiece at the reception. My cheer and fist-pumps during the speeches as we grabbed the winner were not well received. I don't see my cousin anymore.

***

NOBBO ROBBO

I have interviewed countless bands over the years, which is something that requires preparation, concentration and professionalism. So, when I discovered that my phone conversation with Stereophonics coincided with an Albion match at Huddersfield Town, I knew that it wouldn't be one of my finest pieces of journalism.

As I was in my Sydney flat on the phone with the band's bassist, I was simultaneously watching the BBC's scrolling text commentary of Brighton's match. Never mind that I was supposed to be engaging in conversation about Stereophonics' upcoming tour of Australia, I was more concerned with the fact that the Albion were a goal behind and under the cosh. While I should have been asking probing questions about the band's tumultuous relationship with the press, or their recent change of record company, I was instead studying the matter-of-fact commentary that appeared on the screen in front of me. My already shamefully poor concentration completely dissipated when the following appeared on my screen: 'GOAL – Huddersfield 1 Brighton 1'. When I later transcribed the recording of the interview, I heard myself let out a stifled yelp of celebration. At this point in the conversation we were discussing Stereophonics' five consecutive number one albums, and I suppose my interviewee must have thought that I was just really happy about his band's commercial success.

Similarly, I interviewed a band called Starsailor on the same night that Brighton had their most important game of the season. It was the Johnstone's Paint Trophy semi-final against Luton Town. And yes, this did count as the biggest game of the season back then. I've got nothing against Starsailor, who at the time were pretty popular (they had top-ten records and supported The Rolling Stones), but my focus was never going to be fully on the interview when, at that exact moment, Brighton were so close to Wembley. So, while Starsailor's James Stelfox was enthusing down the phone line about his band's new album, all I could think about was the match in Bedfordshire. I wrapped up the interview in time to rush to the TV and watch Luton beat us on penalties. Nowadays, on the rare occasions that I hear Starsailor on the radio, I always think of that defeat to the Hatters.

For much of the Withdean era, my two favourite things, music and Brighton & Hove Albion, were linked by the fact that the team's shirt sponsor was Skint Records. There aren't many times when you could justifiably describe a club's shirt sponsor as being cool, and supporting a football team isn't considered hip unless you are one of the bearded 20-somethings who go to watch Dulwich Hamlet. Being sponsored by your local record label, however, is pretty awesome, and of course the word 'Skint' being written across the middle of the shirt was apt at the time. Having Skint as a sponsor was a dream to a music nut like me, and certainly better than when NOBO was our sponsor back when I was a kid. Walking through town with NOBO emblazoned across my shirt in large red letters wasn't much fun, nor was being called 'Nobbo Robbo' by my peers.

A special-edition strip, released to celebrate a Fatboy Slim album, had the LP's title, *Palookaville*, written in graffiti-style letters across the front and was the rarest of garments, namely a football shirt that I could wear to the pub at night without feeling like I had made a fashion faux pas. I still wear it these days, although usually just when I'm at the gym or out running. I'm guessing many of your old replicas have succumbed to a similar fate; worn in bed, while exercising or when doing jobs around the house. Still, whenever you pull it on, it's like greeting an old friend. The peeling sponsor's logo, the frayed stitching; each imperfection evoking a distant memory of a journey somewhere northern and cold.

Talking of northern and cold, in late 2007 I was on a tour of the UK with Eastbourne-based singer/songwriter David Ford, helping him out by manning his merchandise table (my Priestfield experience finally becoming applicable elsewhere). When I learnt that I would be hitting the road, I did what all football fans do before they travel; I checked the fixture list to see if there were any appealing matches in the cities we were visiting. On this occasion there weren't, and it in fact transpired that I would be in a tour bus heading towards London from the north of England at the exact time that the Albion were travelling in the opposite direction to Hartlepool United. I had long-since promised myself I would never go to Hartlepool again after seeing that dismal defeat in the biting wind back in the 90s, but were I already in the broad vicinity, attending would have been a no-brainer. However, I left the chilly north the day before and instead found myself having to keep up with the action on Sky Sports' *Soccer Saturday* programme in the dressing room of the Shepherd's Bush Empire in west London.

I'm sure you're familiar with the premise of *Soccer Saturday* and its barrage of goal flashes and updates, fired with increasing exuberance by an affable presenter and his merry posse of ex-pros. To those who don't follow football, it is a show so unintelligible that it might as well be in another language, but to the ardent football lover it is a delicious frenzy of statistics and excitement. Sometimes I prefer it to watching a game. I find it weird though, that it uses the word 'soccer' in its name, as not a single person in the UK who has any interest in the sport would ever call it that. I suppose it has a better ring to it than *Football Saturday*, and the logistics of moving every weekend game to Friday nights just so they can rename it *Football Friday* would be a step too far, even when you take into account Sky's flagrant disregard for away fans' travel convenience.

When *Soccer Saturday* revealed that eccentrically-haired Brighton striker Bas Savage had just struck a 94th-minute winner at Hartlepool, I leapt from the sofa and punched the air. Mimicking Savage's often-used celebration, I even attempted (and failed) to moonwalk around the room, much to the bewilderment of the non-football enthusiasts in my company. At this moment, I was probably the only person in history to have been in the unlikely situation of drinking red wine in a comfy dressing room at the elegant Shepherd's Bush Empire, yet wishing I was in Hartlepool. No disrespect, Hartlepool.

***

NEVER A FROWN

A few years later, David Ford and I were on the road again, this time travelling around the country with the former lead singer of The Stranglers, Hugh Cornwell, who was playing a series of solo acoustic gigs, with Ford as his support act. This meant that, while Brighton visited the home of FA Cup holders Wigan Athletic, I was in a van between Bromsgrove and London. We arrived at the venue, the lovely old Union Chapel in Islington, in time for the second half, and I managed to watch the remainder of the game via a stream. David was busy soundchecking and Hugh is more into cricket than football, so I took in the action on my own in a cold, empty dressing room. There is something very strange about watching football completely alone. Shouting encouragement at the screen is futile, yet still a completely involuntary action. When Albion created an opening, I yelled 'GO ON!' Immediately after the chance was missed I felt silly and self-conscious as my cry echoed around the large room and out of the open door into the corridor. It made me realise, more so than ever, that football is a sport that demands to be consumed with other people, whether it is with a couple of mates in your living room, at a pub or, infinitely preferably, in a stadium. Having said that, the elation that immediately overtakes your body when a goal is scored remains the same, regardless of your surroundings, so when Albion hit a late winner I momentarily forgot the self-consciousness I had previously felt and danced a solo jig around the room. Remembering where I was, I soon gathered myself. When the final whistle blew, I shut the laptop and, in doing so, immediately disconnected from the drama and the excitement that, of all the people in the building, only I had experienced.

David and I have done many tours together, and there have been several occasions when we've been able to attend live matches on our route. Well, I say they were 'on our route', but in truth we have taken time-consuming, fuel-guzzling detours to get to games. We've seen Premier League matches, Championship and League One games, and we even watched Chesterfield take on Rochdale in the Johnstone's Paint Trophy (that was the game where the only vegetarian food was Maltesers). In 2025, we took an almighty detour to watch Dunfermline Athletic beat Raith Rovers in the Scottish Championship on a cold Friday night. One time, Ford and I were on tour with Texan artist Jarrod Dickenson and we found ourselves facing a journey from Ayr in Scotland all the way back to Sussex on a Saturday. Keen for a weekend football fix, we decided to break up the long drive by stopping off at Elland Road to watch Leeds United play Bolton Wanderers. Our Texan friend had never been to a football match (his idea of 'football' is that strange armour-wearing thing they play in America), so we saw it as an opportunity to educate him. My old mate at Leeds, Katie Holmes, who by now had presumably escaped the clutches of Tom Cruise, kindly put some tickets aside for us. Once inside the famous old stadium, we witnessed the worst defensive display I have ever seen at Championship level. Leeds were horrific. Their attempt to play offside for the first goal wasn't so much a trap as a guard of honour for the Bolton striker to saunter through. Four more Bolton goals followed as the away fans sang, 'How bad must you be? We're winning away!'

As was always the way when David and I went to a game, it was an enjoyable rarity to have absolutely no investment in either team. In order to fit in with the home fans and not to reveal myself as a southern softy, I feigned fury as Bolton's goals flew in, yet I was happy in the knowledge that none of it meant anything at all to me. It was like being at the theatre, or at a wrestling bout. Whilst it was an enjoyable paradox to be at a football match and not care about the result, it's not something I would want to do on a regular basis. Without those usual gut-wrenching feelings of nerves, passion and excitement, live football is little more than a fun distraction for a couple of hours.

***

THE ARGUS

My life within the music scene, all late nights, gigs and parties, was enthralling, but I soon started to miss being ensconced in a football industry of which I had previously grown weary. The grass is always greener, I suppose, and because I'd been behind the scenes of football in some form or another since I was ten, to be completely on the outside felt disconcerting. I decided, therefore, to try to find an avenue back into the footballing world. I dropped a letter to *The Argus* asking if they were looking for writers. I explained that I was splitting my time between England and Australia, that I was a former employee of the Albion and that I could perhaps come up with some interesting articles about following the team from afar, as well as sharing some anecdotes and memories from my years at the club. Soon after, the sports editor called me and offered me my own weekly column. It was that simple. Or, at least, it seemed that simple. The proviso was that, due to the financial struggles that the print media was suffering (and continues to suffer), I wouldn't be paid for my contribution. Whilst this wasn't ideal, the prospect of having my own weekly newspaper column about the Albion was too good an opportunity to turn down so, failing to play it remotely cool and with no attempt to barter for even a few quid, I gushingly agreed to the editor's terms on the spot. I would go on to write my column for ten years, never receiving a single penny for the 200,000+ words I penned. And do you know what? I loved everything about it: every Tuesday morning spent scratching my head trying to work out what to write about, every letter the newspaper received about my words (either positive or negative), and every person who approached me for a chat at a game or, as happened to me once, when I was buying Quorn nuggets in Sainsbury's.

Because I wasn't getting paid by *The Argus*, I still sometimes did a few shifts in Albion's ticket office when I was in the UK. It was nice of the club to offer me work on a casual basis when they needed an extra pair of hands. Remarkably, despite the passing of so many years since we returned from Priestfield, the tickets we sold at this time were still for our supposedly temporary Withdean home. I wonder how many people, back when the new Millennium dawned, would have believed we'd be waiting to move to a new stadium at Falmer when the decade ended. Actually, considering how terrible much of the 90s were, it probably wouldn't have come as a huge surprise to learn that building a new stadium was going to be problematic. One thing history has taught us is that, when it comes to the Albion, nothing is ever straightforward.

It was a strange decade. In its first half, the club was still hungover from the loss of the Goldstone and from the Priestfield years, and was getting tangled up in red tape with the Falmer application. Money was too tight to mention and the new stadium wasn't even on the horizon, yet the team was unstoppable. As fans marched for Falmer, the players marched to two successive titles. There was a siege mentality at Withdean as we were galvanised by off-field dramas of the recent past and the very much present. A gallant and almost successful fight against relegation had been followed by instant promotion via that memorable play-off final in Cardiff, and then we'd punched above our weight in the Championship for a couple of years. Planning permission for the new stadium was eventually granted to much celebration and relief, but almost as soon as ground was broken at Falmer, things started to go a bit wrong on the field. Crowds fell, form was patchy and the advantage we had once gained by playing at Withdean became a distant memory. It was, of course, fantastic that we ended the decade with plans to move into a beautiful, permanent home, funded by brilliant new owner, chairman and lifelong Albion fan, Tony Bloom, who took over from Dick Knight and, just like Knight, truly loves the club. I don't think it is a coincidence, though, that the team had enjoyed so much success when times were hard. Brighton & Hove Albion and its fans were always at their best when battling against the odds. As soon as there was nothing to fight for or against, the spark temporarily fizzled out a bit.

By the end of the 2008/09 season, the team seemed doomed to be relegated to the league's basement, which would have been an absolute disaster considering there was a massive new stadium about to be built. Enter, Russell Slade. Just as the balding Steve Gritt masterminded Albion's astonishing Great Escape in 1997, another shiny-headed manager would do the same 12 years later. It would be harsh to say that the team hadn't previously been giving their all until Slade was appointed, but there now seemed to be a renewed 'never say die' belief about them which had been lacking for some time. In particular, long-standing striker/winger/full-back Gary Hart came into his own during this run-in.

Hart was an honest professional and a true Albion hero. He had suffered injury and had been out of favour to the extent that he was released the previous summer before returning, after which he was stuck in the reserves for long periods. Yet at no stage did he sulk; rather, he just got on with his job. The priceless boost he gave the team upon his return to the first team wasn't solely due to his fine form in the last few games, but because of his tireless effort. He would have played in any position on the pitch (indeed, he pretty much did) if it meant he could get a game in the blue and white stripes, and he always ran himself into the ground to the point that he ended matches absolutely caked in mud, somehow even on a dry, sunny day. If there were a footballing personification of the dedication of Albion's supporters, it was Gary Hart. His passion and commitment seemed to rub off on the entire squad and, under the level-headed tutorage of Slade, the players somehow dragged themselves to within one win of safety with a game of the campaign remaining.

Stockport County were the visitors on the final day of the season. It was a sunny afternoon and the atmosphere at Withdean was a throwback to the stadium's infancy, before we had grown tired of squatting there. The ground looked like a postcard; all blue and white shirts framed by green trees and a cloudless sky as Nicky Forster scored the only goal of the game to secure a vital win. At the final whistle, fans ran on to the pitch to celebrate at the remarkable survival. Slade was carried from the field shoulder-high, joyfully waving his baseball cap as he went. It's curious how a 'new manager bounce' can transform an entire squad, even though the playing personnel remains the same.

After a sticky start to the next season, however, Slade left the club. His replacement heralded an exciting new era for Brighton & Hove Albion.

***

WE ARE FAMILY

Gus Poyet's first game as manager of Brighton was a Sunday afternoon League One fixture at Southampton's St Mary's Stadium, which was played in front of live television cameras. I was in Australia at this time, living in a warehouse building in the centre of Sydney. It was six storeys of cockroach-infested, graffiti-ridden bohemia shared by bands, artists, filmmakers and rich kids pretending to be poor kids. There was always something happening there. Ed Sheeran played in my neighbour's apartment once, there were regular fashion shoots on the rooftop, live jazz sessions every Monday, and massive raves were shut down by the police pretty much every weekend. It was a wild place to live. Across the road from this listed building was a pub. It had grey carpets, fruit machines (or pokies, as they are called in Australia) and a few TV screens. It was a sterile, soulless joint with the aura of an office breakroom, but it was open at stupid o'clock and was a minute's walk from my front door, making it a convenient place to position my tired limbs at 3am on a Monday (due to the time difference) in order to watch my football team.

When pubs show Premier League games in Sydney, they are usually packed with soccer-loving Aussies and British backpackers. However, it was no surprise that, at the witching hour on a Monday morning with a League One tussle on the menu, this pub was mostly empty. I entered the establishment hoping yet not expecting to find any Albion or Saints fans, but thinking there might at least be a couple of late-night/early-morning football followers with whom I could watch the game. Alas, not one of the handful of wan, hunched, lonely insomniacs in the pub was even looking at the screen. As the barflies stared into their drinks, it was obvious that they weren't there to watch Gustavo Poyet's first game in charge of Brighton, but simply because they had nowhere else to be and nobody to advise them against drinking alone so early on a Monday morning.

Some of them looked as though they were one beer away from crying, fighting, or possibly both. I too, of course, was drinking alone early on a Monday morning, but my demeanour was more upbeat. I ignored the gloom that wafted through the place, instead immersing myself in the game and cheering exuberantly as striker Glenn Murray put Albion one and then two goals in front. Then, after Southampton pulled one back and hunted for an equaliser, I nearly hit the ceiling with delight as the third goal clinched it against the run of play. At the final whistle, as the sun unapologetically peeked from behind the city skyline, I stepped out of the bar and walked the short journey home, surprised that Monday mornings could be such fun. The Uruguayan's reign as manager was off to a fantastic start and, throughout his time at the club, he cultivated a style of passing football that would help Albion climb the league ladder.

It took a while for fans to get used to two aspects of

Brighton's success under Poyet. Firstly, some supporters found his brand of keep-ball frustrating, groaning as defenders passed amongst themselves in never-ending triangles as they waited for gaps to open in the midfield. 'Just get it forward' would often be the cry from individuals in the stands. I enjoyed this patient style of play though. I'd never seen a Brighton side who looked especially comfortable in possession for long periods. In the past, defenders were always intent on getting rid of the ball as quickly as possible, so to see them hogging it, waiting for the right moment to play a forward pass, felt new and progressive. I certainly wasn't alone in my admiration of this style of play. Voices of dissent were drowned out by cheers of encouragement as the Albion back line knocked the ball around. It was a learning curve for the fans as much as the players, but by the time the Seagulls were embarking on their final ever season at Withdean before the big move to their new stadium, everyone was reading from the same page. Withdean was an exciting place to be once again and the team were destroying opponents. On the road too, results were excellent. Consecutive away games in October at Charlton Athletic and Peterborough United ended 4-0 and 3-0 to the Albion, who now topped the table. Oddly, this brought with it the second problem. You'd think that, for the first time in decades, there was absolutely nothing to be annoyed about, yet internet message boards were peppered with people who were upset that the away end at Charlton was filled with glory-hunters.

I've heard some Manchester City fans say they were happier before their club became super rich. They used to stumble from one catastrophe to the next, but it was a world they understood and to which they felt integral. Similarly, it seemed as though Brighton & Hove Albion were at a crossroads. With the new stadium on the horizon, lapsed and new fans flocked to the club, which meant that existing supporters had two ways to react to the fact that they would, for instance, sometimes end up with worse seats than a less deserving supporter. They could either stamp their feet and demand to be afforded reverential status because they went to Gillingham/used to sponsor Garry Nelson's shinpads, or they could embrace this surge in interest in their beloved football team. As for me, although I understood fans' frustrations at the bandwagon-jumpers, I didn't begrudge a few fair-weather fans being part of that amazing atmosphere at Charlton. I knew I'd played a small part in the club's history and was there when it mattered, and that was enough for me, because if we were going to fill a new stadium every week we needed the whole of Sussex to feel as though they belonged, rather than clinging to a fan hierarchy built on bygone days. Whether people were able to attend one game a season or 46, we were all part of the same family.

***

THE STUFF OF DREAMS

Carlisle United at home doesn't have the sound of a classic, does it? However, the Cumbrian side's visit in March 2011 was one of the most exciting contests Withdean hosted in the dozen years Albion played there. Many teams arrived determined to defend, but Carlisle came and attacked, pressing high up the pitch to disrupt Brighton's passing game. This led to a glut of goals. In a topsy-turvy encounter, the home side were 3-2 up as injury time ticked away. With 92 minutes on the clock, Brighton conceded a demoralising equaliser in front of the tiny cluster of away fans, who gleefully celebrated an unlikely away point. Or so they thought. Albion weren't done. In the 94th minute, midfielder Liam Bridcutt hit a dipping, venomous volley from outside the box. As the ball flew into the net, the moment immediately entered Withdean folklore and joined an illustrious collection of glorious late strikes at our temporary home. The win, and the way it was achieved, was unquestionably the catalyst for Albion's leap towards the title. Poyet's team won nine of the next ten matches, sealing promotion with another seven-goal roller-coaster victory at Withdean against Dagenham & Redbridge. The title was wrapped up with victory at Walsall a few days later.

I'd been back in the UK for the majority of the season and had seen most matches, including the Carlisle thriller and the promotion-clinching win over the Daggers. However, because I wasn't able to make it to the Walsall game, there was a little part of me that secretly hoped it would end in a draw so that I could actually be there to witness Albion seal the title at the next home fixture. I think this underlines how much better Brighton were than the rest of the league. There were still four games left when we sewed up the title. Remember, this was a division with Southampton in it, whose squad included Alex Oxlade-Chamberlain, Rickie Lambert, Michail Antonio, José Fonte and future Seagull, Adam Lallana. Usually, battling for the title would be a nail-biting experience, but it became apparent by the end of March that it was going to be a case of when rather than if the Seagulls lifted the trophy. Hoping your team doesn't win the league one weekend because it'd be better if they did it the next week? Sounds like a good season to me. And that's why the 2010/11 campaign was like none that I had witnessed before.

It was unique in that there weren't any gut-wrenching moments as the conclusion neared. In previous promotions there was the tense Chesterfield game, the last-gasp headers against Bristol City and Swindon Town at Withdean and late play-off final penalty drama. What we'd never seen was a team that seized the initiative so early in the campaign and powered their way confidently to the finish line, never meandering, never doubting. It was a strange feeling, and one which many football fans won't ever experience, to have been so certain of promotion for so long. The team was at the summit for months and, unusually for a Brighton fan, I didn't for a minute think they would let their lead slip.

When I look back on that season, it feels so different to previous glories. When I recall winning the title with Micky Adams as boss, I think of Danny Cullip's header. When I remember finishing top of the league under Peter Taylor, it's Lee Steele's late goal that pops into my head. The recollection of our play-off triumph stirs vivid memories of Leon Knight's penalty. But when I reminisce about the 2011 title-winning campaign, rather than recalling individual moments of excitement, I reflect fondly and proudly on nine months of pure dominance, of turning Withdean back into the fortress it once was, of passing the life out of teams, of absolute professionalism and quality from start to finish. I suppose if there is one moment that sits above the rest, it is Liam Bridcutt's volley in that Carlisle game. When you consider that it happened with 14 games of the season still to play, you get an idea of how much of a stroll it turned out to be.

***

WITHDEAN AND I

Not many football fans say goodbye to three home stadiums in 14 years. If Albion's departure from the Goldstone was emotional and their sign-off from Priestfield was more of a good riddance than a goodbye, then the atmosphere as the players took to the Withdean field for the final time fell somewhere between the two.

It's strange to think that I spent more years watching football at our supposedly temporary home than I did at the Goldstone. I wasn't anywhere near as sad about leaving though. For a start, we weren't being forced out with the prospect of going to Gillingham, and we weren't fighting for our lives at the foot of the league. We were signing off from the Theatre of Trees with a trophy presentation as we made our way to a glorious new stadium down the road. It couldn't have been scripted better.

Although I wasn't upset to be leaving, I'll always think affectionately towards our time in the weird little stadium. Sure, playing there held the club back, the rain got us down, the atmosphere was often rather tranquil and there were seasons when we couldn't buy a win, but we also experienced fantastic times. Some fans won't see their team finish top of the table three times in their entire lives, let alone within such a short time frame. Along with the titles, we also enjoyed play-off drama and a last-day survival in the Championship. Those are memories to cherish and they go hand-in-hand with our silly temporary home.

Withdean was the place where I first felt old, specifically when I realised that my hero, Bobby Zamora, was younger than me. What a depressing discovery that was. His goals were responsible for many of my favourite moments at Withdean, not least his rocket against Halifax. That goal was just one of countless happy times watching football there, such as goalkeeper Michel Kuipers' amazing saves, winger Kazenga LuaLua's celebratory somersaults, and veteran centre-back Simon Morgan playing an entire season without making a single error. Images leap randomly around my mind, like when the wealthiest club in the world, Manchester City, were beaten on penalties in the League Cup, or when midfielder Steve Sidwell hit two goals in the last two minutes to snatch a draw against Burnley.

The tiny stadium's idiosyncrasies summed up Brighton & Hove Albion, as did the last match there. Defeat to Huddersfield Town was a fitting way to leave Withdean. The fact that Albion played well, somehow lost the game and then lifted a trophy perfectly demonstrated our bizarre existence there. Indeed, Albion fans voted another home defeat, the Swindon play-off game in which the team performed fairly poorly, as the greatest ever Withdean match, which says it all really. The dozen years we played there were baffling, bizarre and brilliant. Equally, whilst working for the club during this period was sometimes frustrating, it was also rewarding and bonkers in a way that most jobs aren't. For instance, when Albion signed Argentinian striker Federico Turienzo on a two-year contract in 2005, I got a call from our administration office asking if I could help with something. I made the short walk from the ticket office to find Turienzo waiting in reception with one of the members of the club's finance team. It transpired that our new striker needed to open a bank account but he barely spoke a word of English and nobody at the club spoke fluent Spanish. I remained confused as to what role I could play until it became apparent that my mum, who was office manager at the time, had been bigging up my Spanish skills and suggested that I could act as a translator at the bank. I was flabbergasted. I know that parents are inclined to overplay their kids' talents but, in truth, my Spanish vocabulary stretched about as far as loudly asking where the beach was. It was the language I was third best at, behind German and French, and I wasn't very good at either of them. Despite my protests, it was nonetheless decided that I was the most suitable person to head to the nearest bank with Albion's new striker. Predictably, Turienzo barely understood a word of my translation, setting up his account took forever, and the experience was like something from an unfunny and swiftly decommissioned sitcom. Imagine if, today, Premier League Albion signed a Spanish striker who was immediately packed off to the local branch of HSBC with some twerp from the ticket office who barely spoke his language. With our multinational team, it's unthinkable. Remarkably though, I'm pretty sure that a new debit card plopped through Turienzo's letterbox the following week, meaning that our trip to the bank was a decent metaphor for how the club, its players, staff and supporters successfully muddled through the Withdean years.

With the Seagulls moving up a division, it was the perfect time to part company with the athletics stadium. Although the new ground would prove to be better in every possible way, it was still hard not to love Withdean. I guess, no matter how nice your home eventually becomes as you move up the property ladder, you'll always have rose-tinted memories of the dodgy little bedsit where you lived when you were a teen, and of all the happy times that you had there regardless of the mould on the ceiling, the paper-thin walls and the dodgy plumbing.

Well, Withdean was our bedsit and we took some great memories with us when we left. Even though the club has moved on to bigger and better things, there's no denying that watching football there was often more fun than it ever had any right to be.

Me at the Goldstone, seemingly on a non-matchday at the end of the 1970s. I don't remember this but I guess it was my first visit to the ground.

I'm sure I'm not the only person who has ever felt like crying while sitting in the home dugout.

The North Stand at the Goldstone.

Me walking off the Goldstone pitch as a ball boy in 1988.

Having my photo taken with Albion midfielder Robert Codner, around 1989. I loved meeting the players and getting their autographs.

The view from the back of the club shop at the Goldstone.

Wearing the home shirt on the Goldstone pitch in 1995 for an advert which appeared in the club programme.

Anti-Bellotti graffiti in the Goldstone dugouts in 1996.

Fans made their feelings clear by painting SACK THE BOARD on the Goldstone pitch ahead of the abandoned York City match in 1996.

Having a kickabout with my dad, Brian (in goal), on the pitch after the penultimate game at the Goldstone in April 1997.

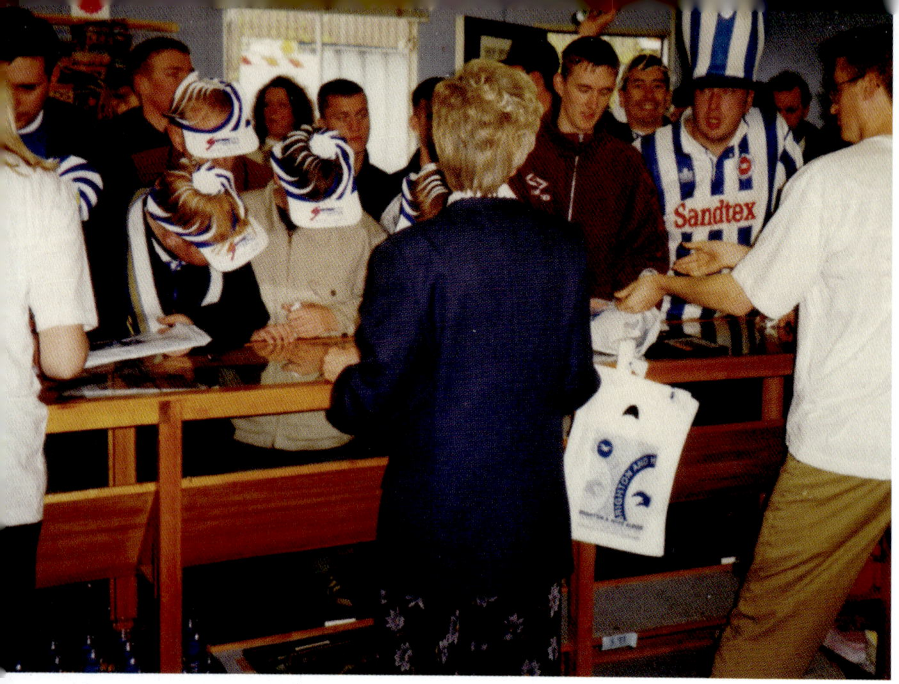

Serving customers with my mum, Sally, in a packed club shop at the last ever match at the Goldstone in April 1997.

With my mum in the new club shop in the centre of Brighton in 1997, after the Goldstone had been bulldozed.

Processing mountains of ticket applications in the office above the club shop in the early 2000s.

My mum multitasking in the Albion's main office in Brighton town centre in the early 2000s.

Posing with the Division Two and Division Three trophies in 2002. Please excuse the awful shirt.

Celebrating European qualification with my wife, Jayne, at the Amex in 2023.

PART FOUR: THE AMEX

A BEAUTIFUL SIGHT/SITE

I'VE BEEN very fortunate to have seen some astonishing sights over the past few years. I've trodden the rusty red sand of Australia's Northern Territory. I've gazed in wonder out of a plane window at illuminated streets flowing like lava through the blackness of the New York City night. I've stood in the Colosseum and imagined its brutal Roman history. I've studied tombs in the Valley of the Kings in Egypt. I've been dwarfed by the steel magnificence of the Eiffel Tower in Paris and strolled the gothic backstreets of Barcelona. I've experienced bustling Indian markets, breathed in the history of Pompeii, played football with local kids on the streets of Soweto and watched the mesmerising tumble of Niagara Falls. However, towards the end of 2009 during my humdrum daily routine in familiar old East Sussex, I saw something that topped all of these. I was on the train from Brighton to Eastbourne when the vista made my stomach turn somersaults and the hairs on the back of my neck stand up. It was a fleeting moment, yet a meaningful one. I was vacantly staring out of the window as the inevitably late train crawled past Falmer station when I spotted, poking up behind some trees and next to one of two universities in the area, the tiniest glimpse of a metal structure. This may not seem like anything to get excited about, but this skeletal framework represented so much more than the sum of its parts. It was a phoenix finally rising from the ashes, an embryonic vision of what would eventually become Brighton & Hove Albion's stunning new stadium.

Because the quest for a new home had been so long-winded with countless hurdles, I'd half-resigned myself to it never actually being built. I was convinced that they'd discover an ancient burial site or something when digging, and tools would be downed. Simply, I refused to believe that the new stadium was going to be a reality until I saw the first brick being laid. Well, with a simple glance over the trees from the train window, I had finally witnessed the evidence with my own eyes.

Throughout the stadium's construction, there were regularly updated photo galleries on the club's official website. Watching it take shape was the best thing I'd seen on the internet since I typed 'Christian the lion reunion' into YouTube (seriously, do it). And by the winter of 2010, during Albion's League One title-winning season, I was witnessing the stadium being built first-hand on a daily basis, as I was working at the club on a full-time, temporary basis, selling season tickets at Falmer, in what was still a building site. A team of us talked supporters through the ticketing options at the new ground and assisted them in selecting seats that were most suitable for their needs and preferences. We worked in a cabin in the car park at the south-east end of the stadium, which felt like being back at the Goldstone (only without David the Rat). The best part of my day, and some of my happiest moments ever at the club, involved pulling on a hard hat and fluorescent jacket and walking through the crunchy snow which blanketed the car park to take fans down to a viewing platform so they could have a look at the ground's progress. Although they were staring at little more than a concrete shell, without exception people's faces lit up when they gazed upon the half-finished structure. It was obvious that we were all simply counting down the months, weeks and days until we could finally set foot inside the completed stadium.

After an eternity of it being a messy building site, the final stages of construction seemed to be completed in fast-forward and, 14 long years after Brighton & Hove Albion said goodbye to the Goldstone Ground, the club had a permanent home within Sussex again. Over the summer, staff migrated from their cabins and from the city centre offices into the lovely new facilities at the north end of the ground. It smelt of new carpets and optimism.

The first league opponents were, in a pleasingly romantic piece of scriptwriting from the Football League, Doncaster Rovers, the final team Brighton played at the Goldstone. Before then though, there were two warm-up matches – the Sussex Senior Cup Final between Brighton Reserves and Eastbourne Borough and a friendly against Tottenham Hotspur. I wasn't sure if I wanted to attend either game. Like many fans, I wanted my first match there to be Doncaster. Both pre-season fixtures would take place in front of reduced capacities and I wanted my debut experience to be a full house. I soon changed my mind, though. Heck, I'd spent every day there all summer when the stands were completely empty, eating my packed lunch in a North Stand seat and gazing out in awe at the beautiful new surroundings, so there seemed no harm in also attending these pre-season kickabouts. The funny thing is that I only recalled going to either game when I was researching this book. I had completely forgotten that I'd seen Gary Hart score the first goal at the new stadium in the local cup final and I even forgot about the five-goal cracker with Spurs. It's funny how the human brain works. I suppose my mind defaulted to telling me that Doncaster was my first game there. That makes for a better story, I guess.

I do, however, recall some of the magnificent complaints that the supporter services team received at this time. It was the busiest pre-season I'd ever known at Brighton & Hove Albion and, inevitably, the big migration saw a handful of small glitches regarding seating, season ticket cards and so on. This was understandable, considering the club had gained about 15,000 new season ticket holders. A handful of people were scathingly unsympathetic though, shouting furiously down the phone and hitting send on ALL-CAPS emails. My two favourite complaints were:

1. The pies at the stadium were too hot.
2. We shouldn't have been playing Tottenham in a friendly because their manager was Harry Redknapp and he had connections with Southampton and Portsmouth (I still don't understand this one).

I think, like all of us, the complainants were just so desperate for their Amex experience to be perfect that they were fretting over every single problem which had occurred or had the potential to occur. This was fair enough, because Brighton fans had been forced to make do for so many years. They'd tirelessly fought Archer, Stanley and Bellotti, travelled 70 miles to attend 'home' matches and sat in a little athletics stadium for 12 years. At long last, their matchdays could represent perfection. They'd certainly earned it, and they didn't want anything to be wrong with their new home.

Pleasingly, by the day before the Doncaster match, most of the glitches had been solved as staff buzzed around the stadium on a cocktail of caffeine and adrenaline. Fans readied their vocal cords and planned their new matchday routine. We were one sleep from the moment we had all dreamed of and fought for. It was like 14 Christmas Eves rolled into one.

***

JUST A PERFECT DAY

On 6 August 2011, beneath an overcast sky, fans disembarked from trains and buses and walked wide-eyed towards the newly named American Express Community Stadium in Falmer, five miles outside of Brighton. Those beaming faces I witnessed on the viewing platform when giving people a glimpse of the stadium's construction were on display again, in their thousands. Once inside, supporters marvelled at concourses which showed Sky Sports and served beer (luxuries of which we could previously only dream), before locating their new seats. Padded seats, no less. Ooh la la. As the two teams took to the field, fans who had journeyed to that stadium in Kent and who had frozen in sodden clothes at Withdean raised their flags and sang 'Sussex by the Sea' with pride in their hearts and fire in their bellies. What was just a muddy field a couple of years ago was now our home, an absolutely stunning stadium. I cried when these two teams walked out of the tunnel at the Goldstone back in 1997 and here I was, shedding a tear once more.

During the first half, I felt a strange sensation, as though I were watching an exhibition game rather than a Championship match. Everything was so unfamiliar. I noticed that people around me were spending as much time staring at the new surroundings as they were paying attention to the action on the field. When Doncaster took the lead towards half-time, it didn't really deflate the mood. To be honest, we could have lost 4-0 and it would still have been a fantastic day. Besides, I think most people half-expected the match to end in defeat. Fans generally understand that things rarely go to plan when it comes to their football club. On this occasion though, a new signing by the name of Will Buckley was on hand to provide the dream end to a wonderful event. When he arrived as a substitute to smash home an equaliser seven minutes from time, he wrote himself into the history books. By the end of the match, his contribution would be etched into Albion folklore. With the game entering its closing moments I think most supporters would have been happy to settle for a draw against our old mates from up north, but Albion's players had a *Roy of the Rovers* ending up their sleeves. Just like when Dean Wilkins curled Brighton into the play-offs in 1991, what happened on this grey afternoon would have been criticised for being far-fetched were it a fictional tale. Diminutive winger Craig Noone shimmied past two Doncaster players on the halfway line before delivering a slide-rule pass with the outside of his boot. It was a piece of skill so exquisite that it cut the visiting team in half, unleashing Buckley, who found himself through on goal. It was the 98th minute.

The coolness of Buckley's finish contrasted the jubilant scenes that followed. As he slotted the ball into the goal, he did so with a calm assuredness more in keeping with a training session than an historic occasion such as this. Players bundled atop the scorer. Gus Poyet, who had earlier been sent off following a typically fiery reaction on the touchline, celebrated in the stand. This wasn't your normal injury-time goal celebration; this was entirely different. There wasn't the same wave of adrenaline-fuelled relief that accompanies an everyday late winner, but rather an extension of the sense of joyous disbelief that had been present all day. We waved our flags and sang songs and high-fived and hugged the people to our left and to our right. This was the Hollywood finish that we all deserved and that none of us imagined we would get. It had been 14 years in the making.

Long after the final whistle had signalled a winning start to Albion's time at their new home, I sipped on a cold pint in Dick's Bar, a lounge in the north-west corner of the stadium which was open to all supporters. It was rammed and noisy. Just like when we played Doncaster in 1997, no one wanted to go home. Every other aspect of our lives was on hold while we enjoyed an afternoon we'd waited so long for. The club's former chairman and now life president, Dick Knight, was there. It was only appropriate really that the man after which the bar was named should be present, accepting every pat on the back and every appreciative handshake. Without him, the backroom staff, directors, fans and, of course, new chairman and owner Tony Bloom, all of whom worked so hard to drag the club from the gutter, Brighton & Hove Albion would have died long before this most wonderful of occasions.

'What a day,' Knight said to me, puffing his cheeks.

Many beers later, as the sun made its descent over the South Downs, I sat on a train to Eastbourne with images of the afternoon montaging in my mind. What a day indeed. Football, like life, can rarely be described as absolute perfection, but when it is, you simply must ride that wave and try to enjoy and memorise every nanosecond of it.

***

SIMPLY THE BEST

Albion's first season at the Amex was an odd one. Ultimately, it was successful, with a tenth-place finish representing a decent return to the league's second tier, and finishing above Crystal Palace was particularly pleasing for banter enthusiasts. Early in the season, a player by the name of Vicente Rodríguez signed from Valencia. I wasn't overwhelmed by his signing, nor was I underwhelmed. I was, I suppose, whelmed. To my shame, considering by now I was doing a lot of football writing and was supposedly knowledgeable about the game, I had never heard of him. A look at his highlights reel on YouTube suggested he was something special, but football fans have been bitten many times by getting excited about video montages of incoming players. Their YouTube compilations, which incidentally always seem to be soundtracked by appalling Eurodance, showcase a world-beater when the reality is invariably somewhat disappointing. As it turned out though, Vicente proved to be just as good as his highlights reel. For example, Brighton's game at home to relegation-threatened Pompey was an ugly, bruising affair, seemingly not suited to the Spaniard's silky touch but, when he came off the bench, the away side simply couldn't cope. He moved across the pitch so fluidly that defenders might as well have been trying to tackle water. With the match still level as the final whistle drew near, three defenders illegally prevented him from running into the box and a free kick was awarded. He picked himself up and placed a left-footed strike into the bottom corner of the north goal. He didn't blast it, but rather passed it in with consummate ease. As he ripped his shirt off and raced towards the crowd, I'm sure I wasn't the only person in the crowd swooning. In injury time, he put the game to bed with a second goal.

As if a brace in a fiery clash with our semi-local rivals wasn't enough to endear him to Albion fans, it was against Derby County a few days later that he really shone. He provided two assists in the win and was breathtaking to watch throughout, with his combination of elegance and the purpose with which he carried the ball. When in possession, he never looked anything other than completely in control. Such poise. Such grace. At one point he embarked on a diagonal run from within his own half which resulted in him taking seven opposition players out of the game before smashing a shot against the crossbar. It wasn't an especially mazy dribble, he just breezed past the Derby defenders as if they were statues. No one even got close enough to him to try to put in a tackle or a foul. The goalkeeper didn't see the shot as it fizzed past him, and the crossbar shook for an eternity as the ball rebounded high into the night sky. Had it struck the bottom of the bar instead of the top, it would have been Brighton's all-time greatest goal. There is a famous picture of Diego Maradona with the ball at his feet in front of a row of six terrified Belgian defenders. That's what it was like watching Vicente take on Derby County on that March evening in 2012. It was one of those rare occasions where it felt as though I was there solely to watch one man. This wasn't a Championship match; this was a Vicente masterclass in football at its most elegant. One moment he had a cluster of opponents around him and then, as if by magic, he was in yards of space. I couldn't take my eyes off him.

I once went to a Lou Reed gig in Sydney where Anohni (of Anohni & The Johnsons) was a backing vocalist. After barely featuring during the show, Anohni took over the lead vocal during a song in the encore with a voice so mesmerising it was as though it had been summoned from some otherworldly place. I will never forget the moment that the beautiful sound caressed my soul. Football is rarely so ethereal, but watching Vicente float effortlessly across the Amex, Dennis Bergkamp turn Newcastle United defenders inside out and Maradona single-handedly win matches comes close. Players like this can free football from its sporting shackles and raise it into a genuine art form, and it feels like a privilege to watch them.

Sadly, in his two seasons at the club, Vicente seemed to spend longer on the treatment table than he did on the pitch, but there is no doubt in my mind that he was the most gifted footballer ever to have played for the club.

Sure, there are countless players who have contributed far more to Brighton & Hove Albion over the years but, in terms of natural ability, nobody tops him.

With Vicente gracing our state-of-the-art stadium, it's fair to say that we were a world away from watching Division Three sluggers churn their way around a muddy Withdean. And even when the team wasn't performing brilliantly, it was still a pleasurable novelty going to matches because of the venue rather than in spite of it. The best way to explain the feelgood factor of the Amex is to recall a 1-0 home defeat to Burnley in mid-December. That might seem like a misnomer, but there was something quite glorious in defeat that day. Brighton had two players harshly sent off in the first 12 minutes, after which the visitors took the lead. From then on, nine players and thousands of supporters battled to try to rescue the game. The men on the field threw their bodies in the way of shots and chased down every loose ball despite their numerical disadvantage, while fans sang the theme tune to *The Great Escape* non-stop, on a loop, for the rest of the match. The atmosphere was incredible. Alas, there was not to be an equaliser, but the afternoon was exciting nonetheless and showcased Brighton supporters at their best. When the fans were fighting the club's owners in 1997, and helping the players punch above their weight at Withdean, they showed tremendous loyalty, invention, wit and passion. It was nice to get a reprisal of it once more on that dreary December afternoon.

The manner of the Burnley defeat will have stirred a familiar feeling to those that supported the club in the 80s and 90s. Back then, Albion always seemed to be the gallant losers. It was built into our collective consciousness that we should expect the club to fail. The FA Cup Final in 1983, the play-off final in 1991, the breathless Liverpool FA Cup replay the same year – we seemed to be forever clapping players from the pitch with a mixture of pride and disappointment. That's why I naturally assumed we'd lose to Hereford United on that fateful day in 1997. Having clawed back the 12-point deficit, it would have been very Brighton to fall short when it mattered. That game proved, however, to be the turning point in the club's history, and not just because it saved us from dropping into the abyss. When the final whistle blew on that emotional afternoon in Herefordshire, not only were we saved from extinction, but our mindset altered too. It was proof that we could emerge victorious from a do-or-die occasion. It was an attitude which we carried forward to Withdean and then to Falmer. Now, Brighton & Hove Albion had a genuine winning mentality. Titles have been won, relegations staved off, planning permission granted. Since the Hereford match, we've been a club that can. And does.

***

SHOUT

I think the atmosphere is generally pretty good at the Amex, but sometimes, as with most stadiums, certain parts of the ground can be a little quiet and, after a run-of-the-mill Sunday afternoon fixture against Barnsley, some fans took to social media to share their concerns about the lack of noise. I think it's important, however, to remember that not everyone goes to the football to spend 90 minutes shouting and singing. When I was a teenager, I liked nothing more than getting amongst it on the terraces, but nowadays I don't sing that much. I'll obviously shout encouragement, involuntarily yell something not very complimentary about the referee and join in with 'Sussex by the Sea' and the thunderous 'Albion' chant, but you're unlikely to hear me singing along with too many other songs from my seat in the East Stand. Some fans, when discussing the Amex's sometimes subdued atmosphere, talk of how amazing the Goldstone's was. I think they are misremembering it. Admittedly the old North Stand's noise was awesome, but, over in the West Stand, aside from a 'Seagulls' chant a couple of times a game, it was fairly quiet. Sure, when it was full, and under lights, the Goldstone had a special atmosphere, just as most old football grounds did with their terraces packed, but all-seater stadiums, by their very nature, are a different proposition. And let's be honest, would the atmosphere for mid-table Albion's Sunday afternoon game against Barnsley have been any better had it been played at the Goldstone? Unlikely. Having said that, safe standing is a great innovation. The first time I experienced it was watching the Albion at the impressive new Tottenham Hotspur Stadium. It made for a great atmosphere that night and I'm delighted that it has been introduced at the Amex.

One thing that is consistent at all stadiums around the world, regardless of the atmosphere, is that some fans don't seem to be able to attend matches without targeting a scapegoat within their team. For a few people at the Amex when the club first started playing there, it was striker Ashley Barnes. Barnes had first found success with Brighton in League One, scoring crucial goals to help the team gain promotion, but some supporters didn't think he was good enough for the Championship and were unwaveringly vocal in their dislike of his performances. Personally, I was a fan of Barnes, and I found it bewildering that a section of the crowd couldn't see his qualities. First things first, I don't believe that any Brighton player, assuming they are trying their hardest, should be given anything other than unequivocal support. Of course, it's perfectly natural to grumble when a pass goes astray, or to vocalise displeasure when the team is playing badly, but Barnes certainly didn't deserve the incessant barracking he received from some. He worked hard, often getting battered by centre-halves or being played out of position on the left by Gus Poyet. Despite having his back to goal for much of the game when Poyet used him as one of the most defensive forwards I've ever seen, his scoring record remained very good. Of course, if a fan pays their admission fee, they are entitled to an opinion, but I genuinely do not know what they hoped to achieve by giving him a hard time, other than to agitate other supporters around them and to knock the player's confidence. Secondly, don't these people think that club managers might be slightly more knowledgeable about team selection? Barnes was a mainstay under two Albion bosses. It's possible for one coach to perhaps have a favourite who doesn't always warrant their place, but for two managers in a row to do the same thing with the same player over a prolonged period of time feels beyond plausible.

Booing Barnes was nothing new, of course. There were scapegoats before and there still are now, but the absolute nadir of the weird relationship between sections of the home crowd and Barnes came in the match against Blackburn Rovers in 2013 when he stepped up to take a penalty at 0-0. He'd been having a barren spell in front of goal and, as he grabbed the ball and put it on the spot, there were audible groans and even a few boos. Astonishing, right? Why would you boo your own player as he is about to take a penalty? I just don't understand some people. He scored from the spot and went on to grab another in a 3-0 win.

Eventually Barnes moved to Burnley. I was sad to see him leave but, were I him, I would have been happy to get away. Despite the player going on to score plenty of goals for Burnley in the Premier League, I'm sure his detractors still find reasons to justify why they gave him such a hard time during his spell at the Albion, but the simple fact is that anybody who couldn't see that Ashley Barnes brought value to the team really doesn't know as much about football as they think.

***

SHOULD I STAY OR SHOULD I GO?

The move to the Amex intensified an issue which always causes heated debate amongst fans. Leaving early. As was the case at Withdean, public transport is the only way for most people to access the stadium, which doesn't really pose a problem before the game, as supporters arrive in dribs and drabs over a few hours, but when leaving at the match's conclusion, you are faced with a queue at the train station or for the park-and-ride buses. Therefore, it isn't surprising that some supporters make the decision to duck out of matches a few minutes ahead of the final whistle in order to avoid getting caught amongst the masses. This leads to criticism from other fans, who don't like the empty seats, the annoyance of having to move as people squeeze past them, and the apparent lack of loyalty.

Personally, I don't leave games early. At the Amex, I have learned that if I absolutely leg it as the final whistle blows, I can get on a train platform really quickly. After the Albion lost on penalties in the FA Cup to Nottingham Forest in 2025, I was on a train to Lewes within three minutes of the match ending. I realise, however, that I am lucky to have long legs and to be a keen marathon runner. I understand that not everyone is able to sprint for a train, but there is also the option of hanging back for a drink for an hour or so, after which you can usually then walk straight on to the platform at Falmer station and board the first available train without any need to queue. Having no kids and only the burning embers of an active social life, I rarely have anywhere to be on a Saturday night, so it makes no difference to me what time I get home.

Equally though, I'm not one to criticise others for leaving a few minutes before the end of a game. If your team is 3-0 up or 3-0 down and missing the last few kicks means you can shave a large chunk of time off your journey, then that's understandable. Fans have any number of reasons for leaving early. Some have mobility issues, lots of people work hours other than 9-5, others have young children, and plenty live long distances away. I moved to London about a decade ago and taking unreliable trains after evening games can be a long and painful process; I can see why people would want to avoid it. Everybody has their own reasons for arriving and leaving when they do. Having said that, I don't really understand why anyone would leave before the final whistle for no good reason. When the Seagulls played Forest back in the Amex's first season, the game was by no means a thriller. For 90 minutes on a bitingly cold December day, very little of note happened, and people started drifting towards the exits before the match had concluded. They would, however, have been frustrated to learn that they missed the game's only memorable moment, a 92nd-minute Brighton winner. If you are going to sit through 85 minutes of a game and you don't have any reason to leave, aside from that you don't fancy queuing for a train or bus, then you've only got yourself to blame when you miss the only action of note. Still, as I said, you buy a ticket, you do what you want.

The one time I remember choosing to leave a match before its conclusion was in Sydney. For a few seasons I did some writing about the A-League in Australia, creating hype pieces about upcoming matches with the aim of boosting ticket sales. Essentially, I tried to make Adelaide United against Brisbane Roar sound as exciting as Real Madrid v Barcelona. I vomited out superlatives about how unmissable the games were going to be when, in truth, they were often slow-paced affairs played in incessant heat to relatively small crowds. Coming up with new and inventive ways each week to essentially say 'this game might not be terrible, you should watch it' was an enjoyable test of my literary skills and it meant that I got a press laminate which allowed me to turn up to any A-League game whenever I wanted. Living a 20-minute walk from Sydney Football Stadium, I would often wander up the road to watch

Sydney FC play, despite having zero affection for them. On one occasion, I snuck out on 88 minutes because the game against Central Coast Mariners was brain-meltingly pedestrian and my mates messaged me to tell me they were at the pub. I nipped off early and as soon as I left the stadium Brett Emerton (remember him?) scored the only goal of the game. In injury time, two Central Coast Mariners players were sent off. Having sat through 88 woeful minutes, I missed an intense and exciting ending, all for the sake of getting to the pub five minutes earlier. It felt like a lesson learned.

As well as barely ever missing the end of games, I try not to ever arrive after kick-off either. I mention this not because I want to be applauded as a 'superfan', but because I find it odd that many supporters seem entirely happy to amble to their seat ten minutes in. Having missed every kick-off when I worked in the club shop at the Goldstone and at Gillingham, I'm in my seat nice and early these days so that I can truly immerse myself in the whole occasion. When I go to the cinema, I'm one of those people who is settled in for the start of the trailers, as opposed to the mavericks who casually stroll in five minutes after the film has started. Come to think of it, unlike at football, people never leave the cinema before the denouement, do they? I guess there aren't 30,000 people at a film screening though, unless you live near an unusually large cinema complex.

Anyone who avoided the final scene of Albion's second season at the Amex may have been glad they did. Gus Poyet's team secured a play-off place at the end of an enjoyable campaign, meaning they would play a two-legged semi-final against the old enemy, Crystal Palace.

After a 0-0 draw at Selhurst Park, two late goals from Palace at the Amex ensured that the Eagles would head to Wembley and eventually secure promotion, while Brighton would face another season in the Championship. We were back to being gallant losers again and, to be honest, it took a long while for the sadness to wear off. As I shuffled out of the stadium at the end of the game, I felt empty. Not only had we lost to our rivals, but nine months of toil had evaporated, just like that. I sat alone on a busy train home and used the tried-and-tested 'look how far we've come' clichés as a crutch. By now I'd been around the club for over 25 years and there had never been times as good as these. Okay, so we'd just lost to Palace, and their fans were going to Wembley and then to the Premier League but, I reminded myself, we'd just faced them on a level playing field in an electric atmosphere created by 30,000 fans. It may not have ended happily, but it was the kind of proper footballing drama that felt a million miles away when Crewe were embarrassing us 4-0 at Withdean in front of 6,000 people just four years previously.

During the summer months, focus shifted away from the bitter defeat and on to who would replace outgoing manager Gus Poyet. At the time, I thought he was the bee's knees, and I think I even called him 'the best manager the club had ever had' in my newspaper column. I lambasted former Albion player Steve Claridge in the same column for his public criticism of Poyet's tactics and apparent lack of a plan B. The idea of progressing without Poyet seemed almost unthinkable to me. He had revolutionised the way the team played and had taken us from the depths of League One to the brink of the Premier League. Of course, once he had gone it became obvious that he wasn't indispensable at all, and that Brighton & Hove Albion could very easily keep moving forward without him. And, in hindsight, it turned out that Claridge's comments about Poyet were actually spot on. The Uruguayan manager's lack of a reactive plan had indeed been a problem; if we went 1-0 down, we rarely got anything from the game.

It's comforting that the football world just keeps on turning despite seemingly seismic shifts. A play-off defeat to Palace? Poyet gone? Not to worry. Despite how it sometimes feels, no individual result and no person is bigger than a club. It's the same when a player chooses to down tools because his head has been turned by a potential transfer. In the 2013/14 mid-season transfer window, Premier League side Sunderland, who by this time were managed by someone called Gus Poyet, wanted to sign Albion's Liam Bridcutt. Brighton's board rejected a bid, after which it was reported that Bridcutt had informed the coaching staff that he wasn't in the right frame of mind to play in a match against Derby County. Eventually the board reluctantly flogged him to Poyet's new club. Bridcutt was a lovely player to watch and had been a fans' favourite. He won Player of the Season twice in a row, yet was his legacy tainted by the way his time at the club came to an end? Maybe. As good a player as he was for Brighton, he certainly got roundly booed the next few times he turned out for an opposing side at the Amex.

During the same season that Bridcutt was sold to Sunderland, Manchester City striker Carlos Tevez seemingly refused to come off the bench during a Champions League game, and it became abundantly clear that the power at football clubs now sat firmly with the players. As you would expect, social media tore into Tevez. People were saying he should be kicked out of the game, but I wasn't so sure about that. I'm not trying to excuse footballers when they behave badly, but think about it; I'm sure that top players are constantly told by fans, the media, their agents and so on, that they are brilliant. Tevez was reportedly earning a quarter of a million pounds a week. My point? Well, if you spoil somebody rotten and inflate their ego, you can't be surprised when they sometimes act like a bit of a diva.

At the time, Bridcutt's departure felt like a disaster. Albion, by now managed by a Spanish gentleman called Óscar García, were once again performing well in the Championship, so to lose their midfield lynchpin midway through the season was worrying. Surely the team would sink down the table without him? Well, they didn't, and looking back at Poyet and Bridcutt's departures, my disappointment now feels entirely out of proportion with the reality of the situation. I suppose, like in many aspects of life, things that seem a big deal at the time turn out to be almost entirely inconsequential in the broader picture.

***

CONTROVERSIAL

I spent New Year's Eve 2013 DJing in a pub in Eastbourne's town centre. My fee was as much rum as I could drink. Consequently, I awoke at 1pm on New Year's Day not feeling my brightest. My tongue was fuzzy, my eyelids felt as though they had been lined with sandpaper and it appeared that the England supporters' band were playing in my head. Brighton were hosting Bournemouth in the Championship in a couple of hours. By the time I had peeled my sorry frame from my sheets, it was 1.30pm. If I was to make it to the game, I would have to leave immediately. It was a half-hour walk to Eastbourne station, then a 35-minute train journey to the ground. I considered crawling back into my warm, comfy bed, but no, I needed the cold January air to blow away the cobwebs so, with the elegance of a reanimated Lindow Man, I made my way to the bathroom, splashed some water on my face, cleaned the layer of fluff from my teeth and pulled on some clothes. I then clicked the front door shut behind me and ventured out into the gloom. The rain drove horizontally and the icy air, rather than blowing away the cobwebs, was a repeated, stinging slap to the face. My fast walk turned into a slow run as I hurried to make the station in time to catch the train. My stomach churned and beads of sweat gathered under my many layers of clothing, meaning I somehow felt both hot and cold as I jumped through the closing train doors like a wheezy Indiana Jones in a woolly hat. I arrived at the Amex ten minutes before kick-off, ate the starchiest food on offer and took my seat. For no reason other than a sense of accomplishment, considering I'd been in bed 90 minutes previously, I was pleased to be at the game. As it turns out, my decision to make my way to the stadium was justified because, within minutes, I had the honour of witnessing one of the most contentious decisions I have ever seen at a football match.

Referee Simon Hooper was well positioned to see Brighton's rugged Spanish full-back Inigo Calderon stretch across the wet surface to perform a perfect slide tackle in the box in the first half. The hearty round of applause which greeted his action confirmed a job well done, so it was entirely baffling when the referee blew his whistle and pointed to the penalty spot. I'd never seen such genuine disbelief from fans and players. It seemed that every single person in the stadium had witnessed a good tackle. Everyone, that is, aside from the referee and presumably his assistants. I was sitting behind the dugouts and I thought the Albion coaching staff were going to spontaneously combust with rage at the decision. Bournemouth scored from the spot as the reaction from the crowd combined confusion and anger.

When Albion grabbed a late equaliser, celebrations in the stands were vitriolic and aimed at the referee, which you don't often see. Once the dust had settled, the penalty became something to laugh about and would eventually become one of those 'I was there' moments. Whilst I was incandescent with rage when Hooper pointed to the spot, it should be remembered that, at the time, officials only got one look at it. Besides, the Bournemouth game would have been immediately forgettable had it not been for his woeful piece of officiating. Conversely, I'm writing about it years later.

Obviously, refereeing decisions can have huge ramifications, but even though Hooper's call ended up costing us a couple of points and would have surely been overturned by VAR, I still much preferred the pre-VAR days of football. At least then you were able to celebrate a goal without that little nagging voice in the back of your head telling you not to get too carried away because it might be disallowed in four minutes' time for an infinitesimal offside. I know I'm not alone in thinking that in tainting the purest, most enjoyable and irreplaceable part of football, the goal celebration, VAR has sucked some of the life out of the game I adore.

Another piece of officiating which was almost as frustrating as Hooper's also came against Bournemouth. It happened at Withdean as the Seagulls were pushing for promotion from League One a few seasons earlier. The match was moving into injury time when the visitors were awarded a penalty for a handball which occurred outside the box (proved conclusively by TV cameras). If you're thinking that the referee simply made a bad call, you'd be incorrect. The referee awarded a free kick but then the referee's assistant incorrectly alerted him that the incident had happened inside the box. Bournemouth scored and the game ended 1-1. As I watched the Bournemouth fans celebrate, I wondered why the man with the flag felt the need to get involved at all. I imagine, as the ball was handled, the referee's assistant's inner monologue went something like this:

'Wait. The ref has given a free kick but I'm sure the handball was in the box. I'm 100 per cent certain in fact. From this perfect vantage point of seven yards behind the line of play and 40 yards away from the incident, I can't possibly be wrong. Now's my big chance to make a name for myself. And the TV cameras are here too! Perfect. The whole world will be saying, "Wow, isn't that linesman an eagle-eyed fellow?" This is brilliant. Shall I get the referee's attention and alert him to his error in giving a free kick and not a penalty? Yes! I'm going to wave my little yellow flag and let him know. This is definitely the correct thing to do.'

Another official who many Albion fans will remember is a certain Kelvin Morton. The referee was in charge of a match between Crystal Palace and Brighton & Hove Albion in 1989 and he ensured that fans of both clubs would never forget him. I was sitting in the home end at Selhurst Park with the Junior Seagulls. As I mentioned when talking about the infamous 'Keith Cuss match', it was fashionable to bring inflatables to matches at the time and I'd jumped all over the fad. Before kick-off, I puffed life into seagulls, a frog and even a full-size skeleton wearing an Albion scarf and hat. I didn't deal in half measures. Just as he would be many years later, my mate Gary the Palace fan was also in attendance, on the home terrace behind the goal. We waved at each other before kick-off and prepared for a cracking match. What followed was an extraordinary afternoon in the south London sun, with one man at its centre. That man was Morton.

With clouds of hair sitting either side of his bald pate, Morton looked every inch an archetypal 1980s referee. Brighton, in their yellow away kit with snazzy shadow stripes, soon fell behind to a blockbusting half-volley from a dynamic young striker called Ian Wright. Shortly afterwards, Morton gave an indication of his intentions by awarding Palace a very soft penalty for a defender climbing in the box. Mark Bright stepped up and scored. Then, the referee sent Albion's Mike Trusson off for an industrial challenge. Straight red cards were rare in those days, but Morton had no hesitation. The Seagulls were down to ten men and two goals behind and it was still the first half.

The Palace fans around us were having a lovely old time. My inflatables weren't getting waved around much.

Before the first period ended, Morton awarded another penalty for a clear foul by Dean Wilkins. Bright stepped up again but this time his kick was saved by John Keeley. Moments later (literally moments), the referee gave a third penalty to Palace. This one wasn't as dubious as the first nor as clear-cut as the second. Wright stepped up and blasted the ball against the post. Brighton would go in at half-time 2-0 down and with only ten men, yet still happy enough in the knowledge that they were somehow still in a contest that should have been out of sight.

Early in the second period, Albion's Kevin Bremner chased a high punt into the Palace box, as did a defender. The man in red and blue put his arm over Bremner's shoulder, which the official saw as reason enough to point to the spot for a fourth time, this time in Albion's favour. It was very soft indeed. Cultured midfielder Alan Curbishley put it in the top corner and, astonishingly, Brighton were in the hunt for an equaliser. I waved my inflatables and waited in anticipation of the fifth penalty of the game. Sure enough, a few minutes later, a cross into the Brighton box deflected on to left-back Ian Chapman's arm. He didn't move his arm towards the ball and he didn't have time to shift it out of the way. Morton was going spot kick crazy though and gave the penalty. Having seen Bright and Wright miss, defender John Pemberton tried his luck. He hit it hard. Really hard. Happily for Brighton, he also hit it miles over the bar in the vague direction of Royal Tunbridge Wells. The Palace fans in front of us took it all in good spirits. They turned to us, shrugged and laughed.

The usual level of bitter rivalry had been overridden by this bizarre story unfolding in front of us and, for now, we were united in our bewilderment. Despite being a man down, Albion did their best to grab an unlikely equaliser but they just couldn't force the ball into the net. Eventually Morton blew the final whistle and we all got to go home and try to make some sense of what we had just witnessed.

So, to recap, Morton awarded five penalties in one game, which at the time of writing remains a British record. Four of the penalties went to Palace. They missed three. Morton also gave one red card and a mountain of yellows. Absolute madness.

I have a very foggy memory of this but, sometime in the mid-90s, Hull City visited the Goldstone and were the victims of some odd officiating. We are constantly informed by pundits that there is no point arguing with a referee as they will never change their mind. Well, anyone who was watching that Hull match can tell you otherwise. Hull launched an attack into Brighton's area, during which the ball may or may not have crossed the goal line before being scooped away by the Albion keeper. The referee decided the ball had gone in and awarded the goal. Albion players surrounded him as the Hull fans celebrated. Meanwhile, City's players congratulated each other and made their way back to their own half, ready to restart the match, but the Brighton team refused to stop protesting. They were insistent that the wrong decision had been made and vehemently appealed for the referee to consult his linesman who, up until this point, had made no attempt to tell the ref he had reason to believe the goal shouldn't stand. He hadn't raised his flag and, like the

Hull team, he had started to make his way back to the half way line. Rather than stand by his original decision, the referee approached his assistant for a brief chinwag. Astonishingly, two officials conjured a reason to disallow the goal. Whether they had decided that the Brighton goalkeeper had been impeded or that the ball had in fact not crossed the line wasn't clear, but the goal was chalked off. Hull's players were incredulous. It was like VAR but without any technology being used, just two blokes having a chat and deciding to reverse the decision. Inevitably, it was now the Hull players' turn to circle the referee. If we learnt one thing that day, it is that a referee won't change his mind twice. The goal remained rescinded and Brighton went on to win 1-0.

You would think, considering the amount of errors that we have all seen officials make over the years, that VAR would have been welcomed into the game with open arms. Let's be honest, its introduction was necessitated by the level of scrutiny of refereeing decisions within TV coverage over many years. It's fair to say though that, although the standard of refereeing remains cause for concern, the implementation of VAR to the Premier League has not really improved things; in fact, it's been disastrous at times. One of the biggest issues, aside from it destroying the immediacy of the game, is that it can still be so subjective. VAR is supposed to offer a definitive, black and white decision, yet in reality it's just another referee watching a bunch of TVs. As a Brighton fan, I would have a different opinion to a Palace supporter on whether something was or wasn't a penalty in the Kelvin Morton game at Selhurst Park. Referees can still make baffling calls after having watched replays from countless angles. Equally, players now know that if they get the slightest touch in the box, they can theatrically fall over and it might look like a penalty when replayed in slow motion. Forgive me if I'm mistaken but that seems like the exact opposite of what VAR was brought in for.

Simply, I feel that VAR in its current incarnation is ruining football as a live experience. Often, supporters inside the ground are clueless as to why the game has been halted for minutes at a time and, as I mentioned before, you can no longer celebrate a goal without worrying that it is going to be chalked off because of something minor that happened in the build-up or because, as happened to Brighton at Palace one time, the hopeless VAR team have somehow contrived to draw the offside lines in the wrong place. It often feels as though VAR actively looks for any possible reason to disallow perfectly good goals rather than double-checking that there weren't any clear and obvious errors which need rectifying. And if you are taking the fun out of celebrating goals and inhibiting the enjoyment of the people who pay to attend games, then what's the point in any of this?

Talking of enjoyment, I can't count the number of times I've felt frustrated during games at the Amex, and not by the Albion. All too often, teams time-waste. One of the things that irritates me most about modern football is the sheer level of cynical time-wasting to which we are subjected. I'm not talking about game management, whereby players try to wind the clock down in the last few minutes when they have a narrow lead. Every side does that, including the Albion, and it is entirely understandable. I'm referring to the teams that, from the first minute, are intent on slowing the game down to a standstill. Before a goal kick, the keeper back-heels the goalpost with each foot, picks some grass off his studs, has a sip from his water bottle, adjusts his gloves, pulls up his socks, gives an instruction to one of his defenders, back-heels the goalpost again, watches the entire *Gavin & Stacey* boxset and phones his mum, before finally walloping the ball up the field. The full-back is sure to carefully wipe every speck of mud, grass and moisture off the ball on his shirt before throwing it, and so on. The seconds tick away.

When Albion were flying high at the top of the Championship, I was often left wondering why opposing teams didn't show more ambition. Parking the bus and time-wasting at the Amex worked on far fewer occasions than it failed. Brighton usually had the wherewithal to find a way to ensure that visiting teams left with nothing, so why didn't opponents just have a go from the kick-off? It's a team's prerogative to play, however, they want, I suppose, but it seemed a shame to employ such a dull and provenly unsuccessful approach to something which is supposed to be entertaining.

It feels like cynicism is eating away at football. One time, I was at a clash between Sydney FC and Melbourne Victory in the A-League, and the most noticeable theme of the match was the sheer level of gamesmanship that went on. At one stage, two balls were on the pitch. A Sydney player went to kick the superfluous one off but then realised that Melbourne were on the attack and, if he left the other ball where it was, the referee might have to stop the match and therefore halt Melbourne in their tracks. The same thing happened a few minutes later, when Sydney were pushing forward and a Melbourne player decided not to remove the extra ball. Every time a throw-in or free kick was given, you would see the defending player kick the ball away, not with sufficient force to get a yellow card at the time, but just enough to slow down the attack. I'm pleased that yellow cards are now given for even causing the slightest delay to the restart, not least because when Declan Rice received his second booking of the game against Brighton in 2024 because of this, the Arsenal fans' meltdown was delicious.

You might be thinking, 'get over it, gamesmanship is just part of the game'. But my point is that it shouldn't be. It has gradually seeped in and is now ingrained in football to the point of acceptance. Wouldn't you love to see an away team not take an age with every goal kick and every throw? Call me crazy, but I'd like the ball to be in play for as many of the 90 minutes as possible and to watch a game played with integrity. I want to witness an occasion where honour is as important as winning, where to be caught diving is embarrassing, where kicking the ball away is not only a yellow card, but a shameful act. Maybe I'm not living in the real world, but all I know is that I'm growing increasingly weary of the game's cynicism.

***

A COLLECTION OF MOMENTS

In ten years of writing a column about Brighton & Hove Albion, I rarely predicted the outcome of upcoming games correctly. For instance, I once suggested that a match against Wycombe Wanderers would be 'pedestrian'. It ended 4-4.

In keeping with the theory that if you sit enough monkeys at typewriters and give them an infinite amount of time they will eventually write the works of Shakespeare, I sometimes did get things right. Under Óscar García. Brighton went into the final game of the 2013/14 season with a slim chance of making the play-offs. Unlike the fantastic day in 1991 when Dean Wilkins scored in the last minute, this time our fate wasn't in our own hands. We had to better Reading's result to squeeze into sixth place. If Reading won, Brighton couldn't qualify. Albion travelled to Nottingham Forest in hope more than expectation.

When I was writing my column the week before the match, I dreamed up a scenario in which Reading's opponents Burnley did us a favour and Albion scored an injury-time winner to make the play-offs. I wondered, though, who would be the 2014 version of Dean Wilkins? Would talismanic striker Leonardo Ulloa deliver a deadly strike? I suggested that it was all set up for Craig Mackail-Smith to mark his recovery from long-term injury by coming off the bench and being a hero.

As well as focusing on Brighton's match in Nottingham, attention was also firmly on what was happening at Reading, making it one of those breathless afternoons where you are acutely aware that the match you are watching only makes up part of a bigger jigsaw. When Albion fell behind in the first half and Reading took the lead in their match, it seemed that our season was over. We would need a three-goal swing to make the play-offs. In the second half though, things started looking up. Burnley turned the game around, not only equalising, but taking the lead. So, when Albion made it 1-1, the Seagulls momentarily leapfrogged Reading into sixth place. If there were no further goals, it would be Brighton who secured the last play-off spot. Reading soon hit an equaliser though, to put them back in the driving seat and drop us down to seventh again. Albion needed to score another goal. Chances went begging. At Reading, the full-time whistle blew on a 2-2 draw. Their fans poured on to the pitch in celebration, just as Barnsley's had back in 1991 before Wilkins scored his majestic free kick. The match in Nottingham went into injury time as Mackail-Smith checked inside, looked up and sent a peach of an inswinging cross into the penalty area. It connected with Ulloa's forehead eight yards from goal. He didn't have to do anything other than give the ball the deftest flick to redirect it into the net. It was the 92nd minute of the final game of the season and, behind the goal, thousands of Albion fans completely lost it. I don't think there are many purer sights than a stand full of people rising as one in celebration, and when I see replays of that goal, I don't watch Ulloa heading the ball, but rather I concentrate on the throngs of Brighton fans going from static to ecstatic in a split second. All over Sussex, people were doing the same, as TV cameras showed Ulloa ripping off his shirt and running to the corner flag. In Berkshire, Reading's pitch invasion fell flat. Brighton were in the play-offs for the second successive season. It was like a low-budget version of that Sergio Agüero goal which won the title for Manchester City while their rivals, United, were preparing to celebrate.

Just as they had been a year previously, the play-offs were a letdown. Derby County dispatched Albion 6-2 over the two legs, meaning we were stuck in the Championship for another season. Incidentally, Derby lost the final at Wembley, with a certain Bobby Zamora scoring a last-minute winner against them for QPR.

Ultimately then, Ulloa's goal led to nothing but almost immediate disappointment. Yet the fact that it is still remembered with such fondness by supporters after all these years clearly demonstrates how football is just a collection of moments. No amount of subsequent disappointment can diminish the delight we felt for those few seconds, nor can it taint our memories when we watch the goal back.

***

RETURN OF THE KING

Do you think anyone is as interested in transfer speculation as the media tell us we should be? Personally, I find it to be a tedious construct, designed to provide rolling content on Sky Sports and online. However, when rumours started doing the rounds in the summer of 2015 about the return of The King, I was all over the internet forums, trying to garner if there was any truth to the whispers that Bobby Zamora was set to re-sign for Brighton. The week prior to this news breaking, I had suggested in my *Argus* column that I wasn't remotely ready for the new football season. The previous campaign had been a real slog. Liverpool legend Sami Hyypiä had taken over as manager and he had not been successful. His stewardship was short-lived, and we only avoided relegation when former Norwich

City and Newcastle United boss Chris Hughton took his place and steadied the ship. After an uninspiring and stressful nine months, I was rather enjoying the break. My outlook changed, however, when I heard that my favourite footballer of all time might come home.

Thrillingly, the hearsay proved to be true and, after a distinguished career which had seen him play for Premier League clubs and represent England, Zamora returned to the place where he was most worshipped. Sure, he was over a decade older and rather creakier in the knees than when he was terrorising defences at Withdean, but I was convinced he would be a success again. Sometimes a player and a club just click and there was no doubt in my mind that Zamora belonged at Brighton. As if it wasn't going to be spine-tingling enough to hear his name chanted when he first stepped on to the Amex pitch in the blue and white stripes, the thought of seeing the ball leave his left boot and arrow into the net was almost too dizzying to contemplate. His first goal for the club would represent an emotional moment for both the player and for everyone who sat watching him weave his magic in that little athletics stadium all those years ago. It would seal the glorious homecoming of a true Albion legend.

His first start was delayed due to injury and he also ended the season on the treatment table. Not long after that, he announced his retirement but, for a few months in between, the team thrived with Bobby as part of it. His first goal was typically dramatic. In the last minute of a game against Leeds United at Elland Road, he deftly chipped the winner with the composure of a man who had spent his career doing just that. Three days later, he was the cause of teary-eyed joy at the Amex as he scored his first home goal. When the ball rebounded to him in the box, the speed of thought to get it under control and then smash it inch-perfectly into the bottom corner rolled back the years to when he was doing the same thing at Withdean.

When Zamora first left the Albion over 12 years previously, the idea of him returning to Brighton when we were playing in our beautiful new stadium seemed implausible. Yet here he was, scoring a late winner to keep the team top of the Championship, and the emotional reaction that this strike prompted on the pitch, in the dugout and in the stands proved just how much he meant to the club and the city.

With his playing days behind him, he later became an official club ambassador and a striker consultant. Seeing such a long-standing, meaningful relationship between a player and a club felt wholesome, particularly in an age when top-level football is often corporate and detached.

***

SEAGULLS DOWNUNDER

I spent the whole of the 2015/16 season in Sydney, meaning I only got to see Bobby Zamora's return on unreliable internet streams and by venturing to the pub at ridiculous hours of the morning. I regret not being there to see Bobby in person, but that's the kind of thing exiled fans are forced to deal with. A supporter's loyalty is generally measured by how many matches they attend, but when that isn't an option, people show an entirely different yet equally valid form of dedication. Quietly watching a match in a dark living room in the dead of night and trying to mute your celebrations when a goal is scored so as not to wake your family takes plenty of commitment, especially considering that the rewards aren't tangible. You don't experience the atmosphere in the stadium nor the camaraderie of being at the game with mates. You don't get the thrill of being there on the big occasion. You tune in every week simply because you love your club. Maybe once a year you will be back to attend a game or two, but largely, being an overseas supporter is a lonely pursuit. The Covid pandemic gave fans in the UK an insight into the surreal alternate reality of only being able to watch their team from the sofa. Well, that's how Australia-based fans have to do it year upon year, which is why local supporters' group Seagulls Downunder is great for Brighton fans in that country.

I'd previously heard of Seagulls Downunder but to my chagrin I didn't get around to meeting up with any of its members until the 2015/16 season. Albion were pushing for promotion to the Premier League and I felt a strong urge to enjoy the games in the company of others, so I reached out to the group's founder and organiser, a lovely bloke called Steve, who told me what Seagulls Downunder was all about. There's no official membership, but rather it is made up of Albion fans who have swapped Sussex for Australia or New Zealand. Their numbers are strong, as is their sense of community and their passion, and they meet up whenever they can. The first time Steve phoned me, we talked for over two hours. I don't even spend that much time on the phone to my family. From our conversation, it was clear that distance had not tempered his love of the Seagulls. If anything, the frustration of not being able to go to matches had made his passion greater. We discussed mutual friends, the old days, the current team, and an upcoming charity match which was taking place in Sydney for the Robert Eaton Memorial Fund. Named after the Brighton fan who died in the Twin Towers attack in 2001, the Robert Eaton Memorial Fund (REMF) was founded to raise money through an annual football match in Sussex between fans of Albion and Crystal Palace. The charity grew to the point that there were all manner of fundraising events each year across Sussex and, as I was now learning, as far away as Australia. The REMF raised hundreds of thousands of pounds, with the money giving a helping hand to underprivileged junior football clubs in the UK and US as well as football-related charity projects in Africa and Albion's powerchair football team.

As we chatted, Steve informed me that he organised this annual match between Sydney-based Albion and Palace fans and, as luck would have it, there was one due to take place in a couple of weeks, so I offered up my services as a barely competent left-back, and I was excited to learn that I'd be on the same team as some real-life professional footballers. Former Seagulls Paul Reid and Lloyd Owusu would be lining up for the Albion.

A fortnight later, Reid kindly picked me up en route to the game and we talked footy as he drove to the venue, a fancy boys' school in the Sydney suburbs. He spoke about playing for Sydney FC alongside the legendary Alessandro Del Piero, and about memories of matches against Crystal Palace for the actual Albion team.

'The one match I always remember is when Albion played Palace at Selhurst Park,' he told me. 'The atmosphere there was brilliant. We won 1-0 and that always sticks in my mind. Selhurst Park is just such a tight stadium and our supporters were unbelievable.'

The upcoming few hours would certainly offer a different vibe to that night at Selhurst. On this blisteringly hot Sydney morning, Reid would instead be turning out with supporters of different ages and sizes, and none of us held the talent of any of his former Albion team-mates, let alone Del Piero. Upon arriving at the school, I saw that the pitch was lush and perfectly mowed. For someone who grew up avoiding dog turds on bobbly, muddy parks across East Sussex, this would unquestionably be the best surface on which I'd ever played. The turnout from both Brighton and Palace fans was also impressive. Scores of people arrived, whether to play or cheer from the sidelines. There was, as you would expect, some light banter, but the overall mood was friendly and inclusive. When you live so far from England, you're just happy to chat with any like-minded football fan, whether they support your team or your arch-rivals. If you are a Seagull or an Eagle who still follows your team from the other side of the globe, then you clearly care greatly about them and about football in general. There were no plastic fans in attendance here.

The welcome that Reid and Owusu received from the Brighton contingent landed somewhere between friendship and hero worship. The former professionals posed for photos with some folks and had long conversations with others as the sun relentlessly beat down. It was over 30 degrees and the clock hadn't even hit midday, causing supporters to shelter under gazebos as the rest of us took to the field. What followed was a roller coaster of a match which saw Palace 5-3 up with just a couple of minutes to go. After the fifth goal, the Eagles' coaches and subs raced on to the pitch to celebrate what seemed like a certain victory. It would be their first ever win in the annual fixture; all they had to do was see out the final few moments. However, within a minute, Owusu scored to make it 5-4 and then, with almost the last kick of the game, his cross was buried by Reid, who wheeled away jubilantly. It might not have been the same as winning at Selhurst Park, but the happiness on his face proved that it still meant something to him. It did to the rest of us too. It doesn't matter at what level you are playing, or how friendly the occasion is, when you score an injury-time equaliser, the delight is entirely real.

The goal proved to be the last action of note and, layered with sweat, I shook hands with my red-and-blue-shirted counterparts, happy to have navigated the match without making a fool of myself. Every time I passed the ball to either Reid or Owusu, I got the slightest feeling of what it might have been like to have been a professional. That was enough to make the day an absolute triumph for me.

After the game, with boots long since removed and socks rolled down to ankles, we all enjoyed drinks and a barbecue, chatting about our respective clubs' fortunes and about living so far from home. As the afternoon sun grew hotter still, Reid drew the raffle, and over $1,500 was raised in total for the REMF.

It felt especially appropriate to be raising money for the Robert Eaton Memorial Fund at this time as, just a couple of months previously, another awful tragedy befell people close to Brighton & Hove Albion and indeed the

REMF itself. In August 2015, an ex-military aircraft crashed during a display at the Shoreham Airshow. The plane became a ball of fire upon hitting the A27, killing 11 people and injuring 16 others. Two of those who died were Matthew Grimstone and Jacob Schilt. Matthew was a member of the ground staff at the Amex and Jacob was a fundraiser and player for the main REMF team. A minute's silence was beautifully observed at grounds across the country in midweek, and messages of support poured in from supporters of all teams. Words of condolence from fans of Crystal Palace were especially touching; the general tone of them was that rivalry is fun but, at times like this, we all need to stick together. Equally, the Albion as an organisation was brilliant in the aftermath of the tragedy. The way that ever-eloquent chief executive Paul Barber spoke to the media was heartfelt and perfect in its tone, while goalkeeper David Stockdale proved himself to be a kind, thoughtful ambassador for the club throughout the aftermath. Representatives of Worthing United, for whom Jacob and Matt played, spoke with dignity despite struggling to come to terms with the loss. Meanwhile, Sussex as a community, and particularly a sporting community, showed great strength. Football's reaction to the Shoreham Airshow crash was a reminder of why the sport is so important in times of tragedy and crisis. Whenever I step into the Amex, I feel a sense of belonging that I simply don't get anywhere else.

It was hard to be overseas while my friends at the Albion were grieving. Watching the tribute to the victims before the next home game, against Hull City, on the internet was very moving, as thousands of people came together to pay their collective and individual respects to the 11 victims, and especially Jacob Schilt and Matt Grimstone. The most touching thing for me was that, although some people at the Amex knew the deceased, most of those sitting in the stands did not, yet everyone was united in their grief and in a genuine outpouring of affection. The event once again showed how supporting a football club is like having a huge extended family. When someone connected with football dies, their memory is honoured on a scale that rarely happens away from the sporting world. There is something profoundly heartening in that.

I seemed to write with painful regularity in my *Argus* column about the loss of members of the Albion family. I suppose something we can be thankful for is that, without football, many people would never have known the likes of Matthew Grimstone and Jacob Schilt, or other loyal Albion supporters, such as my old mate Marie from the ticket office, all of whom were taken from our football family too soon. They have touched countless lives through the beautiful game, and while Worthing United and Brighton & Hove Albion continue to exist, their memory will also live on.

For instance, when it was announced in 2025 that another former colleague of mine, Hannah Deacon, had sadly died at the age of 45, I instantly thought back to the Withdean days. Before she left the club and became a brilliant mum and tireless campaigner in overcoming barriers to medical cannabis in the UK, Hannah was an absolutely hilarious member of staff at the Albion's offices in Queens Road. Whenever I think of her, I think back to how she constantly kept everyone's spirits up. Without

Brighton & Hove Albion, she wouldn't have come into our lives.

Several hours after I had played in the REMF game against Crystal Palace, I laid in my Sydney bed with aching legs and sunburned skin, watching a live stream of Brighton's Championship match at Leeds United. As the clock ticked past 3am and Bobby Zamora won the match in the last minute, I leapt from the bed in celebration, causing my aching thigh muscles to silently scream. As the final whistle blew, I thought about how, dotted around that great Southern Land, there were people like me celebrating. It made me realise more than ever that football has the ability to not only bring people together, but to make a person feel closer to home. When Zamora hit the net at Elland Road, an entire network of people all over the world jumped for joy, their hearts beating as one.

***

WANDERING

An interesting and unexpected bonus of living in Australia for such large chunks of time over the course of a decade was that I was able to take a genuine interest in an A-League club without the same sense of guilt that would come from supporting another professional team in England (which, as we know, is a cardinal sin). Whilst my shiny press laminate gained me entry to any A-League game, it was inevitable, given my then-partner, now-wife Jayne's affinity, that I would eventually land upon Western Sydney Wanderers as my Aussie club of preference. On home matchdays, we would pull on our red-and-black hooped replica shirts and make our way to games. In lieu of being able to go to the Amex, I soon grew to love my new matchday ritual in Australia. We'd take the train to Parramatta, devour a veggie burger in one of the local fast food joints on our way to the ground, and be in our seats in time to watch the teams warm up. Given how much I missed the routine of going to watch football back in Blighty, this was a consoling substitute. The actual matches in the A-League, however, offer a markedly different experience to those in the UK. For a start, it is usually over 20 degrees warmer, meaning the pace of the game is far slower. Also, supporters can drink alcohol in their seats, so there's always an annoying, constant flow of people getting up and down to buy beer. I know there have been tentative rumblings that drinking within view of the pitch might be introduced in England, but I sincerely hope it doesn't happen. I don't want to be constantly moving for people who can't go 45 minutes without a drink, and I don't want to be showered with beer every time a goal goes in. Call me boring, but spending the rest of the day in sticky, booze-stained clothes does not appeal.

Anyway, back to the A-League. Another difference is that, while there are designated home and away areas, there are no barriers separating the fans really, and away supporters can purchase tickets in home sections should they so choose, even in games between big rivals. Usually, the geographical distance between clubs means that there are only a small number of away followers in attendance anyway. All of which creates a less intense atmosphere than you would experience in England, and the banter is, for the most part, light and breezy rather than as full-on as it can be in other parts of the world. It feels relaxed in a way that reflects the laid-back

Australian lifestyle. Rather than violence, someone might just call you 'mate' in a slightly aggressive way.

Having said all that, most A-League clubs have a group of very vocal, passionate fans who do their best to create a vibrant atmosphere, with drums, chants and tifos. However, whenever I was at games, it seemed that they sang their songs in the exact same order and at the exact same time every match. Having grown up on the terraces in England, where funny chants would instantly be created in reaction to what was happening on the pitch, it felt more formulaic in Australia. That's not intended as a criticism, by the way. I understand that the A-League is comparatively very young, and that football's popularity in the country falls way behind cricket, AFL and NRL. The active supporter groups put a lot of time and energy into getting behind their teams and they should be applauded for being at the forefront of creating a culture of football fandom in their country. Without these fan groups, football in Australia would be dour, but it undoubtedly felt different to watching matches back home.

Following Western Sydney Wanderers is a strange experience. I obviously want them to win, but it is never with the same level of desperation that I feel when watching the Albion. And when they invariably lose, I am pretty much over it by the time I'm queuing at the gelato shop on the way back to the station. I definitely consider myself a Western Sydney Wanderers supporter, but the simple truth is that you just can't replicate the passion and commitment you have for the club you truly love.

To be honest, Wanderers' fortunes rarely crossed my mind during the 2015/16 season, as Brighton's promotion push well and truly took centre stage. Albion were excellent throughout the campaign and, with a game to play, we were in third spot, level on points with second-placed Middlesbrough. The final match of the season was away to, you've guessed it, second-placed Middlesbrough. It would be a straight shoot-out for automatic promotion to the Premier League. Boro were above Albion on goal difference, which meant the home side could afford a draw but Brighton needed to go to the Riverside Stadium and win. The media had a field day with this fixture. They called it the £180 million game, as that was apparently how much it would be worth to the winning club. If anything summed up the vulgarity of modern football, it was this. To fans and players, the game was about glory and achieving a lifetime's ambition, yet every article on websites and in newspapers focused on the financial implications. I suppose that's just the landscape these days.

There was clearly no better time for another Seagulls Downunder meet-up. The midday kick-off in the UK meant the game would take place on Saturday night on the other side of the world, making it perfect for boozy gatherings in Sydney, Melbourne, Perth and various other places across Australia and New Zealand. And so, at 8.30pm in Sydney, I walked through Darling Harbour and into the sports bar at the city's huge casino, The Star, where the game would be shown on a big screen. There I would join approximately 130 Albion fans, as well as Paul Reid, who was wearing his actual team shirt from back in the day. Even before a ball had been kicked, I felt overwhelmed. I thought back to when I arrived in the country a decade previously and spent a Sunday night walking the streets alone, trying to find a pub in which to watch the game. Now, as I entered the vast, noisy bar, there were Albion fans everywhere. As I parted with far too much money for a schooner of decidedly average beer, I could have been in any bar in Brighton and it felt magical. We sang songs and banged on tables as the game got underway, making such a din that, whilst we couldn't be heard in Middlesbrough, the rest of the venue certainly knew we were there. Cue baffled looks from tourists and probably a few annoyed gamblers as they tried to concentrate on not losing all of their money.

Brighton's first-half performance was muted and Boro led 1-0 at the break. Really, they should have been further in front but the Seagulls were still in the game as the second half got underway. Then, from nothing, Albion midfielder Dale Stephens popped up to equalise. The away fans at the Riverside went crazy and 130 supporters in Sydney did the same. Songs were sung, more tourists wondered what on earth was going on. We were one goal from the Premier League.

Before we had even regained our breath though, referee Mike Dean essentially ended Albion's bid for automatic promotion. Stephens went in for a challenge on Boro's Gaston Ramirez and caught him with the bottom of his boot. Dean reached for a yellow card but then, astonishingly, he allowed the card to be knocked from his hand by Ramirez and decided that the best course of action would be to change his mind and instead show Albion's midfield lynchpin a red one. Stephens was shocked, as was everyone in the casino. To this day, I think it was a poor decision. I wonder if referees ever lose sleep over such things? I know I would. Brighton's best player on the day and their goalscorer was gone and Chris Hughton's team faced the mammoth task of breaching an impressive home defence again with a numerical disadvantage. The journey from delight to confusion and frustration had taken just a couple of minutes.

There was to be no glorious late winner. The game finished 1-1 and Middlesbrough were promoted. As their fans streamed on to the pitch in delight, I skulked out of the casino and into the Sydney night. A good number of Albion fans stuck around to drink away their sorrows, but I just wanted to get some air into my lungs and to gather my thoughts. The reflection of the city skyline twinkled in the harbour as I made a sobering trudge through weekend revellers towards the train station. I told myself that, even though it was gut-wrenching to miss out on promotion, there was no point dwelling on it. At least we still had the chance of promotion via the back door of the play-offs. Controversial refereeing decisions happen to every team throughout a season, so whining about it would do no good at all. We just had to dust ourselves down and focus on the upcoming task, a semi-final against Sheffield Wednesday. The spirit and determination that the players showed in the second half against Boro, despite being a man down, gave me great hope about our chances in the play-offs. Stephens now being banned so unfairly was a massive blow but maybe the other players would use the injustice as fuel for their fire. Even though we'd failed in our previous two play-off attempts, I felt that this was our year. After all, we'd finished miles ahead of the other contenders and had only missed out on automatic promotion by a whisker. I was due to move back to England at the end of June, but I looked into the possibility of bringing my flight forward in order to attend the final at Wembley.

Whoever said that luck evens itself out over the course of a season needs to re-evaluate their statement. I don't recall Albion being particularly fortunate throughout the 2015/16 campaign yet, from the moment Dean had the yellow card knocked from his grasp in the Middlesbrough match, it felt like the team was cursed. In the first leg of the play-off semi-final with Sheffield Wednesday at Hillsborough, four key Albion players were forced off injured. Four! And teams were only allowed three substitutions back then, so we played with ten men for the final half an hour. Superstitious readers will be interested to note that the game was played on Friday the 13th. The 2-0 defeat was seriously damaging and, despite a fantastic atmosphere at the Amex for the return leg and a gallant effort from the players, a 1-1 draw saw Wednesday make it to Wembley, where they would lose to Hull City in the final. The time difference meant that the play-off semi-final games took place early in the morning for those of us in Australia, so I don't think Seagulls Downunder members arranged any big meet-ups for them. I certainly just watched both matches on my laptop in bed. As the final whistle blew at the Amex, I turned off my computer, got up and readied myself for work. There would be no post-match sorrow-drowning. It was an odd feeling to stand on a busy commuter train having already had an extraordinarily stressful and disappointing morning. Nobody should start their day with a crushing semi-final exit. At work, it was almost impossible to stop my mind wandering back to how close we'd come. The season was over and, anticlimactically, within an hour of the final peep of the referee's whistle, I was in my office filing paperwork.

***

GOODBYE TO ALL THAT

In his magnificent book, *Fever Pitch*, Nick Hornby correctly states that football fans count the passing of time in seasons, not years. Using this metric, the final whistle of the Sheffield Wednesday play-off semi-final represented the end of my tenth season writing a column about Brighton & Hove Albion in *The Argus*. In that time, I had penned over 200,000 words, and I decided that my tenth anniversary was an appropriate juncture to bow out. In the game before my first column, Albion lost 5-1 at home in front of 5,859 fans. The result meant they finished bottom of the Championship with seven wins all season. Now, here they were knocking on the door of the Premier League in front of huge attendances at their beautiful stadium. It had been quite the journey.

I spent the close-season fuming about Mike Dean's Middlesbrough intervention, but the strange truth is I should have been grateful to the referee for sending Dale Stephens off. Why? Because the following season was one of the best and most exciting in Albion's history and, having returned from Australia before the campaign kicked off, I was there to witness the whole glorious spectacle in person. Oddly, this would be the first time since I was ten that I would be attending Brighton matches without any responsibilities other than to support the team. I'd been there as a ball boy, a club employee and a newspaper columnist. Now, I was going to games as a fan and nothing else. In a strange way, I felt as excited as I did the first time I headed to the Goldstone in 1986. There can't be many 40-year-olds who have been watching their team for three decades yet feel like going to a game is an almost entirely new experience.

Expectations were high. Brighton had been superb during the previous season, playing thrilling, counter-attacking football, and there was no reason to think that Chris Hughton's team would perform to a lower standard this time round. Former Albion hero Glenn Murray had re-signed as a replacement for Bobby Zamora and defensive rock Shane Duffy soon arrived to pair up with the best centre-back I'd ever seen play for Brighton, Lewis Dunk. If asteroids had been hurtling towards Earth, Duffy and Dunk would've simply headed them back into outer space.

We had also signed French wing wizard Anthony Knockaert. When Knockaert played for Leicester City at the Amex a couple of seasons previously, he terrorised our defence every time the ball was at his feet. He was a tricky left-footer who played on the right wing, cutting in and causing chaos with every jink and shimmy. He was the kind of footballer that gets supporters' pulses racing whenever running towards goal, the sort of player for whom anything seemed possible. I think every team needs someone like Knockaert. Sure, he threw a strop about once a game and could be frustratingly inconsistent sometimes, but watching a player like him with the ball at his feet as a wide-eyed defender backs off in panic is about as exciting as it gets for a football fan.

As the 2016/17 season progressed, Knockaert provided several seminal moments, including when Sheffield Wednesday visited the Amex for a Friday night fixture. I caught a bout of man flu a couple of days before the game and wasn't well enough to attend, so I instead watched it on Sky from my living room. Knockaert opened the scoring with a brilliant individual goal but, with the score at 1-1 in the second half, Brighton conceded a penalty after Murray handled in the area. He was red-carded. I sank into the sofa. We were set to go 2-1 behind at home to a promotion rival and were a man down. Was this the moment that our season went off the rails? Wednesday's enigmatic forward Fernando Forestieri side-footed the penalty towards goal. Albion's David Stockdale dived to his right and blocked the shot. I leapt from my chair, spilling my Lemsip as I did so. But wait, the ball rebounded directly to Forestieri, who scuffed a shot towards the opposite side of the goal. Stockdale, still on the ground after his initial save, somehow stretched his body back across his area, extended his arm and got a fingertip to the ball. It trickled oh so slowly towards the right-hand post and, gloriously, dribbled inches wide. Albion's keeper leapt to his feet, roaring like a lion. A wave of relief swept through the Amex while, in Eastbourne, I was letting out a cheer which further reddened my sore throat. We were still level and, if we defended well enough, would escape with a hard-earned point.

Wednesday banged firmly at Albion's door, but there was simply no knocking it down. Then, with a few minutes remaining, Brighton launched an attack. Full-back Sébastien Pocognoli delivered an inviting cross to the back post, where Knockaert stuck out a leg and diverted the ball into the back of the net for his second goal of the game. A celebration born out of joyous disbelief reverberated around the Amex while, in Eastbourne, I sank to my knees in my living room and hugged the dog, who had not the slightest idea what was going on but was nonetheless enjoying the attention. Wednesday had blown a huge chance to overturn one of their promotion rivals and they consequently lost the plot, receiving two late red cards and ending the match with nine players. Albion, meanwhile, rose to the top of the table. I fell into bed that night feeling decidedly less ill after watching such a resilient, battling performance in which my team took three points when it seemed they wouldn't get any. The healing power of a win. Strange as it sounds, considering there were still 20 games remaining in the season, it was at that moment that I became 100 per cent confident Brighton were going to be promoted.

***

WELSH ZOMBIE

When Albion were due to play Cardiff City at home on a Friday night just after Christmas, Jayne and I were cat-sitting for some friends in Brighton, staying at their house and looking after two slightly loopy and permanently hungry felines. Being one of those overly cautious people who likes to leave plenty of time to get anywhere (airports, doctors' appointments, football matches, etc), at about 6pm I fed the cats, pulled on my winter coat and hat, and stepped into the misty night to make my way to the Amex. It had been the first time I'd been outside all day and I had no idea that such a layer of grey was blanketing the city. As soon as I clicked the front door shut, my phone buzzed. It was a message from Jayne, who was at work in London. In her text she said she'd heard that the game might be called off because of the fog and that I should perhaps not leave home until a decision had been made. Too late. Checking my pockets, I realised I didn't have keys to the house on me, so I made my way towards Brighton station in the hope that the game would in fact go ahead. By the time I got to the station, the match had indeed been postponed. The concourse, usually abuzz with fans, was deathly quiet, the yellow lighting combining with the misty air to create an eerie atmosphere. I now had three hours to kill until Jayne arrived back in town with her set of keys. I didn't have enough money, post-Christmas, to go to the pub and none of my friends were around anyway, so I forlornly wandered around the few shops which had remained open late. I cannot explain the bleakness of trying to keep warm by walking around the men's section of TK Maxx when I should have been at the Amex cheering my side on to another victory. The ridiculousness of the situation did, however, spark a memory of another time a game against Cardiff had been called off, many years previously.

Brighton's match at home to the Welsh side some time in the late 80s or possibly early 90s had been postponed in the morning due to the pitch being waterlogged. By 3pm, the Goldstone was deserted. Most supporters had heard on the radio that the game was off, or had turned up at the ground, shrugged disappointedly and headed home. In this pre-internet age though, a handful of Cardiff fans weren't aware of the news. The group of about a dozen men (shaven-headed, bomber jackets, you get the idea) arrived in Hove expecting to see a match, but were greeted with empty streets and a silent stadium. They bowled down the road and started banging on the window of the club's main office, demanding to know what was going on. By now, the torrential morning rain had cleared, the sun was shining, and it felt like the perfect afternoon for football. Typical.

I don't know about you, but when a group of angry blokes are aggressively banging on a window, opening the window would be quite low on my list of actions. Inexplicably, Albion's chief executive at the time, a lovely man called Ron Pavey, considered it to be the most appropriate thing to do. Always unfailingly polite, Mr Pavey turned the handle and pushed the window open. Upon explaining that the match had been postponed, he was greeted by a barrage of profanities. What happened next surprised everyone, not least our chief executive. Realising he wasn't going to have the genial exchange for which he had hoped, he tried to close the window. Only, as he did so, one of the Cardiff fans leaned in and bit his hand, just like a zombie would. Mr Pavey immediately managed to free himself from the jaws of the Cardiff fan and pull the window closed before saying, with a look of utter incredulity on his face, 'He bit me! He bit my hand!' The Cardiff fans eventually dispersed, and Albion's chief executive didn't subsequently become a zombie, but the image has always stuck with me, perhaps because it shows how football can prompt such stupid instances of aggression. I suppose when you combine toxic masculinity, alcohol and direct competition it's inevitable that some people will want to swing their fists at each other (or, in this case, bite someone). Take it one step further, and you get organised hooliganism, which is an even more bewildering way to want to spend your spare time. Why would anyone actively plan to spend their weekend down suburban back streets, duffing up strangers and/or being duffed up themselves? Madness. It's sad that healthy competition and rivalry can so easily boil over and be replaced by violence. Thinking about it objectively, it's ridiculous that grown men will fight because of football. Not once in my life has watching football caused me to want to attack a fellow human. I'm sure that mega-tough guys will tell me I'm a wimp, but if being a wimp means not having the desire to punch someone in the face because my team has lost, that's fine with me.

***

ON OUR WAY

Because Brighton & Hove Albion are Brighton & Hove Albion, there were inevitably bumps along the road towards promotion, like the desperately unlucky home defeat to Newcastle United. With Albion 1-0 up going into the closing stages, a Newcastle player completely misfired his shot. It wasn't even going towards goal until it hit a team-mate on the ankle, ballooned into the air and somehow, somehow, nestled into the top corner. Buoyed by their slice of good fortune, the Geordies went on to grab a late winner. It was a hugely important result in terms of where the league title was heading and showed that, no matter how hard you train and prepare, sometimes football is simply about luck.

For the time being though, nobody involved with the Albion really cared that much about the title. Getting promotion was all that mattered. The problem was that, regardless of how many games Brighton and Newcastle won, and no matter how many promotion rivals fell away, there was still one team that would not say die. That team were one of the favourites for relegation at the start of the season, Huddersfield Town, who nibbled at the heels of the division's top two long after they had been expected to slide down the table. Considering this was gearing up to be one of the best seasons in Brighton's history, I spent an inordinate amount of it worrying about Huddersfield's fortunes. I studied their fixtures, checked their socials for injury news and probably took almost as much interest in them as their own supporters did. It became a mild obsession. They were a proper nuisance, but they became slightly less so on an afternoon when they faced lowly Burton Albion and Brighton took on Blackburn Rovers.

Albion's home showdown with Blackburn was an ugly affair which Albion won by a single goal. Three more points. When the final whistle blew at the Amex, Huddersfield were still playing and, surprisingly, were being held at home by lowly Burton. As fans filtered from the stands at the Amex into the concourses below, news came through of a goal in the Huddersfield match. Expecting the worst, I looked at one of the TVs on the concourse. Adjusting my vision towards the rolling scores at the bottom of the screen, I saw that it wasn't in fact Huddersfield that had scored. In their desperation to beat their lowly opponents, they had left huge gaps in their defence and, with the referee checking his watch, Burton raced up the other end and delivered a classic sucker punch. It was a goal that would help ensure Burton's eventual survival in the Championship and, down on the south coast, was celebrated heartily. Huddersfield were still in the hunt, but they weren't breathing down our necks anymore. The cheers that went around the emptying Amex caused everyone to stop in their tracks and, as news quickly spread, an impromptu party started on the concourses and in the sunshine outside the ground. The North Stand concourse was the epicentre of the celebrations, and a fine example of the culture of post-match mingling that takes place around the ground. All concourses are open, meaning fans can meet up and have a drink, and it's nice to see home and away supporters mix amicably while kids in replica kits belt a ball against the wall. Almost immediately, the tribalism that is experienced over 90 minutes diminishes over a pint. As afternoon turned into evening, the North Stand concourse remained full of fans who were by now singing raucously. Half-finished cups of beer were thrown and bins were used as makeshift drums as fans sang about a promotion that was now pretty much within touching distance.

***

ABSOLUTE BEDLAM

I wasn't able to go to Brighton's away match at QPR. The previous time I went to Loftus Road, the game was a 0-0 draw, I couldn't really see anything from my seat and the coach broke down on the way home. And when I went to a pre-season friendly there in 2024, an absolutely wasted teenager projectile vomited near me before kick-off and his puke went all over my shoes. Safe to say it's not my favourite away ground.

Missing this game in 2017 was annoying, but at least it was on Sky. Jayne, once again, was working, so I ended up watching the match at home with just the dog for company. When Glenn Murray calmly slotted the ball into the net to give the Seagulls the lead, I jumped from the sofa and let out a cheer. As had become the norm in this situation, the dog started barking uncontrollably and I had to spend the next few minutes trying to calm her down. Then, Albion got a free kick just outside the box. Anthony Knockaert and Sébastien Pocognoli engaged in a discussion about who was going to take it. It seemed strange. Knockaert was a free-kick expert and I don't think I'd ever seen Pocognoli, a loanee from West Bromwich Albion, even take a shot in his short Brighton career. But, no, it was Pocognoli who struck it. The defender wrapped his left foot around the ball and whipped a deadly strike off the bottom of the crossbar and into the top-right corner of the goal. The away end, directly behind the strike, was a sea of limbs. It was 'absolute bedlam', as the radio commentator so perfectly put it. It was bedlam in my house too. One-man bedlam. Or, to be precise, one man and one dog bedlam. I bounced around the front room, before eventually collapsing in an exhausted heap on the floor. The dog, baffled and excited, jumped on top of me, barking and howling. As happy as I was, it was one of those moments that I look back on now with regret that I wasn't amongst the madness in the two-tier away end at QPR. It must have been amazing to be there when that free kick went in as the players, surprised at what they'd just witnessed, celebrated ecstatically with the fans. Experiencing the same thing in Eastbourne with a confused cocker spaniel wasn't quite the same.

Brighton's next game was also on TV. Back in the bad old days we were lucky if one game a season was televised, but now it felt like we were on the box more regularly than *Coronation Street*. This time Wolves were the hosts as football fans around the world saw Knockaert score two goals in a comfortable victory. This meant that, 34 years after relegation from the top flight, Brighton & Hove Albion were one win away from promotion to the Premier League.

Almost a year after the Middlesbrough disappointment, I was once again nervously making my way to my destination. This time though, I wasn't heading to a casino in Sydney. Rather, I had just disembarked from a train at Falmer's modest station and was walking to the Amex. Jayne was alongside me. This was her first season as a Brighton supporter, having only moved over to England with me when I returned the previous summer. Remembering that her Australian team of choice, Western Sydney Wanderers, won the AFC Champions League within two years of forming, I was starting to think she was something of a lucky charm. As we took our seats in the back row of the lower tier of the East Stand, the atmosphere was like nothing I had ever experienced. I'd been at the ground for play-off semi-finals, big cup games, and that amazing first league match, but this was something entirely different. There were four games remaining and we needed three points. We were going up, of that there seemed little doubt. If it wasn't today, it would be next week or the week after. Whatever was to happen over the next 90 minutes, today was when the party started. Besides, we were playing a relatively poor team in Wigan Athletic, and we were irresistible at home.

However, Brighton's players were clearly nervous and unable to get into any sort of rhythm at first, while Wigan were trying their best to stifle Albion's attacking play and were making a pretty good fist of it. They'd won the toss and opted to make Brighton kick towards the North Stand in the first half, when the players generally preferred to do so in the second period. Little things like that can really affect a team. Former Seagulls captain Paul Rogers once told me that it completely threw players off when they lost the toss and were made to switch ends before kick-off at Withdean. Whatever the reason, Albion continued to struggle against a limited Wigan side. That is until a long Lewis Dunk pass was knocked down on the edge of the box for Murray to arrow a shot into the bottom corner. It instantly felt as though the shackles had been removed.

Midway through the second half, Knockaert danced into the box between two Wigan players and laid the ball off to local lad Solly March, who had made a fabulous impact in recent weeks upon recovering from long-term injury. Now, here he was, after enduring months on the sidelines, with the chance to score the goal which would surely secure his team's promotion. He took a touch eight yards out and then belted a right-footed shot through the goalkeeper's legs and into the net. For the next 20 minutes, the singing from all four sides of the stadium was non-stop. 'We're on our way to the Premier League,' was the cry.

With five minutes remaining, Wigan pulled one back. Of course they did. After the goal, it was squeaky bum time, as Alex Ferguson might say, as the visitors threw all they had at Albion's defence in the hope of getting an unlikely equaliser. They came close, but they didn't get it and, at the referee's final whistle, approximately 20,000 people brazenly and brilliantly ignored the club's pre-match pleas to remain off the pitch and galloped gleefully and naughtily on to the turf. Who could blame them? Only a couple of decades ago, the club was bottom of the entire league, one game from oblivion. After years of hurt, of being homeless and penniless, of fighting their own board, and of battling for a new stadium, their club was in the promised land with a brilliant team of honest professionals, a fine human as manager and an ardent fan as chairman and owner. If now wasn't the time to invade the pitch and to let out all of those pent-up emotions, when was? I thought back to the pitch invasion at the dilapidated old Goldstone in 1996, when enraged supporters snapped the crossbars in desperation. Back then, it was impossible to even dream we'd ever see a day like this.

Like nervous jaywalkers, Jayne and I waited a few moments before tiptoeing on to the pitch in the slipstream of others for the obligatory selfies and to join in with the celebrations in front of the West Stand, where the players had appeared, shirtless, six-packed and tattooed in the press box, while Tony Bloom, the man who had made all of this possible, joyously waved a scarf above his head in the tier above. Something that sticks in my mind is just how strong the smell of cut grass was. It's funny the things you notice. It also felt strange to stand inside the centre circle. As Knockaert commandeered a microphone and led a series of singalongs, I was once again taken out of the moment by swirling memories from years gone by.

The stadium was different and I was much longer in the tooth but, just for a second, I was a 12-year-old kid again, treading down divots at the Goldstone.

Having saluted every one of their heroes, the swarm of fans on the Amex pitch gradually decreased, as people vacated the turf and made their way to the concourses to continue their celebrations and to watch the unfolding Derby County v Huddersfield Town match. Oh yes, I should probably have mentioned that Albion hadn't officially been promoted just yet.

On this most wonderful of days, Brighton's promotion to the Premier League wouldn't be mathematically certain unless Huddersfield failed to win at Derby. Their game kicked off at 5.30pm and, by the time Seagulls fans started to pay attention to it, Huddersfield were already 1-0 up. Make no mistake though, to all intents and purposes, Albion *were* up. Although Huddersfield could still equal our final points tally, their vastly inferior goal difference meant they'd have to win each remaining game by an avalanche of goals and Brighton would have to lose all of their matches equally emphatically. Simply, it wasn't going to happen. Still, the Huddersfield game was worth keeping an eye on because, if they didn't win this match, Brighton could call themselves a Premier League club. It may have only been a case of dotting the 'i' and crossing the 't' of the word 'promotion', but it was a juicy enough prospect to ensure that thousands of supporters, plastic cups of beer in hand, remained at the stadium to watch the Huddersfield game unfold.

It was shown on the main scoreboards at either end of the ground and on TVs on all concourses. As I wandered around the stadium in something of a haze, I bumped into several old friends and acquaintances, including a fine man called Andy Mac from Skint Records. Skint had obviously been really good mates to the club for a long time and I was so happy to see Andy for the first time in years. We shared an exuberant yet exhausted hug and talked about what an amazing day it had been. I think this kind of interaction was happening all around the stadium. If people were watching the Huddersfield game, they were only doing so with one eye while embracing friends old and new. We were up and we were going to enjoy it; we were just waiting for the cherry to be placed on top of the cake.

As the Huddersfield match petered out, seemingly towards an away win which would mean our promotion wouldn't be made official until the following week, I found myself alone on the otherwise packed and noisy North Stand concourse. Jayne had headed to London to meet a visiting pal from Australia, so I stood by myself, caught my breath and attempted to make sense of the day. I bought another pint and watched the activity going on around me. People were drinking, singing, embracing, shaking hands and smiling. Then, two minutes from the end of the Huddersfield match, a shot from the edge of the box took a slight deflection and suddenly I was hugging a total stranger and was covered from head to foot in beer, as plastic cups went flying in every direction. Derby had scored! Whilst we'd all only been half-watching the game until this point, it had suddenly become very interesting indeed. We were a few minutes from officially being a Premier League team. On this occasion, I didn't mind being showered in booze.

The clock ticked into injury time. Anticipation built as Huddersfield piled forward in search of a winner. They were unable to find one though and, when the final whistle blew, the scenes on that concourse were genuinely special. Considering the Huddersfield game was, in reality, of no genuine consequence, the outpouring of joy and emotion was greater than I imagined. People were crying, young kids were placed atop their parents' shoulders and then, something odd happened. I noticed that neither of my feet were touching the floor and I was moving forward. The second pitch invasion of the day was taking place and I was literally being swept along with it. After bottlenecking through the large exit gate on the north-west corner of the ground, my feet touched green terra firma and I found myself once again looking up at the West Stand where, in the middle tier, the club's directors had stepped out of the boardroom to join in the celebrations. Out of the corner of my eye, I spotted a familiar face in the lower West Stand. It was my mum.

More than three decades after she started working at the club, she was still part of the furniture. She'd retired from full-time employment a couple of years previously but assisted in the commercial department on a part-time basis and worked with my dad on the North Stand reception every match. Watching her celebrate alongside my dad and sister was a lovely sight. She waved her arms in the air and sang along with the songs which were emanating from the thousands of fans on the pitch, and I found myself reflecting on just how much she'd been through since she started working voluntarily in the club shop in 1986. She'd been an unsung hero for years. During the Withdean era, my mum and a handful of other loyal staff members had been the beating heart of the club, working tirelessly to ensure the everyday survival of Brighton & Hove Albion. Sure, these days she was a part-timer in a huge operation, but the commitment that my mum showed when the club was operating on a shoestring meant that this was as much her day as anybody's.

That evening, I found myself drinking glass upon glass of red wine with my family in manager Chris Hughton's lounge in the West Stand. As the players sprayed champagne in the East Stand before literally crowd surfing on the train on the way to a deserved drunken night in Brighton town centre, their manager enjoyed a quiet drink, humbly accepting the congratulations from friends, colleagues and well-wishers. That perfectly sums up Chris Hughton, I think.

Long, long after the stadium had fallen quiet and Falmer had gone dark, I made my way home, walking through the car park alongside my mother who, also a few glasses of wine down, was swaying slightly while waving an Albion flag. It was a perfect moment.

***

THE COMFORT IN BEING SAD

Once the dust had settled and the hangovers had abated, a look at the league table told us that one more victory would secure the title ahead of Newcastle United. Equally, if Newcastle dropped any points at all in their final three games, Albion would win the league.

The next match was on a Friday night in Norwich. After the extraordinary high they'd experienced, the players were struggling to come back down to earth and compete in an away game just a few days later. It was hardly surprising that they were looking slightly jaded. The 2-0 defeat was remarkable only because both goals came about in bizarre fashion. Alex Pritchard (a player, incidentally, who was reportedly supposed to sign for Brighton but apparently changed his mind on his way to the stadium and high-tailed it to Norwich instead) hit a good shot from the edge of the box which bounced off the crossbar, hit Albion keeper David Stockdale on the back and rebounded into the goal. Not long later, Pritchard curled an effort towards goal, it hit the post and bounced off the diving Stockdale into the net. Two identical own goals by a keeper in the same game. I doubt that has ever happened before or since. This freak double occurrence meant the Norwich game was a write-off. We would instead have to look towards the next one, Bristol City at home.

If the pre-match atmosphere was fantastic against Wigan, then it went to the next level for the final home game of the season. The club put blue and white flags on every seat, and they were being waved with glee by a sold-out crowd who looked forward to seeing Bruno lifting the trophy by the end of the afternoon. This was what worried me. Everyone seemed so certain of beating Bristol City that many people had spent the previous week discussing whether or not to invade the pitch again. You know sometimes you just get a feeling that things aren't going to go to plan? Well, that was my mindset from the moment Jayne and I arrived at Eastbourne station to discover that trains were at a standstill due to an electrical issue, or some other vague excuse. There was panic as scores of Eastbourne-based football fans tried to work out how they were going to get to Falmer for this massive game. Every member of train staff seemed to be saying something different. Catch a bus to Brighton. Wait for announcements. Nobody knew what action to take. Eventually the trains started running again and we just about got to the Amex in time to take our seats, wave our flags and join in with a big old chorus of 'Sussex by the Sea' before kick-off. Still though, it had been enough of a stress to leave a nagging feeling that the day would go pear-shaped. And so it proved. City defended resolutely against a Brighton attack which seemed uncharacteristically bereft of ideas. When the away team scored shortly before half-time, it felt like it would be a long way back. 'One-nil on your big day out' sang the visiting fans as the rest of the stadium grew increasingly frustrated. There was to be no equaliser.

Shortly after the final whistle blew, the Albion players embarked on a lap of honour. The sell-out crowd remained in their seats to give their team the heroes' reception that this magnificent season deserved. The players warmly applauded the fans, but we should have been seeing them carrying the Championship trophy. The sense of disappointment wasn't overbearing, but it was definitely present. Newcastle had won their latest couple of games. It was slipping away from us. This is probably a good time to revisit my suggestion in the previous chapter that Jayne is a lucky charm. It turns out she is absolutely not. Work commitments meant that Jayne only made it to seven home games throughout her debut season as a Brighton supporter. Albion lost just three home matches throughout their entire promotion campaign and, somewhat impressively, Jayne was in attendance for all of them.

There was still one final opportunity for Brighton to win the league. The last game of the season was at Villa Park the following Sunday. Tickets for the Aston Villa game were like gold dust, so I instead went to watch a beam-back of the match at the Amex. A series of big screens were lined up at the front of two of the stands, offering a perfect view of the action for thousands of supporters not lucky enough to be at the game. The equation was simple. If Brighton matched or bettered Newcastle's result, we would be celebrating the title at the final whistle.

Villa had nothing riding on the game, which allowed them to play with freedom, and they were the better team in a goalless first half. Newcastle were winning though, which meant Brighton had to push on in the second period. In the 63rd minute, Albion striker Sam Baldock was brought down in the box and the defender who upended him was shown a red card. This was our chance. Glenn Murray, cool as you like, converted the penalty. The goal was celebrated wildly at Villa Park and at the Amex. We were 1-0 up against ten men who had nothing to play for. Surely the title was ours.

Despite the numerical advantage, the Seagulls couldn't find a second goal and, with the clock counting down, the players started to defend further and further back. In the last minute, the ball fell to Villa's Jack Grealish, who used his impressive calves to fashion a low, curling shot towards goal from outside the box. He hadn't hit it perfectly though, and it seemed like a straightforward save for David Stockdale but, to the horror of Albion fans, the ball slipped under the keeper's body and into the net. And with Stockdale's error, the title was gone in a puff of smoke. Newcastle cruised to victory in their game and were crowned champions while Brighton's players were left to sit forlornly on the Villa Park turf and contemplate the one that got away. For a few moments, I experienced that all-too-familiar, helpless feeling of gut-churning disappointment. You know the one.

It was such a downbeat way for this brilliant season to end and I momentarily hated football. My disappointment, however, only lasted for as long as it took me to rise from my seat in the stand and walk the few steps down to the concourse. Once there, I was greeted by a long line of lads doing the conga, beers in hand, chanting the song about being on our way to the Premier League. And with that, my gloom lifted. Okay, so we weren't champions, but for the first time since I started following the Albion over 30 years previously, I was going to watch them play in the top tier of English football. I joined in with the song, which grew louder and louder around the concourse. I didn't want to miss the chance to holler those words one last time. After today, we wouldn't be able to sing it anymore. We were no longer on our way. We were there.

When I look back on the season's slightly disappointing conclusion, I strangely take a small amount of comfort from it. Essentially, we lost the title thanks to a combination of a fluke goal that Newcastle scored against us when the ball ricocheted randomly off some bloke's ankle, and Stockdale scoring a couple of comedy own goals and then letting one slip under his body in the last minute of the season. It served to remind me that, despite Albion's inexorable climb up the league and the transformation from a homeless little club into a Premier League behemoth, this was still the same disaster-prone Brighton & Hove Albion that I had always supported.

I sometimes feel emotionally distanced from the super-corporate modern game, so the wrench of disappointment when the title slipped away acted as a timely reminder of how deeply football still affects me. It had been very easy and enjoyable to watch Brighton steamroller teams week after week, but here was proof that the painful moments are just as important and just as relevant. Without the bad times, the good times don't feel half as good. (The rainbow and the rain, remember?)

I don't know what the future holds for Brighton & Hove Albion, but what I do know is that, no matter how big the club becomes, we'll only ever be one rogue ankle deflection or a goalkeeping error away from heartbreak. Football, just like life, has a way of never allowing you to become complacent. Steven Gerrard slipping over? Manchester United thinking they'd won the league only for their main rivals to score two goals in injury time to snatch it from them? Diego Maradona punching one in against England? These are the things that make football the brilliant soap opera that it is.

***

THE EYE OF THE BEHOLDER

On 12 August 2017, Brighton & Hove Albion made their Premier League debut, and played their first top-flight game since 1983. Their opponents? Oh, only Manchester

City, possibly the greatest team in the world at the time. Talk about a baptism of fire.

Jayne and I were in our seats stupidly early, because I didn't want to miss a single second of the Seagulls' introduction to the Premier League. I had, after all, waited my whole life for this day. I knew that City were a team of world-class players, but what surprised me when the game started was just how physical, fast and strong they were. On the rare occasions that Albion managed to steal the ball from them, they pressed aggressively to win it back almost immediately. It was eye-opening. Would it be like this every week? If so, it was going to be a long season. In the end, Brighton held out for over 70 minutes before succumbing to a 2-0 loss but, even in defeat, Albion's players left the field to a rousing reception from the fans. Everyone knew it was going to be a tough season and this game had certainly confirmed it. If we were going to stay up, we all had to be in this together.

It would take three and a half matches for Brighton to score in the Premier League and, when it finally happened against West Bromwich Albion, it was like popping a champagne cork. Solly March crossed to new German midfielder Pascal Gross, who hit a left-footed shot into the bottom corner with the help of a slight deflection. It wasn't an attractive goal, but at the same time it was divine. Beauty is indeed in the eye of the beholder and, while West Brom fans will point to some horrible defending, Brighton supporters saw something magical. We didn't know it at the time, but Gross would go on to become one of the club's greatest signings, having arrived from Ingolstadt for a paltry £3 million.

The first season in England's top division continued to be a lovely novelty. Seeing Albion on *Match of the Day* every week was a Saturday night treat, and every win, every hard-earned draw against one of the world's best sides, felt monumental. The thrill of it all served to conflict with my occasional negative feelings towards the Premier League. Before getting swept up in the excitement of our promotion, I had always considered the Premier League a gluttonous machine; its oh-so-serious nature smoothing over the rather lovely jagged edges that you get in the lower divisions. I had heard of matches feeling more like theatre events, with tourists and glory-hunters TikToking their way through games, while Sky hyped fixtures to the point of parody. And, of course, everything, absolutely everything, in the Premier League ultimately boils down to money. Don't get me wrong though, the day that Brighton got promoted was one of the best of my life. Even though I had contributed nothing towards promotion, it somehow felt like I had achieved a lifelong personal ambition, and watching my team take on some of the greatest players on the planet makes me so proud that, at the risk of reaching the same level of hyperbole as you hear on Sky, it almost feels like an honour.

It's a strange dichotomy to dislike some aspects of the Premier League, yet still be desperate for your club to remain part of it. Indeed, when the Seagulls beat Manchester United at the Amex to ensure our survival at the end of the first season (with Gross again the goalscorer), I certainly wasn't contemplating any of the Premier League's faults. Rather, I was merrily singing from my seat as the players danced on the pitch. If you'd have told any of those hardy individuals who went to Priestfield that, a couple of decades on, we'd be in the Premier League beating Manchester United, they'd have thought you'd lost the plot.

To be honest though, as Albion scrapped for points at the bottom end of the Premier League for a couple of years running, it started to feel a bit like hard work at times. The run of performances at the end of Chris Hughton's otherwise excellent tenure was especially moribund and spirit-sapping. It's a shame that money dominates modern football because I genuinely think that the Championship is a brilliantly exciting league and, sometimes towards the end of the Hughton era, I wondered if it might be more fun for the Seagulls to spend another season winning games down there. Then I looked at the fortunes of some of the clubs who were relegated from the Premier League and that aspired to immediately return, your Boltons and your Blackpools, and I had a very sharp change of mind. And, even though sometimes weeks went by without having anything much to celebrate in our early seasons in the Premier League, the moments of magic far outweighed the disappointments or the negative aspects of the division. The home win against Arsenal in that first season, for instance, is one of my all-time favourite games; if I close my eyes, I'm there now, celebrating Glenn Murray's header with a feeling of glorious disbelief. Similarly, when we smashed West Ham United 3-1, I wasn't weighing up the pros and cons of life in the top division, rather I was going nuts as winger José Izquierdo curled a gem into the top corner.

Equally, when goalkeeper Bart Verbruggen saved an injury-time penalty against Brentford in 2025, I wasn't contemplating whether the Premier League introducing 'squad cost ratio' and sustainability measures was a good or bad thing, I was wildly celebrating three points. I suppose, as much as you can attempt to hold the moral high ground with regard to certain aspects of modern football, ultimately we all just want our team to be as successful as possible. Besides, for every corrupt FIFA official, and for every awful story you hear about the conditions under which construction workers built Qatar's World Cup stadiums, there is Marcus Rashford taking on the government, the annual Soccer Aid match, Jermain Defoe befriending terminally ill six-year-old Bradley Lowery, a fundraising Everton fan in Speedos, Sadio Mané building schools in Senegal, and Albion's excellent ongoing community work, using the power of football for good.

***

I DON'T WANT TO CHEER CHELSEA

Another weird consequence of Brighton being at the bottom end of the Premier League during their first few seasons was that, across the latter stages of each campaign, I found myself doing something that I had never previously contemplated in all my years of being a football fan: namely, cheering the big teams against the smaller ones.

There are few more enjoyable experiences as a neutral than watching one of the traditional big hitters being given a bloody nose by a smaller team, but that dynamic shifted a bit when Albion got promoted. An obvious part of being involved in a relegation tussle is taking a keen interest in the teams around yours and wanting them to lose every game to further your own club's chances of staying up. This means that I now found myself celebrating when, for instance, Manchester United scored against Norwich City, or Chelsea netted against Fulham. Before Brighton were in the Premier League, I had never once celebrated a goal by either of those teams, yet here I was, regularly cheering on some of the richest, most bloated clubs in the world. I won't lie, it felt dirty and I became very grateful when Brighton established themselves as a top-ten club, because it meant I was once again able to root for the underdogs in such matches. Obviously, there are many more important reasons why it was brilliant that Albion became a mainstay in the Premier League, but I certainly appreciated not having to cheer a Chelsea goal anymore.

Speaking of Chelsea, something else I've learned from following a Premier League team is just how entitled many fans are. Since we've been part of the top division, social media posts from fans of the traditionally big clubs have made for depressing reading. Given our many transfer dealings with Chelsea, there has consequently been lots of bickering and abuse between the two sets of supporters online, and the constant insult that comes our way from them (and from fans of the likes of Arsenal, Manchester United, etc) is that we are a 'small club', as though that's a bad thing in some way. I'm immensely proud to support a 'small club' that has been to hell and back, and the fact that they think it is a stick with which to bash us shows how clueless and out of touch these glory-hunters are. I'd wager that many of these keyboard warriors have never even set foot inside their team's stadium. It's made me realise that, even though our traditional rivals are Crystal

Palace, my dislike for these Super League wannabes far outweighs any inherent negativity towards that lot from Selhurst Park. Indeed, Palace fans and Brighton fans are probably more alike than different. They are similar-sized clubs with (and I'm choosing to ignore Palace's recent cup runs when making this statement) similar levels of success. If I had the choice between going to the pub with some Palace fans or some Chelsea supporters, I would choose our supposed rivals every single time.

***

LOCKDOWN

I wasn't feeling quite so warm towards Crystal Palace when they beat us 1-0 at the Amex in February 2020 and, as I trudged miserably from the stadium at full time, I had no idea that I wouldn't be back for a year and a half. With the UK locking down because of Covid, attending football matches, just like visiting family or friends, was outlawed.

Football barely paused though. While we were wearing masks, queuing outside supermarkets and then wrestling grannies for the last pack of loo roll once inside, the Premier League got going again behind closed doors, streaming all matches live. Looking back, watching games being played in empty stadiums with crowd noises overlaid in the mix was utter madness, but I suppose it offered an alternative to Zoom quizzes, jigsaw puzzles and baking bread. And it also brought some much-needed joy in otherwise awful circumstances, such as when Neal Maupay scored a 95th-minute winner against Arsenal.

The conclusion of the season was played sans supporters, as was the vast majority of the 2020/21 campaign. It doesn't feel real now. A victory at Anfield, a game in which we absolutely battered Palace and somehow conspired to lose 2-1, and a match where Manchester United were awarded a penalty after the full-time whistle (don't get me started on VAR again) all just feel like curiosities, rather than actual moments in the club's recent history. These games belong to an unprecedented and odd period of time and I'm not sure that Covid's damage to our collective mental health has been fully recognised yet. My introversion, for example, is far more pronounced than before lockdown. So it was particularly emotional to be able to set foot back in the Amex for the first home match of the 2021/22 season. What was, essentially, a run-of-the-mill 2-0 win against Watford took on much greater significance. It was the first time that 30,000 people had sat together at Brighton's home ground since the beforetimes and, given the misery and uncertainty that we had all experienced, it felt such a relief to be back doing something so cherished.

When Shane Duffy headed in from a corner in the first half, the sense of emotion around the stadium was clear to see, as some of the weight of the previous 18 months fell from people's shoulders. Never underestimate the raw power of football.

***

THE IMPOSSIBLE DREAM

Under Chris Hughton's replacement, Graham Potter, Albion finished ninth and picked up wins away at Arsenal and Spurs. One of the highlights of the campaign came when Manchester United visited Sussex and were smashed 4-0. The game is also notable because it featured one of the greatest footballers of all time, although he wasn't at all great on this occasion. Cristiano Ronaldo sulked his way around the pitch, doing nothing aside from blazing a free kick miles over the bar, before being subbed in the second half. While it was exciting to see him play in the flesh, he was a shadow of his former self, and there was something a little sad about how even superhumans like him can't beat the ravages of time.

With Brighton continuing their fine form into the next season, it was no surprise that other clubs came sniffing around Potter and, after a 5-2 thrashing of Leicester City at the Amex, Albion's boss left to join Chelsea, taking his backroom staff with him. It was a bitter pill for fans to swallow. They had stood by him during a few frustrating runs in his tenure, as the majority understood that his was a project that needed time. So when he upped sticks and disappeared, it was sad and somewhat baffling, because we all knew that a club as mad as Chelsea definitely wouldn't give him the time he needed to achieve anything there.

With Potter and his coaching staff (including club legend Bruno) having been tempted away, Brighton turned to someone that, if we're being honest, few of us had previously heard of. Italian Roberto De Zerbi, with his little beard and spiky hair, took over, and his first game gave an indication of the excitement that we would witness for the rest of the season. A 3-3 draw at Anfield was quite the introduction, but it would be five games before he would get his first win. The opponents? Graham Potter's Chelsea.

It's fair to say that every Brighton fan and player at this Premier League game at the end of October 2022 was bang up for it and Chelsea, with Potter and Bruno looking bereft on the bench, were simply blown away by the urgency of the home team's performance and the vociferous reaction from the crowd. It was 3-0 before half-time and finished 4-1. It is unquestionably one of the highlights of our time at the Amex so far. By the time Brighton did the double over Chelsea with a 2-1 win at Stamford Bridge in April, Potter had been sacked.

De Zerbi had the team playing lovely football and, alongside pushing for European places in the league, they were also having success in the FA Cup. A thrashing of Middlesbrough was followed by Japanese winger Kaoru Mitoma scoring an injury-time winner against Liverpool. Stoke City and Grimsby Town were also dispatched, meaning that the Albion would be appearing in an FA Cup semi-final for only the third time in their history. Having reached the final in 1983, the club made it to the semis again in 2019, under Chris Hughton, only to lose 1-0 to Manchester City. I was overseas for that one, so the game against Manchester United in 2023 would be my first semi-final experience.

Having cheered on some pals in the London Marathon in the morning, Jayne and I headed to Wembley for the match, with the unmistakable combination of excitement and nervousness in our tummies. As we glanced down Wembley Way to witness a sea of blue and red stretching before us, I told myself to remember the moment, as I didn't know when, or indeed if, I'd be back here to see my team again. We strolled towards the ground, made our way in and climbed high up into the top tier and found our seats. The packed stadium looked incredible. I had only seen my team play here once before, in 1991, and as the teams took to the field I tried to convince myself that this time it would have a happy ending.

The game was an incredibly tense affair with few chances at either end and extra time felt inevitable long before the clock hit the 90-minute mark. Sure enough, 30 minutes were added, but brought no goals. So, at the end of a stalemate, the match would be decided on penalties.

Penalty shoot-outs make for fantastic viewing if your team is not involved. They are pure theatre. However, they are an absolute nightmare if you have skin in the game. In fact, I can't think of a more awful, stomach-churning experience in sport. All around me, grey faces watched on as the rain poured down on Wembley's lush pitch and each player made the long, lonely walk from the halfway line. I felt sick and could barely bring myself to watch.

This wasn't the first penalty shoot-out I'd seen Brighton involved in that season. Just after the winter break to accommodate the World Cup in Qatar, I was at Valley Parade to see another 0-0 draw, this time against Charlton Athletic in the EFL Cup. A topsy-turvy shoot-out saw four Brighton players miss, with Gross and Leandro Trossard hitting the woodwork, Moisés Caicedo having his shot saved and Solly March blazing over the bar. We lost 4-3 in sudden death.

Against Manchester United, each successful kick was greeted with less of a cheer of joy and more with one of relief as a place in the FA Cup Final hung in the balance. With all of the first ten penalties scored, it went to sudden death. Just like on that cold December night against Charlton, it was March who missed, hitting the ball over the crossbar once more. Albion were beaten 7-6 and it felt like a punch in the stomach.

As Albion's heartbroken faithful made their way down the million Wembley stairs and stepped out into the miserable evening, they were greeted by United fans on the way to the tube station. A number of them were far from magnanimous in victory, and seemed more determined to mock their defeated opponents rather than just enjoying their win. It was the kind of classless act that made me hope they would lose the subsequent final against their cross-city rivals. I cheered from my flat in London as they did exactly that the following month.

As for the Albion, they were able to take revenge against Manchester United almost immediately. The two sides played each other at the Amex in the Premier League just a couple of weeks later, and it would provide one of the most iconic pieces of footage that the stadium has ever seen. The game was heading towards another goalless draw when, in the last throes of injury time, VAR spotted a United handball in the box and a penalty was awarded to Brighton. It was about time VAR went in our favour, given some of the howlingly bad decisions that had gone against us that season. Now we had the chance for three crucial points in the battle to qualify for Europe and the opportunity to send those smug United fans home unhappy.

Had this been a movie, March would have scored from the penalty spot, but it was actually World Cup winner Alexis Mac Allister on spot kick duty, as usual. The Argentinian midfielder took his time, ran up and then smashed the ball into the top corner in front of an ecstatic North Stand. It was a special moment, made all the more so because the defeat at Wembley against the same opponents still felt so raw. The match was live on Sky and footage filmed from above the stadium shows Mac Allister dispatching the penalty and then pans out to reveal a stadium bursting with life. It's an incredible shot and serves as another reminder of what something as simple as one person kicking a football can mean.

The win was a big step towards securing European football but, as a further indicator that the Seagulls never do things the easy way, the team got absolutely battered at home by relegation-threatened Everton in the next match a few days later. The 5-1 defeat really brought everyone back down to earth. Next? A trip to Arsenal, who were still chasing the title. Surely that would end in another loss? Well, no actually. Albion dismantled the Gunners 3-0 that day, ending the north London club's hopes of winning the league, and causing the Emirates to be almost empty before the full-time whistle. It was the second time that season we'd won there, having dumped them out of the EFL Cup in November.

The mad mix of results kept coming, as we were walloped 4-1 up at Newcastle United, before European football was secured for the first time in the club's history with a 3-1 win over Southampton on a Sunday afternoon at the Amex. The scenes at the full-time whistle were quite something, as the team and management celebrated an achievement that had been unthinkable just a few years ago. Brighton's ascent from the basement division to Europe served as an illustration that, with sensible yet visionary people like Tony Bloom and Paul Barber at the helm, any club can achieve something really special, and the Albion's story should be inspirational to fans of teams who are currently in the doldrums. Jayne and I watched the game from the West Stand, and celebrated each of the three goals with abandon. Fans sang their hearts out as the team and coaching staff embarked on a lap of honour after the game, and a shared sense of pride and achievement reverberated around the stadium. It felt unreal.

The win against Southampton meant that the UEFA Conference League, at the very least, was guaranteed, and a Europa League spot was achieved with a 1-1 draw against Manchester City three days later. There had never been a better time to be a Brighton & Hove Albion supporter.

***

WHY I LOVE FOOTBALL

It felt as though my personal journey reached some kind of conclusion when I stepped into the Amex in September 2023 to watch Brighton & Hove Albion's first ever game in a European competition.

By this point, I had been following the club across five different decades. I'd seen us sit at the top of the Premier League and at the very foot of the bottom division. I'd seen us beat Liverpool and lose to Lincoln, win against Spurs and suffer defeat to Sudbury. I was around when the club was a kick of a football away from disappearing into oblivion. I'd been a ball kid, worked in all manner of roles at the club and had written hundreds of thousands of words about all of Brighton's various travails over the years. Now, having seen the team play in all four divisions, I was about to watch them in the Europa League. It felt like a meaningful occasion and, in a way that is hard to explain, it felt like the end of something.

In literal terms, it wasn't the end of anything at all. Of course it wasn't. After the game against AEK Athens, I'd be back for the next Premier League match, and would then be sitting in the same seat for more Europa League action against Ajax and Marseille, and then the knockout tie against Roma. And when I went to the Fulham match at the start of the 2025/26 campaign, it represented my 40th season attending matches. Because, let's face it, football never really ends, does it? Match follows match, season follows season. If your team is hopeless one week, at least there's next week. The sport marches on relentlessly. There is always something about which to reminisce, something to look forward to, and the symbiotic relationship between you, your fellow supporters and the players will always exist. Every weekend for nine months of each year, your team will thrill you, frustrate you, make your pulse race and your heart sink.

But I can't deny that my relationship with Brighton & Hove Albion has shifted slightly as I've grown older. It's not worse or better, just different. It's difficult to pinpoint exactly how and why it has altered. Perhaps it's simply because my family isn't quite as involved with the inner workings of the club as we once were. Maybe it's because I have spent such a lot of time in Australia and missed so many games, or because I no longer write a weekly column about the club. Perhaps it's because my current domestic commitments up in London mean I get to fewer men's matches per season than I would like, along with only a handful of the Albion Women's games. I do feel as if I am watching from the outside, whereas I was once at the epicentre.

Maybe it's the corporate sheen of the Premier League, and the lack of consideration from the FA and Sky for supporters regarding kick-off times. Maybe it's the cost of tickets for football matches these days. Is it because VAR has genuinely ruined the experience of watching football in a stadium? Or is it simply because it feels like my club has outgrown me, in a good way?

You know how it is. You discover your new favourite band playing in tiny pubs and you feel part of something secret and special. Then you go and see them in bigger venues with a sense of pride and excitement. Better acoustics, a bigger crowd, nicer merchandise. But by the time they are playing sold-out nights at Wembley Arena, you feel like they won't miss you if you don't attend. Indisputably, Albion are no longer the slightly rubbish band that plays in dingy pubs and, maybe for me, their journey to the Premier League and to Europe, with all the obstacles that stood in the way, was the most important thing. Now, with the club being brilliantly run and with the team playing in front of over 30,000 fans in a spectacular home arena, part of me can let go a little, and I'm fine with that. It's the natural evolution of my relationship with a football club that has grown exponentially.

I suppose I can sum up this pseudo-psychology by explaining that, although I absolutely adore watching my football at the American Express Stadium, about once a season as my train from London to Brighton passes through Withdean, I get a strange and unfathomable urge to see the Albion play there again, with its sandpits, rickety stands, hammer net and boggy pitch. These thoughts pass as quickly as they arrive. In reality, it would be a total nightmare to be back at Withdean, and I realise it's just rose-tinted reminiscence, but I don't think that the slight internal conflict of enjoying the exciting present versus an occasional yearning for the past is exclusive to me. Rather, it is probably something that is common in many people's lives, whether they are football supporters or not.

It would be unrealistic to expect my relationship with the Albion to remain the same forever. Times change and circumstances alter and, for now, I'm very happy with my slightly less intense relationship with the club. As I mentioned before, it's no better or worse, just different. That said, whether watching Ajax at the Amex, Wolves at Withdean, Peterborough at Priestfield or Grimsby at the Goldstone, my reaction to goals, bad tackles, whatever, are exactly the same as they ever were, and the primal feelings that football stirs in me will always be there. Take the visit of Marseille in Brighton's final group match in their debut Europa League campaign in December 2023. With the game level at 0-0 going into the final moments, the Seagulls needed to score to win the group. A neat attack found Brazilian striker João Pedro with the ball at his feet in the box, and he blasted it towards goal. There was that beautiful moment of silence before the net bulged, and then I went absolutely bananas as the goalscorer leapt the hoardings and celebrated with fans. As the players eventually made their way back to the halfway line, the entire home crowd sang 'Albion' in unison. Only, they didn't sing it, they bellowed it, summoning the words from the very bottom of their lungs.

I love the fact that, 37 years after my first live game, and after everything that the club had been through during that time, I was still able to experience such pure joy. Sure, as an adult trying to navigate his way through a never-ending cost-of-living crisis, my life is less singularly Albion-focused than when I was a kid, but how many other moments in life give you the same excitement in your 40s as they did when you were nine? The win had the same impact on Jayne in her eighth season and on my mum and dad who had been watching the Albion since long before I was born. It prompted the same emotions from the old chap across the aisle who had been following the team since the 50s, and from the mother and her young daughter sitting in the row in front. Moments like this, an explosion of emphatic delight that you share with thousands of others, will make the hairs stand up on the back of your neck when you recall them weeks, months, years after the event.

When Pedro headed an injury-time winner against Manchester United in the first home match of the following season, I went just as bonkers as I did against Marseille and as when I was a ball boy in front of the North Stand all those years ago. Equally, a few weeks later when Albion had a four-against-one attack in injury time against Wolves and yet somehow managed to *concede* a goal and throw away a win, I was absolutely inconsolable. For days. When we came from 2-1 down with a minute to go to beat West Ham United (managed by a certain Graham Potter) later in the same season, I was just as excited as I was when I watched the team win as a child. And when, in 2025, we scored a last-minute goal to beat Manchester City at home for the second season running, I almost burst.

Regardless of what division they are in and whether I attend one game a season or all of them, Brighton & Hove Albion will always, always stir these emotions in me.

And that's why I love football.

ACKNOWLEDGEMENTS

FIRSTLY, I would like to thank my wife, Jayne, for her unwavering support and love, and for embracing my passion for Brighton & Hove Albion. Whether watching the men's or women's team home or away, she is by my side, even when the temperature is about 20 degrees colder than her Australian bones would prefer.

Also, of course, I couldn't imagine my Albion journey without my mum and dad, Sally and Brian, and my sister, Kay. Three true legends. If you cut them open, they would bleed blue and white. They could not have been more supportive of me as I have made my way through this silly thing called life.

Thanks and G'day to my Aussie family: John, Jenny, Billy, Tim, Clare, Alexia, Finley and Audrey, and to the countless members of my extended family.

Big love to all my pals in the UK, Australia and dotted around the globe. I can't list everyone, so I won't name anyone. You know who you are, and you know how much I appreciate your ongoing love, encouragement and help.

Thanks to everyone at Brighton & Hove Albion, past and present, especially my former colleagues. Again, there are too many people to name individually here (and indeed too many to mention in the book; sorry if you didn't see your name) but I loved working at the club and the friendships I made during my many years there. I'm also sending love into the universe to my old workmates who are sadly no longer with us. And cheers to all the Albion fans who have supported this project.

I must also acknowledge the good people at *The Argus* for giving me my own column and letting me write whatever I wanted for a decade.

A big thank you to everyone at Pitch Publishing for having belief in my book. I am also grateful to Vassos and Matt for their invaluable advice in the earlier stages of the process, and much love to Chris Evans for speaking about me and my book on the radio, even before I had finished writing it!

I am penning these acknowledgements long before this book hits the shelves, but I know there will have been plenty of other friends in the media who have also helped to spread the word about it, so thanks in advance to all of them. Hugs and high fives all round.

Last, but by no means least, thanks to you for taking a chance on this book despite the vast competition for your attention. Whether you know me as Robert, Rob, Bobby, Bob, Bobbo or even Bobbles, and especially if you don't know me at all, I cannot express how grateful I am that you have taken the time to read my words.

Stand or Fall, I love you all.